An Advanced Course in
Communication Sciences and Disorders

An Advanced Course in
Communication Sciences and Disorders

Dennis C. Tanner, Ph.D.
Northern Arizona University
Flagstaff, Arizona

AUTHORS CHOICE PRESS

iUniverse, Inc.
Bloomington

AN ADVANCED COURSE IN COMMUNICATION SCIENCES AND DISORDERS

AUTHORS CHOICE PRESS

Published by iUniverse, Inc.

For information address:
iUniverse
1663 Liberty Drive
Bloomington, IN 47403
www.iuniverse.com
1-800-Authors (1-800-288-4677)

Originally published by Plural Publishing

ISBN: 978-1-4759-5903-1 (sc)

Printed in the United States of America

iUniverse rev. date: 12/04/2012

Dedication

This book is dedicated to the memory of Dr. Larry Sant and Dr. Oscar Tosi, who so long ago, sparked my interest in human communication and its disorders, and gave me the direction I needed.

Contents

Foreword

An Advanced Course in Communication Sciences and Disorders, Dennis C. Tanner's latest book, is a major and unique contribution to the speech and hearing literature. Written in a narrative and academic style, this book explores the field of communication sciences and disorders with a compelling plot and a happy ending. Intriguing, fascinating, but never failing to embrace the facts, the book is filled with relevant information on both normal and disordered communication. Tanner has woven the facts into a tapestry of color and style that he calls a unified model, allowing readers to see everything important about normal and disordered communications in one place. What I admire about Dr. Tanner is that he explores fully the *connections* among all aspects of normal human communication, and the impact on the individual, family, caregiver, and society when this connection is lost. This is what our field is all about. The national organizations of American Speech-Language-Hearing Association and American Academy of Audiology have for many years endeavored to bring a unified view of the professions to every student and clinician in these fields. Dr. Tanner has accomplished this in one textbook.

While reading this manuscript, it kept occurring to me that this is a definitive text that will answer the essential question that every communication science and disorder student must ask: "When I leave this program, how do I put it all together?" These students have been through many courses dealing with various aspects of normal and disordered communication at all levels, from basic introductions to advanced scientific and clinical seminars. These are by design highly specialized courses in both normal and disordered language, speech, and hearing. Before any student can conclude their study in our field, he or she needs to make the connections, to assimilate all the information they have learned into a cohesive whole.

This book is so essential to making these connections that students should read it twice: once upon embarking on their studies in the field of communication sciences and disorders, and again when nearing completion of their academic and clinical educations. The first reading of this book will undoubtedly whet their academic appetites, increase their curiosity, challenge intellectual acumen, and bring them to the decision that they need to explore this field further. The final reading will allow them to become the best consumer of all of the intellectual assets they have accumulated in the field of communication sciences and disorders.

Sadanand Singh, Ph.D.

Preface

Many authors have written books, chapters, and articles about language and thought, the role of language in consciousness, expressive and receptive language, motor speech, acoustics, hearing, and perception. Neither is there a shortage of books and chapters on communication disorders. Several authors have provided models of motor speech, static and dynamic articulation, respiration, voice production, and audition, but none have unified all aspects of communication, and its disorders, into a comprehensive model. The notion of "unification" is borrowed from theoretical physics and is my attempt to unify all aspects of the process of communication into a cohesive whole and to apply this schema to disorders.

I have written about the unified model of communication and its disorders in several books and use it for introducing communication sciences and disorders in my courses at Northern Arizona University. I believe the model successfully unifies all aspects of the process of communication and is sound philosophically, theoretically, and scientifically. This model provides a schema for understanding the complexities of human communication and its disorders. *An Advanced Course in Communication Sciences and Disorders* gives the thoughtful reader relevant philosophical, theoretical, and scientific information about human communication and the myriad deficiencies, diseases, deficits, and disorders that can lay waste to it.

Acknowledgments

I am grateful to several people who were instrumental in helping me write this book. First, thanks to Dr. John Sciacca and Dr. William Culbertson for helping me to work out some of the technical aspects of *An Advanced Course in Communication Sciences and Disorders*. I am indebted to Jody M. Tanner and Stephanie S. Cotton for serving as a sounding-board for some of the controversial issues in this book, and for their insightful feedback. I am also grateful to the reviewers for their helpful comments and suggestions.

To the Reader

Today, most colleges and universities require one course for students that provides them with a capstone to their undergraduate education. This upper division course brings together all of the students' previous education in a meaningful and comprehensive scholarly learning experience. My goal in writing *An Advanced Course in Communication Sciences and Disorders* is to provide the student with a framework and model for this type of course. The chapters in the book are organized to provide students with cohesive exposure to all of the important aspects of the discipline of communication sciences and disorders.

In this book, there are discussions of communication disorders. However, I have referred to disorders only where they illustrate an aspect of the *Unified Model of Communication Sciences and Disorders* or in some way provide additional insight into a function or process. Although there are many references to communication disorders, this book is not a diagnostic or therapeutic treatise on speech and hearing pathologies.

In Chapter 1, there is a general overview of the process of communication and the countless disorders, deficits, diseases, and disabilities that can impair or destroy this marvelous human ability. It is written in narrative form and serves as a segue to the scientific and technical discussions that follow. For visual learners, there is also a model illustrating the process of communication. Chapter 2 reviews the disciplines and specialities involved in study of communication and the treatment of its disorders. There is also a detailed examination of the Code of Ethics of the American Speech-Language-Hearing Association. Chapter 3 reviews the history of the acquisition of knowledge in communication sciences and disorders, and Chapter 4 focuses on science and logic as the foundation of the discipline. Chapter 5 is an exciting examination of human consciousness, thought, language, and communication. Beginning with Chapter 6 and concluding with Chapter 10, the communication chain is scientifically examined tracing the process from expressive language formulation in speakers to receptive language in listeners.

Throughout this book, I have tried to present the material in each chapter in an orderly, systematic way. Each chapter begins with a preview of the information that follows. There is generous usage of headings and subheadings to help provide a context for the material. Each chapter also has a summary, study and discussion questions, and suggestions for further reading. Liberally dispersed throughout this book are sidebars. These are interesting asides to the material presented in the text. There is also a glossary of terms used in the text, as well as additional professional and technical terms you may encounter as you continue your education.

I believe this book is readable, interesting, and provides the foundation for the most important aspect of your education: the capstone experience. At least those were my goals in writing it.

Dennis C. Tanner
Flagstaff, Arizona

CHAPTER 1

The Unified Model of Communication Sciences and Disorders

"Each language is not merely a reproducing instrument for voicing ideas, but rather is itself a shaper of ideas."

Benjamin Lee Whorf

CHAPTER PREVIEW

This chapter describes the intricate process of communication occurring between two college students. Written in narrative form, it is an uncomplicated examination of communication using nontechnical terms and easily understood descriptions. *Connections* begins with the speaker, Andrew, organizing and structuring his thoughts, and traces communication through motor speech planning, the physical acts involved in speech production, transmission of information through the medium of air, sound detection, speech perception, and concludes with the listener, Angela, decoding and associating the transmitted information in her mind. *Connections Lost* is a general overview of the disorders that can impair or destroy this remarkable process. In the chapters that follow, which address the scientific basis of the communication chain (Chapters 6–10), excerpts are taken from *Connections* to serve as a segue into each stage of the process.

Connections

Two college students, Andrew and Angela, sit at a table in the student union. They sip coffee, laugh, gesture, and share revelations about each other. To the other patrons in the union's coffee shop, they are simply two undergraduates sharing time and company before their next class. However, on a deeper level, what is occurring in the coffee shop is a chain of physical and mental events representing the highest functions of which humans are capable (see Figure 1-1). These two students are exploring relationship possibilities and the bridge connecting them is communication, the crowning glory of humanity.

During communication, Andrew's thoughts and feelings are placed in linguistic structures for expression, but language also plays an important role in his thought processes. Some verbal thoughts are simply concrete representations of reality, such as "chair," "coffee cup," and "hot." However, others are intangible abstractions; the words are the units of thoughts, ideas, notions, and concepts such as "thoughtful," "honest," "truth," and "sensible." Andrew's thoughts are based on his experiences and drawn from his personal memories and associations. The linguistic structure

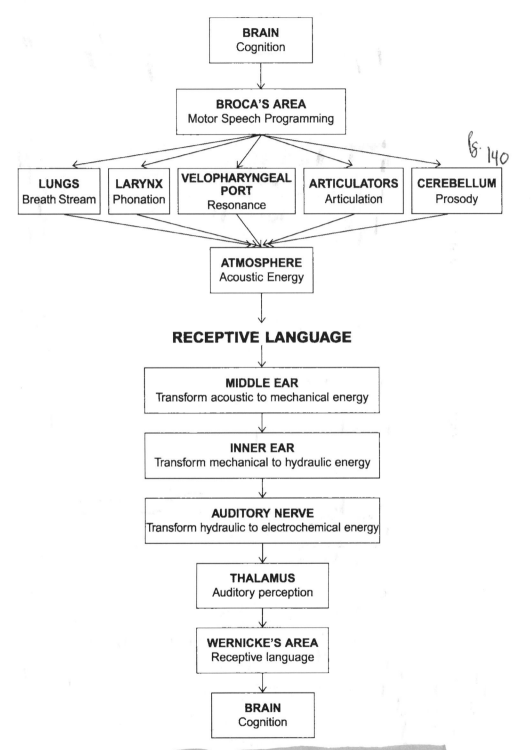

Figure 1–1. The Unified Model of Communication Disorders

includes the grammatic forms all languages take. Speech sounds are arranged in an ordered sequence to form words, and there are rules for stringing them into utterances. These language constructs express Andrew's thoughts and feelings, and they convey his experiences and intentions.

Once the language constructs are formulated, they are routed to the motor speech programming centers of Andrew's brain. The primary motor speech center is in the left hemisphere of his brain where most of the movements, timing, and positioning for the act of purposeful speech are programmed. Programmed are the respiratory support, frequency and intensity of vocal fold vibrations, tongue, lip, and soft palate movements, and the rhythm and fluency required for normal speech production. The plan and sequence of speech involve more than one hundred muscles, and are activated and monitored by thousands of neurologic impulses. They are nearly instantaneously programmed in response to Andrew's ongoing language requirements to express himself. Only rarely does Andrew gives thought to the complicated neuromuscular plans required for each utterance; for the most part, they are done subconsciously.

The language activities occurring in Andrew's mind are a result of thousands of neurologic impulses firing in his brain. The communicating connection of one neuron to another is the synapse, and at this point of contact, chemicals transmit and inhibit nerve impulses. The neurologic impulses are chemically based electrical currents shooting from one brain cell to another, from a group of brain cells to others, and to and from the muscles and sensory fibers of his body. They carry electrochemical information throughout Andrew's brain, and are the physical basis to his thoughts. The electrical and chemical activities in his brain become the words and language constructs in some yet-to-be-discovered way.

Sitting at the coffee shop table, Andrew breathes in and out normally to sustain life; oxygen replaces carbon dioxide to feed the cells of his body. However, when he speaks, the normal breathing ebb and flow of air are interrupted by the respiratory requirements to produce speech. Respiration provides the compressed air from which speech sounds are made. During his speech production, the exhalation phase of breathing is extended to allow for the production of individual speech sounds. Remarkably, when the production of speech sounds results in more airflow resistance in the oral tract, Andrew's respiratory system makes corresponding minor adjustments in muscular force. This subconscious respiratory adjustment occurs on every speech sound. As changes in resistance to airflow occurs in the oral

The idea that one brain hemisphere is completely responsible for a specific mental function in all people is a common misconception. Although it is true that certain mental functions are associated with particular areas of the brain in some persons, there is great variance in the exact location of these areas; the brain operates as a whole; and no single part functions completely independent of the others.

track, Andrew's respiration is correspondingly adjusted so that his ongoing speech has the proper flow, loudness, and emphasis.

Some of Andrew's speech sounds are voiced, for example, "uh," "v," and "b," and his vocal folds vibrate during their production. Other speech sounds are voiceless, for example, "s," "sh," and "h," and are produced with no vocal fold vibration. Voicing creates loudness and gives emphasis to Andrew's utterances. Andrew's vocal folds vibrate, on average, 130 times per second, and this itself is a remarkable muscular and aerodynamic event. The respiratory air pressure blows his vocal folds apart, and they are set into vibration because of muscular elasticity, the tendency of muscles to regain their shape, and a suction effect created by air moving through a constricted space. These principles account for his ability to vibrate his vocal folds rapidly. Frequently, Andrew alters the intensity of vocal fold vibration to add meaning, emphasis, and variability to his utterances, and minor adjustments of the cartilages and muscles in his voice box cause resulting pitch changes. During voicing, acoustic shock waves shoot upward at the speed of sound and resonate the cavities of his neck and head. In effect, Andrew's head and neck become resonating chambers giving him his distinct voice quality that is immediately recognizable by Angela, and his other friends and acquaintances.

The compressed air coming from Andrew's lungs flows through his mouth and nose where it is valved into recognizable speech sounds. Interestingly, Andrew does not produce precise individual speech sounds by making ideal points of contact with his articulators. Because his speech sound production happens rapidly, it becomes a stream of articulatory events. There is overshooting and undershooting of the ideal points of articulatory contact, and the speech sounds preceding and following the one being produced influences its production. Nevertheless, Andrew's tongue, lips, soft palate, and teeth work together to "valve" the compressed air coming from his lungs.

Some articulation valving sites constrict the air such as during the production of "sh," "v," and "th." During the production of stop consonants, such as "t," "d," and "p," the airstream and acoustic energy completely stop for a brief time. Some speech sounds such as "d" and "t," and "s" and "z" vary only by the presence or absence of voicing. Other speech sounds such as "w," "l," and "r" require a gliding action of his tongue to produce them. The nasality of Andrew's speech is maximized or minimized by his soft palate closing or opening the nasal port. When the nasal port is opened, the speech resonance and energy is projected through his nasal cavity and nose, and his tongue or lips block the oral cavity. The syllables spoken by Andrew are the basic acoustic and physiologic units of speech, and the vowels are their central components. Andrew's vowels are produced by minor adjustments in the front-to-back position of his tongue, its height in his mouth, and lip rounding.

All the time Andrew is speaking to Angela, he uses facial expressions and hand gestures to reinforce and describe what he is talking about. He smiles, nods, and shakes his head to reinforce what he is saying, or to signal that he agrees or disagrees with Angela's comments. Andrew uses hand gestures to clarify what he is saying and to show size, distance, location, and other physical aspects of his message. While speaking, Andrew occasionally pauses the flow of speech to sip his coffee and this too is done easily and smoothly, never abruptly interfering with the flow of speech. For the most part, Andrew is unaware of the mechanics of what is being spoken and concentrates primarily on the ideas being shared and the pleasure he is experiencing conversing with Angela.

If the other patrons in the coffee shop could see air at the molecular level, they would see a remarkable acoustic event. Surrounding Andrew and Angela's bodies are billions and billions of air molecules. As Andrew speaks, these air molecules are set into vibration corresponding to his voice and articulation. For example, when Andrew says, "Angela," his vocal folds vibrate on the initial "a" speech sound. Each vocal fold contact sends acoustic shock waves upward and outward through Andrew's mouth and nose as air also slowly escapes from his oral tract. Also, in the production of the vowel "a" in Angela, Andrew's soft palate makes a seal preventing air and much of the sound energy from entering his nose. His tongue moves to a low position compared with his hard palate, and bunched toward the front of his mouth. This creates the articulatory adjustments necessary for the energy to resonant into the perceptual features of the "a" vowel. The sound waves emanating from his head correspond to the molecular disruptions occurring in his speech tract. This energy is transmitted through the air of the coffee shop as sound waves, the back and forth movements of air molecules similar to what occur with water waves. These sound waves are high and low pressure points traveling from Andrew to Angela.

After Andrew has produced the articulatory and voicing movements necessary to say the "a" vowel in "Angela," his articulators rapidly move into the position to produce the nasal "n." The tip of his tongue contacts the ridge of tissue behind his upper front teeth as his soft palate drops. These movements stop the air from escaping through his mouth, and direct it through his nose. Most of the voiced sound energy is also directed through his nasal cavity. Andrew makes the "g" speech sound by briefly stopping the airflow and voiced sound energy through his mouth using his tongue. (Actually, the "g" in Angela is a combination of the "d" and "g" speech sounds). Gliding his tongue from the top to the bottom of his mouth, Andrew makes the "l" speech sound, and finishes the word "Angela" with the "uh" vowel by elevating his tongue toward the back of his mouth. For each articulatory movement necessary for Andrew to say "Angela," there is sensory feedback monitoring the process. Of course, all of this is done subconsciously; Andrew is unaware of the movements and sensory feedback. Remarkably, the articulatory movements necessary to say the word "Angela" is completed in about one second.

As Andrew talks, there is also a rhythm to his speech; it is not choppy or broken. His brain plans and programs speech based on the available respiratory support, and the voicing, nasalization, and articulation are coordinated in a way that produces fluent, effortless utterances. Rarely does Andrew repeat, prolong, or otherwise struggle during speech; all of the neurologic and muscular events are produced with precision and ease. This is noteworthy given that Andrew can produce words very rapidly, more than 500 words per minute, eight to ten per second, and still be understood by Angela.

For an instant, Andrew's utterances are nothing more or less than acoustic energy. His thoughts and feelings are molecular vibrations, sound waves, traveling through time and space, and captured by Angela's ear. Andrew's thoughts, feelings, and experiences, words and their meanings, voicing, and articulatory valving of the compressed air coming from his lungs are reduced to energy transmitted through the medium of air. Through the miracle of speech communication, the depths of Andrew's thoughts, the totality of his experiences, and the joy and sadness expressed by this college student, for a brief time, are informational units encoded on sound waves. The frequency and amplitude of the complex speech sound waves carry information from speaker to listener, and sound energy is the connection between Andrew and Angela.

The sound waves travel at about 1,100 feet per second and reach Angela in a fraction of a second. (Andrew's visual communications, his facial expressions and gestures, reach Angela much more rapidly because they travel at the speed of light.) In contact with the air molecules vibrating in response to Andrew's speech production is Angela's eardrum, a small, thin membrane. Because her eardrum is in contact with the air molecules, this

Knowing the speed of sound can determine the distance of a lightning strike. Sound travels at about 1,130 feet per second. The lightning flash is seen at the speed of light, nearly instantaneously. If you count the number of seconds from the lightning flash to the time of the thunder and multiply it by 1,130 feet, you can figure out the distance of the lightning flash from your position.

extremely sensitive tissue vibrates in concert with them. Consequently, Angela's eardrum vibrates at a frequency and an amplitude corresponding to the source, that is, Andrew's speech production mechanism. Angela's eardrum is so sensitive that it can detect the smallest of molecular displacements. If it were any more sensitive, it could detect the sound of air rushing as people leave the coffee shop or move their hands through the air to swat a fly. Attached to Angela's eardrum are the three smallest bones of the human body, the hammer, anvil, and stirrup collectively known as the ossicles, which vibrate in unison with her eardrum and, in so doing, amplify and transmit energy to her cochlea.

So far in the process of communication, Andrew's words and language constructs have been transformed from electrochemical energy in his brain and nervous system, to the acoustic energy of sound waves, and at Angela's eardrum and ossicles of her middle ear, they become mechanical energy. For an instant, Andrew's thoughts, feelings, and experiences are the mechanical vibrations of Angela's eardrum and the bones of her middle ear. The bones of Angela's middle ear are in contact with a small shell-shaped structure, the cochlea, which contains the hearing sensory mechanism. At the fluid-filled cochlea, there is yet another energy transformation; Andrew's communication becomes hydraulic energy.

The footplate of middle ear bones, the stirrup, is connected to Angela's cochlea and vibrates in response to Andrew's speech. The cochlear fluid moves back and forth, and embedded in the fluid are nerve fibers, or hair cells, that convert the sound pressure waves into electrochemical energy. The electrochemical energy moves along the VIIIth cranial nerve, also known as the auditory nerve, to the base of Angela's brain where the nerve impulses are routed to a structure of her brain, the thalamus, also known as the "gatekeeper."

Acting as a gate, the thalamus allows some sensory information to reach consciousness while denying it to others. In this coffee shop, there is the ever present clanging of cups and saucers, high-pitched scream of boiled water being released, mumbled conversations, and the shuffling of patrons as they pass by Angela and Andrew's table. Through it all, Angela attends primarily to Andrew's utterances and automatically blocks competing sounds from reaching awareness. Although she is aware of the background noise at some level, it does not reach the conscious level to be processed as salient and meaningful information. Also, thanks to Angela's thalamus, other sensory stimulation such as the sights of students entering and exiting the union, taste of the expensive Italian coffee, and the way her new shoes pinch her toes are similarly reduced to background stimuli, and not the focus of her perceptions. (The only sense not routed through the thalamus is smell.) What does reach Angela's awareness are the speech sounds, words, and language constructs being rapidly uttered by Andrew.

The electrochemical signals gated by Angela's thalamus to reach her conscious awareness travel to both sides of her brain. Because Angela is right-handed and left brain-hemisphere dominant, the ones involving language primarily go to the temporal lobe of her left hemisphere. Here the auditory signals are decoded. (In her right hemisphere, Andrew's facial expressions, gestures, and other verbal and nonverbal aspects of communication are processed.) Because they are speaking the English language, Angela deciphers Andrew's acoustics energy into sounds and words they both understand. Her decoding includes the rules by which sounds are strung together to make English words, syntax, and grammar. What is most remarkable is Angela's understanding of Andrew's words, or more specifically, his morphemes, the smallest units of meaning in his utterances. Angela's semantic processors decode his utterances through a process of association involving her thoughts, feelings, and experiences.

During the communication acts in this coffee shop, the totality of Andrew's thoughts, feelings, and experiences are not physically transferred to Angela's brain. There is no neuron running from Andrew to Angela permitting all his images, feelings, and semantic association to be transferred. No matter how clearly Andrew expresses himself, and no matter Angela's listening and understanding, desire and ability, all that he communicates are stimuli with the potential of meaning. In fact, the belief that exact transference of information occurs during verbal communication is an illusion held by many persons.

During the verbal exchange, the words and sentences used by Andrew are drawn from his experiences and learning, and reflect his unique perspective on the world. The semantics of the words, and the way he phrases them, are based on Andrew's life experiences. Once expressed by Andrew, Angela interprets them based on her unique perspective on the world. Angela associates the messages based on her experiences and learning, which may be close or far removed from Andrew's. Although Angela may more accurately decode some information expressed by Andrew, such as the taste of the coffee or its temperature, other ideas are less likely to be precisely decoded. Complex and abstract ideas and notions, particularly those without some physical representation, may require several communication acts to prompt Angela to appreciate Andrew's meaning optimally, and even then, there is rarely, if ever, total sharing of information. As noted above, the absolute sharing of information between speaker and listener during verbal communication is an illusion.

Through the process of communication, the speaker prompts the listener to share associations based on verbal stimuli. Angela and Andrew are semantic reactors engaging in a sophisticated process of sharing common associations where each utterance has only the potential of meaning. The satisfaction of their encounter depends, in no small part, on how well they allow this process to work. A multitude of disabilities, diseases, disorders, and deficits afflicting humans also can dramatically alter the communication equation.

Connections Lost

The form and content of communication between these two college students would be substantially different if Andrew's cognition was impaired (Table 1–1). Physical (organic) and environmental (nonorganic) factors could have inhibited Andrew's mental growth affecting the quality and quantity of his thoughts. During gestation, Andrew could have suffered one or more irregularities retarding his mental development, and several birth complications could also result in impaired intelligence. Genetic abnormalities, and a host of environmental factors, could also have impaired his intelligence. Strokes, diseases, and traumatic brain injuries can also affect intelligence and consequently alter the form and content of communication. Andrew's intelligence, his ability to think rationally and to adapt to environmental changes, dictates the nature of his thoughts and ideas for expression. Reduced abilities to abstract, learn, remember, reason, and problem-solve can affect the substance of the expressed information.

Similar to cognitive impairments, organic and environmental factors also could have significantly altered Andrew's expressive language abilities. Expressive language disorders include the inability or impaired ability to express his thoughts, feelings, and intentions through spoken, gestured, or written symbols. Environmental factors, such as isolation or reduced interaction with others, and a variety of childhood diseases, defects, and disorders could cause Andrew to be unable or impaired in his ability to put his thoughts and feelings into a linguistic social code for expression. Expressive language disorders include phonologic disorders where mastery of adult rules for speech sound production is delayed, and semantic language impairments, namely, absent, deficient, or reduced vocabulary. Expressive grammatic disorders

Table 1–1. Functional Components of the Unified Model of
Communication Sciences and Disorders

Brain	Cognition	Mental Retardation/ Dementia
Broca's Area	Expressive language-motor speech programming	Expressive language delay/Aphasia; Apraxia of speech
Lungs	Respiration	Respiratory disorders
Larynx	Phonation	Laryngeal disorders
Articulators	Articulation	Articulation disorders
Velopharyngeal Port	Resonance	Velopharyngeal incompetence/ insufficiency
Cerebellum (and other structures)	Prosody	Stuttering/Cluttering/ Ataxic dysarthria
Atmosphere	Acoustic energy	Noise
Middle Ear	Mechanical energy	Conductive hearing loss
Inner Ear/ Cranial Nerve VIII	Hydraulic and electrochemical energy	Sensorineural hearing loss
Thalamus	Auditory perception	Auditory agnosia/ Auditory perceptual disorders
Wernicke's Area	Receptive language	Receptive language delay/Aphasia
Brain	Cognition	Mental retardation/ Dementia

involve knowing and using the form, usage, and rules of speaking and writing and can also include pragmatic disorders. Pragmatic disorders are social-communication impairments where Andrew would have problems appreciating the social context of language. Expressive aphasia, the loss of the ability to use language to express oneself, can eliminate or impair Andrew's communication at this stage in the process. Brain damage, such as occurs with strokes, head traumas, and diseases, can cause aphasia.

Motor speech disorders, apraxia of speech and the dysarthrias, are neuromuscular disorders affecting the motor (physical) movement necessary for speech production. Apraxia of speech is the inability to plan the motor speech movements necessary for an utterance. Apraxia of speech would cause Andrew to be impaired or unable to express himself verbally. Although he would know the meanings of words he wants to say, he would have problems planning the voluntary movements necessary for them. In severe apraxia of speech, he would be unable to program any speech into existence. In milder forms of the disorder, he would stumble and struggle during speech production and would have varying degrees of success self-correcting the errors.

The dysarthrias are a group of motor speech disorders impairing speech production due to flaccid, spastic, ataxic paralysis, and/or movement disorders. The dysarthrias can affect respiration, phonation, articulation, resonance, and prosody to varying degrees. Cerebral palsy, strokes, tumors, multiple sclerosis, muscular dystrophy, and Parkinson's disease, or other diseases, disorders, and defects can cause Andrew to have one or more of the motor speech disorders.

Respiration provides the compressed air and driving force for speech production, and any disease, disorder, or defect significantly affecting respiration may also cause Andrew to have trouble talking. Respiratory deficits cause reduced loudness, inappropriate and irregular syllable emphases, and problems with the speed and smoothness of speech. Tied to respiration is Andrew's phonation, the ability to vibrate his vocal folds. Severe voice disorders, such as occurs with cancer of the larynx, can eliminate Andrew's ability to speak. Vocal fold pathologies can cause him to be hoarse, breathy, and/or to have pitch and loudness disorders.

Andrew's ability to articulate could be eliminated by paralysis, and his speech intelligibility impaired by muscular weakness (paresis), structural abnormalities, improper learning, and other causative factors. Neuromuscular disorders such as multiple sclerosis, Parkinson's disease, and amyotrophic lateral sclerosis are a common cause of speech unintelligibility due to articulation impairments. Cosmetic articulation disorders, those speech sound production irregularities not impairing intelligibility but drawing attention to themselves (obtrusive), are caused by immature acquisition of phonologic rules and by perceptual-sensory-motor impairments. Additionally, deafness and psychological factors can cause mutism.

Had Andrew been one of the 700 live births with cleft lip and palate, the resonance of his speech would have been affected. Cleft palates are congenital fissures creating an opening between the oral and nasal cavities. His speech would be produced with an audible hiss of air escaping from his nose and the non-nasal speech sounds produced with too much nasality. Weakness and paralysis of the soft palate also can cause resonance disorders.

The prosody (melody) of Andrew speech involves the pitch and quality of his voice, stress and intonational patterns, and the fluency of his utterances. Although many speech pathologies can cause prosodic disturbances, stuttering is the primary fluency disorder. If Andrew stutters, repetitions and prolongations of sounds, syllables, words, and phrases disrupt the rhythm and flow of his speech. In addition, stuttering blocks, pauses before, between, and within words, further disrupt the flow of his speech. Stuttering is not limited to Andrew's speech repetitions, prolongations, and blocks, accessory features such as eye squints, head jerks, and other indications of struggle punctuate the broken speech flow. Often, Andrew and Angela feel anxiety as stuttering disrupts their communication, making it not an enjoyable, satisfying exchange, but a tense exercise in frustration, and sometimes, futility of expression.

The noise in the union's coffee shop can block verbal communication by interfering with the sound transmission of Andrew's speech to Angela's ears. Other disturbances in the coffee shop can momentarily distract speaker and listener, and require repetitions and less than satisfactory communication. To adapt for ambient noise, Andrew can raise the volume of his voice and Angela can watch his lips for cues about his utterances. The loudness and clarity of Andrew's messages would further be impaired if Angela's suffered from a hearing loss. Of course, to impair verbal communication substantially, the hearing loss would need to be in both of her ears (bilateral).

An obstruction of Angela's ear canal, such as a buildup of earwax, could disrupt the speech signals coming from Andrew. Angela could also have a ruptured eardrum, broken or fixed ossicular chain, or pressure buildup in her middle ear causing the mechanical stage of energy transmission from Andrew to be impaired. Head colds, sudden loud noises, and head traumas can cause pathologies of the external and middle ear, and a consequent conductive hearing loss.

Speech communication between Andrew and Angela would be impaired or impossible if Angela suffered damage to her cochlea or had impairments along the nerve pathways from her inner ear to her brainstem. The acoustic nerve (cranial nerve XIII) transmits auditory nerve impulses to the pons (bridge) structure of her brainstem. Although diseases, strokes, tumors, and traumas

The cochlea is to hearing as the eyes are to vision.

can damage her inner ear, frequent and lengthy exposures to loud noises are the most common causes of sensorineural hearing loss and deafness.

Beyond hearing loss and deafness, auditory perceptual disorders can impair the process of communication. Many areas and structures of Angela's brain are involved in auditory perception. Angela's brain operates as a whole rather than as independent structures but nonetheless, one brain structure, her thalamus, is very important to the process of "perceiving" Andrew's speech. Agnosia is the diagnostic label given to perceptual disorders. Auditory and acoustic agnosia involve the listener's inability to attend to and appreciate the significance of hearing information. Auditory agnosia includes the inability to appreciate speech and nonspeech information. A person with auditory agnosia might answer the telephone when someone knocks at the door or open the door when an alarm clock goes off. Acoustic agnosia is an aspect of auditory agnosia and relates only to speech discrimination; it is difficulty in discriminating the sounds of a language. In acoustic agnosia, the perceptual impairments are greater the more similar the speech sounds. Auditory attention, auditory figure-ground, and auditory analysis are required perceptual abilities for the process of communication to continue between Andrew and Angela.

Auditory attention is the ability to attend to auditory stimuli and includes auditory localization, the ability to know where a speaker is by his or her voice. Basic attention to Andrew's speech is necessary for Angela to process auditory information, and without auditory attention, the process of verbal communication would be interrupted. Auditory "figure" is the salient, and important information in the communicative information, and the "ground" is the unimportant information or nonessential aspects of the message. If Angela has difficulty with this aspect of auditory perception, she will be too distracted by the other sounds in the coffee shop to converse with Andrew meaningfully; Andrew's speech becomes no more important than the background noise. Auditory analysis is the ability to detect and perceive meaning in words, and if Angela were impaired in this perceptual ability, she would be unable to attend to and process the meaning in Andrew's utterances. These and other auditory perceptual disorders can be caused by a variety of diseases and defects, and also by learning disorders.

Angela's receptive language abilities allow her to decode and process Andrew's messages. Receptive language disorders involve the inability or impaired ability to comprehend Andrew's thoughts, feelings, and intentions. They would also affect Angela's abilities to read what Andrew has written. Environmental factors and a variety of childhood diseases, defects, and disabilities can cause receptive language disorders. Isolation or reduced interaction with others can cause Angela to be impaired or unable to understand the meaning of Andrew's words. Receptive aphasia resulting from a stroke, head trauma, or disease could cause Angela to be impaired or unable to decode Andrew's speech sound and grammatic codes, and eliminate or block retrieval of the meaning of his word. Genetic abnormalities, environmental factors, and brain damage could also impair Angela's intelligence, and alter the form and content of their communication. Consequently, Angela's reduced abilities to abstract, learn, remember, reason, and problem-solve would impair her ability to comprehend and relate to Andrew's verbal messages.

CHAPTER SUMMARY

Angela and Andrew are two college students sharing companionship and coffee in a student union. To others in the coffee shop, they are simply two individuals enjoying each other's company. On a deeper level, they are engaging in acts of communication, chains of physical and mental events, born from millions of years of evolution and remarkably capable of connecting their beings. These two humans express and comprehend a multitude of thoughts, feelings, and experiences through separate, but interconnected, mental and physical processes. Like all normal humans, Andrew and Angela were born with this innate ability to communicate, and it is second nature; they rarely give the underlying processes a thought. The rapid exchange of meanings connects them in a way that is distinctly human. This communication bridge will support their relationship now and in the future, and with unlimited possibilities. Unfortunately, a multitude of communication disorders can impair or destroy this remarkable ability.

Study and Discussion Questions

1. What brain hemisphere is associated with logical, verbal thought? What brain hemisphere is associated with creativity, visual, and spatial mental functions? What brain hemisphere do you believe is your dominant one? Why?

2. Provide your definition of language. How does language differ from speech?

3. Did you or a friend have a communication disorder when you were young? If so, what part or aspect of the communication chain was affected?

4. Hearing is sometimes called the second sense. Why? What is the primary sense? Is hearing secondary to other senses concerning learning language?

5. What factors make for a pleasant and rewarding communication experience? What factors make for an unpleasant and negative communication experience?

6. Can you study while watching television or does the distraction impair your ability to learn? Why can some persons study with distractions and others cannot?

7. What is meant when people say, "We are only arguing over semantics?" Is it important to agree on semantics? Why or why not?

8. Why is "lack of communication" listed as the number one reason many marriages fail? What steps can be taken to improve communication between marriage partners?

Suggested Reading

Denes, P., & Pinson, E. (1993). *The speech chain* (2nd ed.). New York: W.H. Freeman and Company.

Tanner, D. (2003). *Exploring communication disorders: A 21st century introduction through literature and media.* Boston: Allyn & Bacon.

CHAPTER 2

Communication Sciences and Disorders: The Discipline

"Originality is nothing but judicious imitation."

Voltaire

CHAPTER PREVIEW

In this chapter, the role communication plays in the 21st century and its importance in today's world are discussed. There is a review of the academic disciplines and specialties that involve communication sciences and disorders. Classification systems are explained providing a foundation for understanding the professionals and disciplines involved in the study of communication and treatment of its disorders. Additionally, several ethical and legal issues pertaining to communication sciences and disorders are reviewed. There is also comprehensive review of the Code of Ethics of the American Speech-Language-Hearing Association.

A Capstone Experience in Communication Sciences and Disorders

Many college students declare communication sciences and disorders as a major after having been introduced to the discipline in an introductory course or because a friend or an acquaintance has recommended it. Some students are in the education or health care fields, and find that their aptitudes and interests are better adapted to communication and its disorders. Other students may have become disenchanted with a major and elect communication sciences and disorders as a viable alternative. Juniors and seniors sometimes select communication sciences and disorders as a general type of major, one that will allow completion of their degrees in a timely manner. An increasingly large number of students are nontraditional in that they are typically older and have returned to college to pursue an alternative career. Many of these students take some or all of their courses online and through other distant learning means.

Several factors may have gone into the student's decision to major in communication sciences and disorders. The study of communication is fascinating. Communication is fundamental to developing and maintaining relationships. Interpersonal relationships are born from communication and thrive because of it; and the failure of communication is often cited for the reason so many marriages fail. In addition, the quality of the relationship between parents and children can often be measured by their communication. Friendships blossom and become long lasting because of easy, satisfying communication. Communication is the glue that bonds relationships, and regular and meaningful communication is necessary for people to grow together rather than apart.

It is also possible that the student appreciates the role communication has played, and continues to play, in the advancement of human civilization. The world would be dramatically different if not for human communication. The human evolutionary rise to prominence is directly related to our ancestors' ability to work cooperatively. Because of communication, early humans could share information that provided a powerful survival advantage. They could cooperatively hunt, gather, farm, and warn of danger. Social order among early humans also benefitted from the ability to communicate. Tribal and family structures more readily adapted to changing environmental conditions because of communication; options could be discussed, examined, and debated, providing more opportunities for them to adapt to a changing world. Primitive tribes and their gradually developing communication abilities sowed the seeds of present-day religious, legal, military, political, and education institutions.

Perhaps the student appreciates the role effective communication plays in business and industry. Communication allows businesses, from small establishments to international corporations, to prosper, and effective communication has never been more critical to their success. Today, communication has become an essential business requisite. In the past, a boss simply told a subordinate when and how to do a task; the job was primarily manual labor and did not involve extensive information sharing among employees. During the 20th century, a major change occurred in the way businesses conduct themselves. According to Ruben (2000), at the beginning of the 1900s, at least 80% of the workforce in the United States was primarily involved in manual labor and effective communication was only occasionally necessary. Today, effective communication is necessary for more than 60% of the labor force, and even the remaining blue collar and farming jobs depend, at least in part, on effective communication. In the modern information age, teams plan, carry out, and evaluate many business activities, and effective and efficient communication is fundamental to their success. Ruben (2000, p. 245) comments about communication and vocational opportunities: "The fitness of the person in the 21st century will be defined, for the most part, in terms of his or her ability to communicate effectively." In fact, in business and industry, the higher one goes up the corporate ladder, the more exclusively the job becomes one of communication. Presidents and chief executive officers do not physically work to produce the goods or services of the company, nevertheless, the company's success is due, in no small part, to their communication abilities.

Scientists and theorists have barely scratched the surface of knowing about the varied mechanisms involved in normal human communication. Consequently, it is not surprising that our understanding of communication disorders is also far from complete. The study, diagnosis, and treatment of communication disorders is a challenging discipline unto itself. Communication disorders can range from inconveniences such as mild stutters and speech imprecisions to complete inabilities to hear, voice, articulate, and use language. For people with communication disorders, they can be mild nuisances or devastating losses that dramatically affect quality of life.

Scientists and clinicians have three classification systems, or ways of classifying communication disorders. First, communication disorders can be classified by the diseases, disorders, or disabilities that caused them. For example, a patient may have the

Communication disorders cost the United States between $154 and $186 billion annually (Ruben, 2000).

slow, trembling speech characteristics of Parkinson's disease or the harsh voice of multiple sclerosis. Second, communication disorders may be classified by the site of the neurologic or muscular damage occurring in a patient. For example, a patient may have a damaged cochlea and the resulting sensorineural hearing loss or the slurred, distorted speech associated with spastic paralysis. The third and most widely used method of classifying communication disorders is by the process of normal communication that has been affected.

Communication Disorders Classified by Affected Process

As Table 2-1 shows, communication disorders can be separated into symbolic and nonsymbolic disorders. The symbolic disorders include language disorders in adults and delayed language acquisition in children. Symbolic disturbances involve the patient's inability or impaired ability to understand and engage in symbolic acts, and disorders include the inability or impaired ability to represent reality using language. Language delay and disorders are frequently divided into predominantly expressive and predominantly receptive categories. Expressive disorders include defective speaking, writing, and the use of expressive gestures. Receptive disorders include deficient verbal comprehension, reading, and the comprehension of gestures. Because mathematics is a language, the ability to perform and understand simple arithmetic may also be impaired.

The nonsymbolic disorders include hearing loss and deafness, and impairments in motor speech planning and execution. Motor speech disorders are nonsymbolic disorders of communication. They do not directly involve language, symbolic encoding, decoding, or manipulation in their symptomatology. The motor speech disorders can affect the five basic motor speech

Table 2–1. Communication Disorders Classified by Affected Process

Symbolic	*Nonsymbolic*
Language delay	Apraxia of speech
Language disorders	Dysarthrias
Language of confusion	Articulation and fluency disorders
Psychotic language	Hearing loss and deafness

processes: respiration, phonation (voicing), articulation, resonance, and prosody (rhythm of speech). Of course, the division between language and motor speech is ill-defined because the language symbol also contains the necessary elements for its production and comprehension.

The study of communication sciences and disorders involves delving into several diverse but related branches of knowledge, each a challenging discipline unto itself. Anatomy, physiology, acoustics, and cognition lie at the heart of communication sciences. The study of the diagnosis and treatment of communication disorders spans several disciplines including clinical neuroscience, psychology, and special education. There are also several medical and dental disciplines and specialties that concern communication sciences and disorders (see Table 2-2).

For the student, this diverse study of several separate but interconnected disciplines can be both exciting and frustrating. Certainly, it is exciting to study synapses, axons, muscle tissue, sound waves, and the thought processes that drive communication. Diagnosing pathologies and establishing treatments for people who suffer from communication disorders is equally satisfying. Yet, it can be frustrating for the student to comprehend each aspect of communication sciences and disorders as a meaningful part of a complete whole. Communication is the highest evolved function of which humans are capable, and the disorders, diseases, and disabilities that damage it sometimes seem hard to comprehend. Understandably, students may feel overwhelmed by the sheer magnitude of their academic and clinical undertakings.

Disciplines Involved in Communication Sciences

The Sciences of Human Anatomy and Physiology

Anatomy is the study of the structure of the human organism and the science of its morphology (form). Several specialties of anatomy are pertinent to the study of communication sciences. (Zemlin, 1998). Cytology and histology are the study of cells and tissues. Embryonic and fetal anatomy concern the development of the human organism from conception to birth and address the morphology of the communication structures in the developing human. Gross anatomy, viewing with the naked eye (as opposed to microanatomy, or viewing parts of the body with magnification), descriptive anatomy, functional relationships of

In 1601, Julius Casserius published the first specialized illustrated text on speech and hearing anatomy and physiology: *De Vocis Auditusque Organis Historia Anatomica* (Kent, 1997).

Table 2–2. Disciplines Involved in Communication Sciences

Communication Sciences	Communication Disorders	Medical and Dental Specialties
Anatomy:	*Clinical Neurosciences and Psychology:*	Dentistry
Cytology	Clinical Psychology	Gerontology
Descriptive Anatomy	Neuropsychology	Laryngology
Embryonic Anatomy		Neurology
Fetal Anatomy	*Special Education:*	Orthodontics
Gross Anatomy	Autism Spectrum	Otolaryngology
Histology	Deaf-Visual Impairment	Otology
Practical Anatomy	Learning Disability	Otorhinolaryngology
Topographic Anatomy	(Resource Teacher)	Pediatrics
	Multihandicap	Psychiatry
Physiology:		Physiatry
Applied Physiology		Radiology
Cellular Physiology		
Special Physiology		
Acoustics:		
Acoustic Phonetics		
Physiologic Acoustics		
Psychoacoustics		
Cognition:		
Childhood Language Development		
Cognitive Psychology		
Cognitive Neuroscience		
Developmental Psychology		
Psycholinguistics		

individual systems, and practical anatomy, the application of several clinical disciplines, are also involved in the study of speech and hearing. However, speech and hearing anatomy is technically a branch of topographic anatomy, which concerns the head, neck, and trunk, and the relationship of two or more systems.

Whereas anatomy examines *structure*, physiology addresses *function*. Human physiology is the study of functional activity and the normal vital processes of cells, muscles, organs, and other structures. Physiology concerns normal vital processes and how living organisms work, but it also can include the effects of disease and other agents. Like anatomy, the specialties of physiology are pertinent to the study of communication sciences. According to Zemlin (1998), applied physiology is the application of physiologic knowledge of problems in medicine and industry. Cellular physiology addresses cellular vital process and functional activities individually or collectively. Zemlin (1998) notes that special physiology addresses the functional activity of some organ, such as the study of individual structures involved in communication.

The Science of Acoustics

"Sounds are the currency of auditory-oral communication" (Plante & Beeson, 2004, p. 40) and the science of acoustics, a branch of physics, concerns the physical nature of sound, hearing, and auditory perception. Speech sounds are constantly changing molecular vibrations, complex sound waves emanating from the speaker. Sound energy is transmitted through the medium of air and the listener's hearing mechanism senses the ever changing frequency and amplitude changes, perceives salient aspects of the auditory signal, and associates the signal with other stored memories. Specialties of acoustics include psychoacoustics addressing the quantification of sensation and measurement of its psychological correlates (Durrant & Loverinic, 1995). It is the study of acoustic stimulation and corresponding psychological responses. Acoustic phonetics addresses the physical properties of speech sounds and their auditory perceptual features. Physiologic acoustics concerns the functions and workings of the auditory system in response to physical stimuli.

The Sciences of Cognition

Cognition and language are inseparable. Broadly defined, cognition is "thinking" and the mental process involved in knowing oneself and the environment. It includes all the processes that go into thinking and knowing including learning and memory. More specifically, cognition includes encoding, decoding, and manipulating verbal symbols as is done with language. Cognitive neuroscience addresses the activities of the brain and their role in how the human mind works (Bear, Connors, & Paradiso, 1996). Psycholinguistics combines psychology and linguistics to explore grammatic rules and psychological functions as they pertain to language competence and performance. Cognitive psychology is a branch of psychology specifically addressing thought, memory, and learning. Developmental psychology and childhood language development are psychological and educational specialties addressing the role childhood experience plays in the development of thought and language. Cognition is the mental foundation of communication sciences and disorders because of the role language has in thought and vice versa.

Disciplines and Specialties Involved in Communication Disorders

Clinical Neuroscience, Psychology, and Special Education

Neuroscience concerns the study of the brain, spinal cord, and nerves of the body and clinical neuroscience addresses neurogenic diseases and disorders, and their diagnosis and treatment. Several clinical neuroscience professions intersect with communication disorders. Clinical psychology is a branch of psychology addressing the diagnosis of behavioral and emotional disorders and the use of psychological principles and techniques to treat them. Neuropsychology is a combination of neurology and psychology, and addresses the cognitive, learning, memory, and behavioral problems experienced by patients with neurogenic disorders.

Special education is an education discipline with several specialties. The specialty as a teacher of children with multiple handicaps addresses the education of children with two or more disabilities. The specialty as a learning disability specialist (resource teacher) addresses a wide range of disabilities seen in the classroom. The specialty as a teacher of the deaf and visually impaired concerns education of children who are hard of hearing, deaf, and/or visually impaired. The autism spectrum specialty addresses the teaching of children with pervasive developmental disabilities.

Medical and Dental Specialties Involved in Communication Disorders

Dentistry and orthodontics are also involved in communication disorders because of the role dentition (teeth) plays in articulation. Speech-language pathologists conduct oromyofunctional therapy, sometimes called tongue thrust therapy, to help orthodontists in the treatment of malocclusions. In dysphagia therapy, sometimes called swallowing therapy, speech-language pathologists are concerned with mastication (chewing), and the role teeth and occlusion play in swallowing. Dentistry and orthodontics are also involved in the diagnosis and treatment of orofacial anomalies, for example, cleft lip and palate.

Radiography, sometimes called cineradiography or fluoroscopy, is the use of X-rays to depict images of the body's internal structures. The video swallowing study (VSS) is integral to the diagnosis and treatment of dysphagia. Other brain scanning techniques, such as computed tomography (CT), magnetic resonance imaging (MRI) and functional magnetic resonance imaging (fMRI), single photon tomography (SPECT), and positron emission tomography (PET) are also used in communication disorders research, diagnostics, and therapeutics.

Communication disorders also intersect with otology and laryngology which are involved in the diagnosis and treatment of diseases and disorders of the ear, larynx, and related head and neck structures. Otolaryngology and otorhinolaryngology are combined medical specialties addressing the ear and throat, and the ear, nose, and throat, respectively. Pediatrics and gerontology are involved in special medical issues in children and the elderly many of whom have age-related communication disorders. Medical specialists in physiatry, sometimes called physical medicine and rehabilitation, address rehabilitation issues involving communication disorders. Neurology is a branch of medicine concerned with the brain, nervous system, and their disorders, and psychiatry is a branch involved in the diagnosis and treatment of mood, personality, and behavioral disorders. In addition, nursing has several specialties that concern the care and treatment of patients with communication disorders.

Given the complicated multiple processes involved in communication sciences and disorders, it is not surprising that this discipline spans many medical, dental, educational, psychological, and academic fields. Communication is a highly sophisticated mental, physical, and neurologic process involving the brain and nervous system, muscles of the head, neck, and trunk, the physics of sound, and the highest cognitive abilities humans perform. In addition hundreds, if not thousands, of diseases and disorders can affect this sophisticated process involving the educational, medical, and rehabilitation specialists charged with their diagnosis and treatment. The study of communication sciences requires a broad-based interdisciplinary education, and the diagnosis and treatment of communication disorders are health care and educational professions.

The American Speech-Language-Hearing Association

In the United States and many other countries, there are two general types of speech and hearing service models. The first involves the free enterprise system, capitalism, and the private sector. The second, the socialistic model, involves the social welfare system and government-sponsored programs.

The scientific study of communication explores the highest human function known on this planet, and the diagnosis and treatment of its disorders is no less a profound undertaking. As seen by the above discussion of related disciplines and specialities, communication sciences and disorders is a broad-based, all-encompassing scientific, educational, and health care discipline. In the United States, the primary national association that represents scientists and practitioners in communication sciences and disorders is the American Speech-Language-Hearing Association (ASHA). It was founded in 1925 and currently has approximately 120,000 members.

The propagation of scientific research into communication disorders is one of the major activities of the American Speech-Language-Hearing Association. The Association funds research, publishes several journals, and sponsors annual national conventions. ASHA also sets and enforces ethical standards for practicing speech-language pathologists and audiologists.

Ethics and Law

Ethics is a branch of philosophy. It is also the foundation of most religions, and every profession, more or less, is concerned with the concepts of right and wrong, and the goodness or badness of individual and collective actions. Ethics are sets of moral principles, and morals are standards of individual behavior. Laws, on the other hand, are a collection of rules created by a state to govern the conduct of its citizens. Laws are enforced by state-imposed penalties, and professional ethics are regulated by professional associations and sanctions. Professional ethics, while also an aspect of law, are generally defined rules involving the degree to which a person conforms to accepted standards of professional conduct. Certainly, ethics and laws overlap, but what is legal may or may not be ethical and vice versa.

Laws and Ethical Standards in Communication Sciences

The scientific pursuit of knowledge in communication sciences and disorders requires attention to many of the same ethical, legal, and moral issues faced by researchers in other scientific disciplines. Ethical and legal issues related to subject selection, research design, statistics, interpretation of results, and so forth, addressed by neuroscientists, biologists, psychologists, linguists, and other scientists are also addressed by speech and hearing scientists. However, speech and hearing scientists also address ethical, legal, and moral issues uniquely related to the scientific study of communication and its disorders. As will be discussed, the study of communication and its disorders poses several unique ethical and legal issues not confronted in other social and behavioral sciences.

Speech and hearing scientists, like all scientists, must abide by laws protecting the rights of subjects. Subjects for speech and hearing research must read (or otherwise be informed), agree to, and sign informed consent documents. They must be told of all foreseeable risks associated with the research, and understand the general purpose of the study. When children (or other dependent individuals) are used in research, their parents or legal guardians must also sign informed consent documents. No person can participate in research without agreeing to it and he or she can stop participation at any time. Because most speech and hearing research is conducted at institutions of higher education, colleges and universities have committees and protocols to govern research practices.

Violations of laws and ethical standards in speech and hearing research have been rare. However, recently some subjects used in stuttering research in the mid 1900s have brought legal action against a Midwestern university in a well-publicized case of alleged subject abuse in children from an orphanage. Some now-adult subjects in the stuttering research project contend that the principal investigators caused them to stutter in an attempt to prove a theory about the cause of stuttering, and that they suffered from the disorder throughout their lives. The theory being tested, the diagnosogenic theory of stuttering (Johnson, 1938), contends that misdiagnosis of normal nonfluencies can have a self-fulfilling effect. The research examined the hypothesis that convincing a child who is simply going through a normal period of disfluency that his or her speech is stuttering, can cause that person to stutter.

All the facts regarding this case have yet to be disclosed, and whereas some of the researchers and subjects are no longer living, the veracity of the allegations is undetermined. However, the university has apologized for the research design, and noted that today, such research would not be possible given the protections for subjects. Although the research design may have been unethical, and using orphaned subjects deplorable, some good may have come from the study. The fact that some subjects believed that stuttering was caused by the study gives face validity to the hypothesis that drawing attention in a negative manner to normal nonfluencies may precipitate stuttering. Today, the Diagnosogenic Theory of Stuttering may help prevent unnecessary stuttering in some children. (For more about this study, read *Ethics: A Case Study from Fluency*, edited by Robert Goldfarb, Ph.D., and published by Plural Publishing, Inc., San Diego.)

Laws and Ethical Standards in Speech-Language Pathology and Audiology

With the establishment of licensure, individual states now have statutes governing the practice of speech-language pathology and audiology and enforce penalties for practitioners who violate them. Although there is considerable variability in licensure laws, states dictate the minimum educational and training levels and continuing education requirements. States also may require background checks for past criminal conduct and require fingerprinting for identification and verification. States may require that licenses be renewed annually and, of course, assess and collect application and licensing fees. Although states vary widely in their enforcement of speech-language pathology and audiology licensing laws, there may be criminal penalties for practicing without a license. Licensees who violate laws governing the practice of speech-language pathology and audiology are also subject to criminal penalties, fines, suspension, and revocation of their license.

In the practice of speech-language pathology and audiology, there are two primary employment settings: medical and educational. Each employment setting has unique ethical and legal challenges faced by the practitioner. While there is overlap in the ethical and legal issues faced by all speech-language pathologists and audiologists, practitioners employed in medical settings face unique issues related to types of patients and disorders seen in hospitals, nursing homes, rehabilitation facilities, and clinics. Similarly, speech-language pathologists and audiologists in public, private, parochial, and charter schools address educational issues not typically seen in medical environments. Although there are several other employment settings, and private practice, the majority of ethical and legal issues faced by speech-language pathologists and audiologists are associated with either the general practice of medicine or providing services in educational systems.

As noted above, legislating ethics and morality, while often inherent in the motivations and objectives of laws and regulations, can sometimes result in incompatible outcomes. There are a wide variety of social and political perspectives on laws and morality. Some extremists believe that laws and regulations provided by a governing body are inherently unethical and immoral; they do not recognize this type of authority. Others argue that only religion can provide ethical and moral guidance, and some believe that only a particular religion can guide ethical and moral behavior. Some persons are ethical and moral relativists and believe that ethics and morality are personal decisions made under specific circumstances; no generalizations can be made to encompass all ethical and moral decisions.

Professional ethics are inherently political statements, relating to the interests of a profession, the status of the professional organization, and the conduct of its members. Most professions create written codes of ethics and update them regularly to reflect the changing times. Most of these codes detail minimum ethical and moral rules by which all decent humans should abide when interacting with other humans. Some however, extend their codes of ethics to include specific political views of the governing body, and not necessarily those held by the majority of the professional association or the general public. They directly or indirectly promote a specific political perspective and political correctness they consider ethical and moral. However, because the creators of professional codes of ethics are usually elected representatives of the greater professional body as a whole, they are democratically based, and more or less, representative of its individual members.

The Code of Ethics of the American Speech-Language-Hearing Association

The preamble of the Code of Ethics of the American Speech-Language-Hearing Association (2005, p. 1) states the importance of professional ethical practice: "The preservation of the highest standards of integrity and ethical principles is vital to the responsible discharge of obligations in the professions of speech-language pathology and audiology. This Code of Ethics sets forth the fundamental principles and rules considered essential to this purpose." The Code of Ethics lists and defines principles and rules of ethical conduct, yet only provides for minimal ethical standards of ethical conduct. The preamble also states that failure to specify particular responsibilities or practices in the code does not deny their existence.

The American Speech-Language-Hearing Association lists four principles of ethics with rules detailing individual conduct regarding them. Below, the Principles of Ethics are listed as well as a summary of the rules pertaining to them. Critical analyses of the controversial ethical principles and the rules that support them are also provided.

Principle of Ethics I: Individuals shall honor their responsibility to hold paramount the welfare of persons they serve professionally.

The Rules of Ethics regarding the above principle state that all services shall be provided competently, clinicians shall use every resource available, not discriminate in the delivery of services, and inform persons they serve of the nature and possible effects of services rendered and products dispensed. While not guaranteeing the results of services or products, clinicians must evaluate and render services only with reasonable expectation of benefit. Speech-language pathologists and audiologist shall not treat solely by correspondence, shall maintain adequate records, and respect the privacy of persons served. Charging for services not rendered is considered unethical as is providing services while the clinician is adversely affected by substance abuse or other health-related conditions.

Although Principle of Ethics I attempts to address the welfare of persons professionally served by speech-language pathologists and audiologists, it is ambiguous with regard to the term "competently." Competent performance suggests that the person has the essential and up-to-date skills and knowledge to complete a task successfully. The question arises whether individuals whose terminal degree is a Master of Arts or Science has acquired the necessary information, learned the required skills, and can competently provide clinical services in diverse employment settings, to a multitude of clients and patients of all ages, and address the communication disorders arising from thousands of etiologies. Even if the terminal degree in speech-language pathology were raised to a clinical doctorate, as is the case with audiology, is it reasonable to assume that a person who has competently practiced the profession in a public school with communication delayed or disordered children can transition to a medical setting, and provide equally competent services for patients with traumatic brain injury, swallowing disorders, aphasia, and so forth? Given the dramatic increase in information about communication sciences and disorders that has occurred in the past 20 years, and the expansion of clinical responsibilities, is it not reasonable for the clinical doctorate to become the terminal degree in speech-language pathology, and specialty certification required?

Principle of Ethics II: Individuals shall honor their responsibility to achieve and maintain the highest level of professional competence.

The Rules of Ethics regarding the above principle state that clinicians shall hold, or be in the process of obtaining, the appropriate Certificate of Clinical Competence, continue their professional development, delegate the provision of clinical services appropriately, and use properly working and calibrated equipment.

This Principle of Ethics, and others, address the evolving role of support personnel in the provision of clinical speech and hearing services. In 2003, the American Speech-Language-Hearing Association attempted to regulate support personnel by certifying Speech-Language Pathology Assistants (SLPA). The Association dropped this certification soon thereafter for several reasons including the costs involved in the certification process. Now, the American Speech-Language-Hearing Association sets guidelines for the training and supervision of support personnel, and has made SLPAs' clinical competency and performance an ethical extension of the supervising speech-language pathologist. In effect, competent clinical performance by a speech-language pathology assistant is the ethical responsibility of the supervising speech-language pathologist.

Principle of Ethics III: Individuals shall honor their responsibility to the public by promoting public understanding of the professions, by supporting the development of services designed to fulfill the unmet needs of the public, and by providing accurate information in all communications involving any aspect of the professions.

Specifically prohibited by the Rules of Ethics for Principle III are the misrepresentations of professional credentials and clinical proficiencies, engaging in conflicts of interest and fraudulent practices, and falsely representing diagnostic information for financial gain. This clause also addresses the relationship between the ASHA member and the public; statements and advertising shall not be misrepresented.

Although misrepresentation for financial gain can be alleged in any speech and hearing clinical practice, this ethical stipulation can be an issue in hearing aid dispensing and the treatment of stuttering. In the past, some hearing aid dispensers have allegedly made untrue or inaccurate statements. For example, they have said that if a patient does not purchase a hearing aid, his or her hearing acuity will continue to decline and that amplification will arrest the decline. Statements were also allegedly made that a hearing aid will improve a patient's ability to hear speech when, in fact, this clinical prognosis had questionable validity. Some speech-language pathology practitioners promised a "cure" to stuttering if a person participated in a particular therapy or wore a prosthetic. Although there are gray areas in determining the value of hearing aids on speech discrimination, hearing aids do not prevent hearing loss. When advertising a particular stuttering treatment, care should be taken to define what is meant by a "cure" for the disorder and making the symptoms more "manageable."

Principle of Ethics IV: Individuals shall honor their responsibilities to the professions and their relationships with colleagues, students, and members of allied professions. Individuals shall uphold the dignity and autonomy of the professions, maintain harmonious interprofessional and intraprofessional relationships, and accept the professions' self-imposed standards.

The American Academy of Audiology (AAA) was founded in 1988. Its mission is to provide quality hearing care to the public, enhance the ability of members to achieve career objectives, provide professional development through education and research, and to increase public awareness of hearing disorders and audiologic services.

Rules of Ethics pertaining to the above Principle prohibits anyone under their supervision from engaging in violations of the Code of Ethics, dishonesty, fraud, deceit, and misrepresentation with regard to clinical practice and research. Specifically prohibited is the provision of professional services without exercising independent professional judgment. Discrimination in professional relationships is also prohibited. The Code of Ethics states that individuals who have reason to believe that the Code of Ethics has been violated must inform the Ethical Practice Board and participate in investigations of alleged violations.

The prohibition of providing professional services without exercising independent professional judgment addresses the distinction between a "prescribed" and "referred" medical or educational services. A prescribed service is one where a professional from another discipline determines the diagnosis and treatment objectives, frequency and duration of services, and exercises professional control over the quantity and quality of the treatment being provided. In the medical setting, a physician may attempt to prescribe the speech and hearing services to a patient. In an educational setting, a neuropsychologist, teacher, or special education director may attempt to detail the nature and extent of services provided to a child in special education. A referred service, on the other hand, is one where a physician or educational specialist brings to the professional attention of a speech-language pathologist or audiologist a specific patient or client. The speech-language pathologist or audiologist determines the speech and hearing diagnosis, treatment parameters, and prognosis. According to the Principle of Ethics IV, upon referral, practitioners must act independently; speech-language pathology and audiology are referred and not prescribed services.

CHAPTER SUMMARY

The rise of human prominence on this planet is due, in no small part, to communication. It has dramatically influenced, and continues to influence, the very nature of human existence. Communication provides the means for human growth and cooperation, whether people are involved in business and industry, law, religion, education, interpersonal relationships, or any other human endeavor. Human communication is complex, dynamic, and multifaceted, and so it is not surprising that many academic and clinical disciplines are involved in its study. Anatomy, physiology, acoustics, cognition, special education, psychology, and the clinical neurosciences are involved in the study of human communication and the treatment of its disorders. State laws and regulations, and the American Speech-Language-Hearing Association, enforce legal and ethical standards for the scientific study of communication and the treatment of its disorders.

Study and Discussion Questions

1. How are students typically exposed to the discipline of communication sciences and disorders? How were you introduced to it?

2. In descending order of importance, list the factors that should be considered when selecting a college major. Discuss the relative importance of each factor.

3. Compare human communication with the types of communication seen in lower animals. Do lower animals have communication disorders? Why or why not?

4. Discuss the "job interview" relative to the importance of effective communication. What are desirable and undesirable messages to be communicated during a job interview? How would a communication disorder, such as stuttering or lisping, affect the interview?

5. How are communication disorders classified? List three examples in each classification category.

6. Compare symbolic and nonsymbolic communication disorders.

7. List and define the disciplines involved in the communication sciences.

8. List and define the disciplines involved in the study, diagnosis, and treatment of communication disorders.

9. Provide an example where a law may be unethical and immoral. Provide an example of an ethical and moral standard that should be covered by law.

10. Discuss professional issues associated with each of the four Principles of Ethics of the American Speech-Language-Hearing Association.

Suggested Reading

Justice, L. (2006). *Communication sciences and disorders: An introduction.* Upper Saddle River, NJ: Pearson/Merrill Prentice Hall.

Kent, R. D. (1997). *The speech sciences.* San Diego, CA: Singular Publishing Group.

Power, G. (2002). Communication sciences and disorders: The discipline. In R. Gillam, T. Marquardt, & F. Martin (Eds.), *Communication sciences and disorders: From science to clinical practice* (pp. 3–24). San Diego, CA: Singular Publishing Group.

Tanner, D. (2003). *Exploring communication disorders: A 21st century introduction through literature and media.* Boston: Pearson Allyn & Bacon.

Tanner, D. (2006). *Case studies in communication sciences and disorders.* Upper Saddle River, NJ: Pearson/Merrilll Prentice Hall.

Zemlin, W. (1998). *Speech and hearing science* (4th ed.). Boston: Allyn & Bacon.

CHAPTER 3

The Acquisition of Knowledge in Communication Sciences and Disorders

"The striking similarities between Indian, Greek and German philosophy are easy to explain. Their languages have a common origin and a similar grammar that unconsciously dominates and directs them. These similarities bar other ways of interpreting the world."

Friedrich Nietzsche

CHAPTER PREVIEW

Because of the massive amount of information being provided to speech and hearing scientists and clinicians in the 21st century, it is necessary to be intelligent information consumers. This chapter explores the two major forces in the acquisition of knowledge: believing and knowing. The theories of the origin of language and language disorders are provided to illustrate the notions of believing and knowing. There is a historical review of the study of communication and its disorders including the contributions of ancient physicians and philosophers. Modern epistemology, the philosophy of knowledge acquisition, is reviewed concerning communication sciences and disorders with an emphasis on rationalism and empiricism.

The Age of Information

In the mid 1900s, a fuse was lit causing an explosion of knowledge, and harkening the current "Age of Information." That fuse was the invention of the silicon chip. During the past 50 years, the silicon chip has gradually altered the very nature of human existence. The silicon chip, and computer revolution it spawned, has substantially changed human interaction. The life-altering changes caused by this small electronic device undoubtably will continue into the 21st century and the discipline of communication sciences and disorders will reap many of its benefits. It will be a brave new world of professional opportunities, but also a future filled with Orwellian pitfalls.

The explosion of knowledge and the technological advances that followed the development of the silicon chip have dramatically influenced industrialized societies. Computers have changed the nature of many time-honored human interactions. Ever more homes have at least one personal computer, and digital high-definition and plasma televisions are becoming commonplace. Schoolchildren spend much of their time talking on cell phones while walking to and from classes, waiting at bus stops, and standing in lunch lines. Telephone numbers are voice-activated, and many are picture and video phones, an invention that was the domain of science fiction only a few years ago.

Directly or indirectly, the Internet reaches into the lives of most people, and every day becomes ever more a part of modern living. Only a few years ago, families got their news and information only from newspapers, books, and the major television networks, played board games, and chatted with friends on telephone land lines. Today, instant news and access to vast stores of information are at the fingertips of every person with a wired or wireless Internet connection. Children play video games so realistic that the military uses them to prepare soldiers for combat, and flight training programs use them for ground school. Internet chat and discussion rooms have created an abundance of opportunities for people to meet and develop relationships completely in cyberspace. No billboard advertisement would be complete without a "dot com" reference, and more and more shopping is done on the Internet. An increasingly large number of the workforce works from home.

The list of information and technologic advances directly and indirectly attributable to the silicon chip is far too great to list. Few institutions have not been dramatically affected by the computer revolution; the silicon chip has altered the military, religion, medicine, business, science, and education. Laser-guided smart bombs, global-positioning technology, and night-vision goggles have changed the way modern military operations are conducted. Churches have Web sites and there are virtual services, weddings, and funerals. The genome project in medicine, and the successful mapping of human genes, have increased understanding of many diseases and are offering cures to the previously incurable. Although the "paperless office" did not come to fruition, e-mails, attachments, and computer file folders are as much a part of business as paperclips, pens, and pencils. Today, scientists use in their research desktop computers having more speed and memory than the early mainframes used to launch astronauts into space. Distant learning technology has enabled many courses to be offered via the Web and most face-to-face ones are Web-enhanced. Most colleges and universities offer some or all of their training in communication sciences and disorders via the Internet.

Intelligent Information Consumption

Today, more scientists are conducting research than the total number of scientists that ever lived. Scientific advances are announced on daily television newscasts, the Internet, and in newspapers. Never in the history of humanity have people been so inundated with miracle drugs, anthropologic discoveries, super-computing marvels, spectacular photographs of distant galaxies, and nearly incomprehensible theories about time, space, and the origin of the universe. Genes are being discovered providing explanations for all that ails humans from obesity to stuttering. Physicists are working frantically on the TOE (theory of everything), unifying our understanding of the atom and the cosmos. Scientists are ringing the massive information bell and there is no way to unring it, nor should there be. The pace of these new and sometimes disturbing breakthroughs is increasing; the future promises more and even greater discoveries. Unquestioned past belief systems that provided explanations about the world seem to be under attack by these unrelenting scientific advances. To many, it seems that past tried-and-true beliefs about mankind's place in the universe, and the meaning of human existence, are undergoing dramatic revisions. Communication lies at the heart of the information age, and the discipline of communication sciences and disorders is not removed from the challenges facing it.

Today, because of the massive amount of near-instantaneously available information, being intelligent information consumers is necessary. Information users, be they scientists, clinicians, or the general public, must become thoughtful consumers; no longer can facts be taken at face value, books believed true simply because they are in print, and the veracity of Web sites go unchallenged. Intelligent consumers of information must recognize the difference between that which is believed to be true and information proven to be factual. A clear understanding of these differences will provide the framework for acting on the massive amount of information available in the speech and hearing sciences and concerning clinical practice.

To know something is to have proof that can be replicated and shared with others, that is, the knowledge is verifiable. The most powerful way to know something in communication sciences and disorders is through the scientific method. However, to know something does not require several scientific studies all leading to the same conclusion. There are other ways of knowing such as logical deduction, reason, and observed consistency of one phenomenon with other observed phenomena. These concepts are discussed in detail in subsequent sections of this book.

Believing, on the other hand, involves accepting or rejecting something in the absence of proof. Belief involves intuition, not reason, and is often the unquestioned acceptance of an existing assumption about the nature of the world. Religions are belief systems where acceptance of information precedes discovery of the facts leading to them. In a belief system, an understanding of something is accepted on face value, and discovery of the process leading to the belief is not relevant or necessary. Often, believing fills the void created by the absence of knowing. In the broadest sense, knowing is a product of science, and believing is a product of faith. By necessity, speech and hearing scientists and clinicians operate on both the knowing and believing levels.

Science and belief systems appear to be at odds in several aspects of understanding communication and in the treatment of its disorders. Science views communication as a knowable series of cognitive, neurologic, muscular, acoustic, and perceptual events allowing the exchange of information between two or more people. Disorders of communication are treated by the provision of counseling, instruction, surgeries, medications, and therapies that have been tested by the scientific method, and proven effective to eliminate, minimize, or remedy them.

Many organized religions, and other belief systems, view communication as a divine creation and essentially as a metaphysical event. Communication, in all its modes, is fundamental to religious institutions and permits the study and acceptance of religious doctrine, ministry, meditation, conversion, and prayer. After all, according to some religions, "In the beginning was the Word." While accepting some scientific tenants, many belief systems also adhere to ritualistic treatments such as prayer, exorcism, healing ceremonies, laying-on-of-hands, and other expressions of supernatural intervention. Belief systems about communication and its disorders can include organized doctrine, intuition, and loosely held spiritual beliefs.

Language: Believing and Knowing

No better example exists between the believing and knowing dichotomy than in the origin and nature of languages, and by extension, language disorders. According to some Christian and Hebraic believers, the biblical parable of the tower of Babel explains the varied languages of the world; to prevent the building of the tower, God created different languages. In this belief system, multiple languages were created to eliminate human cooperation in the construction of the tower of Babel, and to inhibit human curiosity and exploration. Creationists believe this is a literal account for multiple languages of the world. In the Creation view, before attempting to build the Tower of Babel, there was only one language spoken by the people of the world. This language, or tongue, was part of the divine creation of humans, and because humans were created in God's image, it was the language of that deity. Currently, there are about 10,000 languages and dialects in use, and according to this belief system, they exist because of this supernatural event. The word "babbling" grew from this parable. Also, according to this belief system, communication disorders are a result of supernatural forces. In Exodus 4:10, there is a reference to communication disorders: "And Moses said unto the Lord, O my Lord, I am not eloquent, neither heretofore, nor since thou hast spoken unto thy servant; but I am slow of speech and slow of tongue. And the Lord said unto him, Who hath made man's mouth? or who maketh the dumb, or deaf, or the seeing, or the blind? have not I the Lord?"

> The Whorfian hypothesis proposes that the words and structure of a language determine how a speaker of that language thinks.

The evolutionary view of the origin of languages differs fundamentally from the Creation belief system. The evolutionary theory is a result of anthropologic and linguistic research. In the evolutionary theory of multiple languages, early human societies were isolated from each other, and thus developed unique languages because of this isolation. According to the evolutionary theory, there are no pre-existing set rules dictating the creation of words and what they mean. The sound combinations that make up words are purely arbitrary. (Contrary to Einstein's refrain, at least with respect to semantics, God does play craps with the universe.) The semantics of language were agreed upon early in the development of societies. A sound or a series of sounds uttered by people of a language community overtime came to mean the thought, event, thing, or feeling to which they were referring. Because early societies were isolated from one another, there were differences to what the sound combinations referred, and some languages have sounds that others do not use. This isolation of language societies accounts for the many different languages and dialects of the world. The same arbitrary rules of semantics hold true for new words that become part of languages each year. What is most important, according to the evolutionary view of language, is that language is simply a more evolved animalistic function, and not unique to humans or divinely inspired. The evolutionary theory of language includes the role it plays in survival of the species. Language has served, and continues to serve, a powerful survival function. In the scientific view of language disorders, treatment follows the educational and medical models.

Two separate but interconnected ways of understanding communication sciences and disorders are believing and knowing. Certainly, the most powerful force of information is knowing through the scientific method. As discussed in subsequent chapters, there are degrees of power in the scientific method; some types of research provide stronger and more vigorous knowledge than others. Also to be discussed are relative strengths of belief systems and their role in understanding communication and the myriad disorders that can affect it. Both believing and knowing have their place in communication sciences and disorders, but it is necessary for scientists and clinicians to be cognizant of their applications, strengths, and weaknesses. The belief and knowing roads leading to modern understanding of communication and its disorders began about 4,000 years ago with the earliest Egyptian writings on the subject. Before this time, humans had no conception of logic and little need to make sense of the world; existence was reactionary. Spirits, demons, and gods provided what little explanation of the universe that was needed.

The Arduous Journey to Knowing and Believing in Human Communication and Its Disorders

O'Neill (1980) reports a medical reference to speechlessness in an ancient Egyptian surgical text. This text contains about 50 cases beginning with injuries to the head and systematically continuing downward through the human body. Case 22 involves a patient with a "smash in his temple" and a communication disorder. Interesting, this apparently traumatically induced communication disorder was considered untreatable. According to O'Neill, in the text, the word "brain" appeared for the first time in recorded history; the cerebral convolutions were compared with corrugations on a metallic slag; and the meninges surrounding the brain likened to a sack. For the first time in written history, an injury to the brain was connected with speechlessness suggesting a connection between the brain and the ability to speak. It would be nearly four centuries later that Pierre Paul Broca would refine this initial observation with the uttering of his famous statement: "We speak with the left hemisphere."

Approximately 800 years later, the "Gloss" (an account of the passage) explained that the speechlessness of the patient was a projectile-induced open head injury. "Although the patient was speechless, his impairment was not linked to an irrational element, nor was there any indication that this symptom was considered to alter the fundamental nature of the patient" (O'Neill, 1980, p. 13). This ancient observation would harken a great debate that endures to modern times: "What effect, if any, does a communication disorder have on the thought and personality of the patient?" This simple observation would sow the seeds of current controversies involving the brain-mind dichotomy, the role language plays in thought, definitions of intelligence and mental retardation, and the very nature of human symbolism. Although centuries of theorizing, reasoning, debating, and scientific exploration will result in thousands of discoveries and revelations about human communication and its disorders, only the surface will be scratched in resolving them. Today, modern scientists, therapists, and physicians, not unlike their ancient Egyptian counterparts, will examine persons with communication disorders, ponder the rationality of their symptoms, and question what effect the disorders have had on their fundamental nature.

According to *Scientific American* (1999), the first medical textbook written is the Edwin Smith papyrus. It was named for U.S. scientist Edwin Smith, a pioneer in Egyptology, who acquired it in Luxor, Egypt in 1863.

Anaudos, Aphonos, and Aphasia

A consistent problem that will persist throughout the study of communication and the treatment of its disorders are vague or absent definitions of important terms. This definitional ambiguity began early in the study of communication and its disorders, and continues, albeit to a lesser degree, today. Problems with nonexistent and ill-defined terms create unnecessary confusion, inhibit advances in believing and knowing, and limit accurate discussion about important ideas.

The first recorded terminology controversy occurred over references to general speechlessness and the specific loss of voice. According to Benton (1981), Hippocrates, the Greek physician and founder of medicine, first described speech disorders as "anaudos" and "aphonos." Early translators and scholars disagreed about whether Hippocrates used the two words synonymously. Galen, another Greek physician, opined about their differences in meaning and implied that humans have a unique ability to speak. According to O'Neill (1980, p. 22), Galen proposed that aphonos was the complete loss of the voice while anaudos was the loss of the general faculty of speech: "In Galen's discussion of this case is the statement of his conviction that only humans are capable of speech." Reading and writing are certainly only limited to humans, and Valerius Maximus, in about 30 A.D., described a case of alexia that was of traumatic origin (Benton & Joynt, 1960). In 180 A.D., Galen, while practicing in Rome, wrote the *Methodus Medendi* (*Method of Physicians*) that will become the ultimate medical textbook in medieval medicine (*Scientific American*, 1999).

Especially in aphasiology, the practice of not defining or having nebulous definitions of terms has resulted in a "chaos" of terminology and classification. Homer is credited with coining the word "aphasia" to refer to speechlessness. According to O'Neill (1980, p. 14), Homer attributed aphasia to an emotional etiology: "Aphasia was the speechlessness caused by emotion and usually accompanied by lachrymose [tearful] eyes." Many definitional ambiguities continue today as scientists and clinicians wrestle with sometimes controversial and often imprecise terms such as the "mind," "language," "intelligence," "perception," and so forth. These definitional ambiguities extend to the diagnostic labels and classification systems of aphasia. The nature of clinical entities such as "motor aphasia," "jargon," and "agnosia," to name a few, have ill-defined definitions clouding the understanding of their nature, what they encompass, and what they exclude.

Hippocrates and Galen were adherents to the "body humors" theories describing the circulation of the blood. A humor is any body fluid or semifluid. Adherents to the body humors theories believed that a healthy person had these fluids balanced, and that an imbalance caused disease. Therefore, by extension, diseases that cause communication disorders were also a result of humor imbalances. The humor theory led to bloodletting, a common medical practice that persisted into the 1800s. Beyond Galen's adherence to the body humors theory, he believed that nature was an expression of a divine spirit (*Scientific American*, 1999). Although Galen was not a Christian, his philosophy of linking nature to a supreme deity was consistent with conventional beliefs during the early rise of Christianity. Galen's beliefs were the foundation of current philosophies and belief systems attributing human communication as "God-given," and its disorders as a divine imposition.

Hippocratic writings on communication and its disorders did not address motor speech. There was no attempt to explain respiration's role in compressing air for speech production, nor the workings of the larynx and articulators. "One reason for this omission may be that as the Hippocratic physicians ignored the study of anatomy, they were not interested in determining either the instruments or the functioning of the vocal and articulative mechanisms" (O'Neill, 1980, p. 27). However, it is certain that the Hippocratic authors did appreciate motor speech as a direct result of human physiology.

According to O'Neill (1980), Plato and Aristotle are the creators of the "systemic period" of Greek philosophy combining the thoughts of their predecessors into a philosophic synthesis. Plato, Aristotle, and Socrates addressed the role of language in the human condition that triggered the language-thought controversy that continues today: "Is language integral to thought or does it simply express it?" Socrates' dictum to "know thyself" held language not only as a means to self-exploration, but also an end. Plato and Socrates considered thought to be a conversation with the soul, and that speech is the outward expression of it. Interestingly, Plato believed hearing to be the exact reverse or inversion of speech, and the bloodstream conducted sound to the brain. However, according to Bois (1966), Aristotle set the groundwork for science with his introduction of words to describe humankind including key anatomic and physiologic notions such as *category*, *form*, and *principle*. Aristotle, and other early philosophers, established the rules of deductive logic, common sense conclusions about the nature of things based on observations of the real world largely unfettered by mythologic beliefs.

The philosopher John R. Searle distinguished between linguistic philosophy, a method, and the philosophy of language, a subject (Searle, 1969).

Aristotle distinguished between voice and articulation, and addressed several speech impediments (O'Neill, 1980). Aristotle philosophized about the speech disorders of drunken persons, temporary alienation of the mind or psyche because of fright, impeded articulation resulting from excessive cold (tremor), apoplexy (stroke), and the labored speech seen in depression. Terms coined by Aristotle for communication disorders include "ischnophonos," (hesitancy in speech) "traylos," (lisping), and "psellos"(stammering). O'Neill notes that the Oxford translations of the terms do not correspond to modern syndromes.

In Western thought, many early scientific ideas about human communication and its disorders advanced by the Greek philosophers were cultivated into the early 1900s. Certainly, anatomic and physiologic discoveries will refine understanding of the processes involved in speech, hearing, and language, but the basic philosophy of communication and its disorders will remain unchallenged. In 1921, Alfred Korzybski, a mathematician, proposed a new philosophy in dealing with communication: General Semantics. It took a relativist approach to communication, especially language, and defined humanity as a "time-binding" class of life. "General Semanticists make an effort to free themselves of the logic of Aristotle, of the Ideas of Plato, and of the many offshoots of Greek philosophy that have been cultivated all through the ages in our Western world" (Bois, 1966, p. 263). Also in 1921, Edward Sapir, a Yale professor and language theorist broke from the Greek philosophers' view of instinctive language, and proposed that language is symbolic and non-instinctive. According to Sapir (1921, p. 8) "Language is a purely human and non-instinctive method of communicating ideas, emotions, and desires by means of a system of voluntarily produced symbols." Although it will later be proven that other animals possess language, his observation that language is non-instinctive will become generally accepted.

Of course, ancient exploration of communication and its disorders was not limited to the Western world. According to *Scientific American* (1999), in 2500 B.C., the practice of acupuncture was developed in China. This ancient Asian healing and therapeutic procedure uses body punctures with long thin needles to effect anesthesia and other bodily states. The practice continues to today and there is a body of research to support its efficacy. Acupuncture and acupressure are used to effect anesthesia, and to treat conditions and diseases that can cause communication disorders and specific speech disorders such as stuttering. Additionally, many ancient societies of the world, and Native Americans and First Nation Tribes in North American, developed the practice of using herbs, potions, and other medicinal supplements for the treatment of traumas and illnesses. Research has shown many of them to have at least some therapeutic value and to be beneficial particularly in the psychological domain. Even today, peyote is used by some Native American tribes to treat aphasia and related disorders as part of religious healing ceremonies (Huttlinger & Tanner, 1994).

The Dark Ages, lasting about 500 years, were a time of little if any scientific and medical advances. Superstitions about the process of communication and its disorders flourished. "During this time, nothing of significance happened culturally, intellectually, or scientifically, and Greek science was forgotten" (Lum, 2002, p. 36). Religious dogma supplanted reason as to the nature, causes, and treatments for communication disorders. Often, communication disorders were thought to result from supernatural possessions and rituals were performed to return the patient to normalcy. In Western Europe, the Dark Ages resulted in cultural, scientific, and intellectual stagnation, but in Persia and Arabia, learning continued to flourish. The Dark Ages gradually ended with the dawn of the Middle Ages. "The main prevailing and accepted source of knowledge at this time were the works of Aristotle and Plato and the Holy Scriptures. Science, being little more than a branch of philosophy, was declining" (Lum, 2002, p. 36). During the Middle Ages, plagues and mass diseases fed superstitions and some disabled persons were made scapegoats for the widespread death and destruction. In some cities, the disabled dared not venture into public places for fear of being stoned. According to Van Riper and Erickson (1996), the inhabitants of ancient India cast disabled people into the Ganges, the Spartans hurled them from precipices, the Aztecs sacrificed them to the Gods, and the Melanesians buried them alive. Many disabled persons were relegated to the life of beggars and the word "handicapped" may have originated from the practice of disabled people begging for food and money with a cap in hand on street corners.

During the Dark and Middle Ages, disabled individuals were often thought to be possessed by supernatural forces. Their disabilities were believed to be caused by possession of evil spirits or to be a manifestation of being out of harmony with nature. Shamans, and other practitioners of magic, were called upon to treat the disorders by casting out the evil spirits and demons. The Renaissance began in about the 1500s, and eventually brought major scientific revelations with great thinkers such as Copernicus, Galileo, Descartes, and Newton. Observation and inductive reasoning, the basis to the scientific method, were advanced by the great minds of the time. Boyle, Nightingale, Darwin, Einstein, and Pierre and Marie Curie continued the advancement of modern beliefs and knowledge with their discoveries, principles, and theories.

During the Renaissance, discussions about communication disorders became more descriptive and comprehensive. Antonio Guainerio described the symptoms of two aphasic patients and erroneously speculated that the cause of the disorder was "excessive accumulation of phlegm in the fourth ventricle." One of the patients had severe aphasia and he could utter only a few words. The second aphasic patient displayed paraphasic misnaming. Benton (1981) notes that during the Renaissance some physicians began to understand that brain disease could cause nonparalytic types of speech disorders. The physician Johann Schenck von Grafenberg observed:

> . . . diseases of the brain that, although the tongue was not paralyzed, the patient could not speak because, the faculty of memory being abolished, the words were not produced (Benton & Joynt, 1960, p. 209).

The phrenology theory was popular in the early 1800s. Franz Joseph Gall postulated that a person's mental traits and personality could be discovered by palpations of the bones of the skull. According to Sies (1974), Gall believed the cortex to be the organ of the mind and that the human brain is composed of instincts, reason, and animal propensities. Gall and Jean Baptiste Bouillaud were involved in the hotly contested localization versus nonlocalization debate regarding speech and language centers in the frontal lobes (Sies, 1974).

Pierre Paul Broca's coined the term "aphemia" to signify the loss of the ability to combine the movements of the articulatory structures into words (apraxia of speech). He identified the lesion in the third frontal convolution of the left hemisphere based on postmortum autopsies of aphasic patients. As noted previously, Broca, in 1865, identified the left hemisphere, and particularly the frontal lobe, as the site for speech expression.

At about the time of Broca's discoveries, Karl Wernicke, a German physician, identified the receptive language counterpart to Broca's area and the disorder "sensory aphasia." Wernicke also identified conduction and total aphasia (Sies, 1974). In the early 1900s, Henry Head criticized researchers and theorists who would attempt to localize all speech and language functioning and diagrammed the human brain with the publication of *Aphasia and Kindred Disorders of Speech*.

In the late 1800s, John Hughlings Jackson addressed the patient's "psyche" and communication. Addressing patients with communication disorders, Jackson did not include the artificial separation of thought, language, and the patient's psychology. Jackson explored propositional and nonpropositional speech acts, and related them to thought, language, and communication disorders. Jackson, in an article written in the neurology journal *Brain*, capsulized his theory:

> To speak is not simply to utter words, it is to propositionise. A proposition is such a relation of words that it makes one new

meaning; not by a mere addition of what we call the separate meanings of the several words; the terms of the proposition are modified by each other. Single words are meaningless, and so is any unrelated succession of words. The unit of speech is the proposition. A single word is, or is in effect, a proposition, if other words in relation are implied (Jackson, 1878, p. 311).

According to Sies (1974), Jackson also addressed "inner speech" and suggested that it occurs with the same structure as other propositional utterances. Jackson believed it was artificial to consider externalized language, the language constructs expressed to others, as basically different from internal monologues.

The modern period of communication sciences and disorders began in the early 1900s with Weisenburg and McBrides' scientific study on aphasia and later with Wendell Johnson's research on stuttering. Kurt Goldstein postulated the abstract-concrete imbalance and the loss of the "abstract attitude" in aphasic patients. According to Sies (1974), Macdonald Critchley proposed the idea of the "preverbitum" (the silent thinking process that differs from inner speech) and a grammar of verbal thought. Penfield and Roberts (1959) engaged in extensive brain mapping studies leading to discovery of supplementary speech production areas. In 1925, the American Speech-Language-Hearing Association was formed stating as its primary objective the scientific study of communication disorders.

The late 1900s were a remarkable time of scientific discovery about communication and its disorders. The theoretical and scientific foundations set by Broca, Wernicke, and others into the neurologic substrates of aphasia provided the bases to current localization research conducted with new generations of brain scanning technology. Hearing science discovered the workings of the cochlea, and audiology, which got its start as an independent profession after World War II, developed scores of reliable and valid hearing tests. Digital hearing aids and cochlear implants dramatically improved the hearing of deaf and hard-of-hearing individuals. Hermann Von Helmholtz's work on speech resonance, Henry Sweet's pioneering efforts in phonetics, and others such as Ilse Lehiste, Grant Fairbanks, Karl S. Lashley, Oscar I. Tosi, Franklin Cooper, Alvin Liebermann, and Melville and Alexander Graham Bell contributed to hearing science, speech pattern recognition, speech sound spectrography, and general acoustics. Specialists in childhood language development and disorders, building on Piaget's observations in the early 1900s, identified the cognitive underpinnings of language and provided milestones of linguistic and social-communicative (pragmatic) development. Using play in therapy for language-delayed and

Most scholars consider the research conducted by Weisenburg and McBride in 1935 to harken the modern period of aphasiology. Unfortunately, their conclusions about the performance of aphasic subjects were questionable because of a flawed research design; their subjects were not neurologically stable at the time of testing.

disordered children, and behavior modification for children with articulation disorders evolved in theory and treatment methodology. Improved understanding of laryngeal functioning provided the foundation for current voice therapies for vocal nodules, polyps, and contact ulcers. Pharyngeal flap surgeries and resonance therapies improved communication abilities for children with birth defects. Although stuttering remains stubbornly resistant to a cure, medications, therapies, and auditory feedback therapies and devices show promise in helping many people who stutter to manage their disfluencies. After decades of research, the efficacy of aphasia therapy has been clearly demonstrated for non-globally-involved individuals.

In 1988, the Human Genome Organization was established in the United States to compile a complete map of the human genes (*Scientific American*, 1999), and the project was completed at the turn of the century. In physics, string theory is proposing several dimensions of reality and that the universe consists of vibrating strings of energy so small that it is likely they will never be physically observed, only hypothesized. In the early 2000s, computer chips are so efficient and capable that unlimited storage memory exists for most personal computing. Access to the World Wide Web is only limited by the capacity of Internet connections and not the speed of the computers; computer chips now can compute more than 400 million computations in 1/50th of a second (Tanner, 2001).

> Computers operate in nanoseconds, billionths of a second, and picoseconds, thousand-billionths of a second.

The Philosophical Foundations to Speech and Hearing Knowledge Acquisition

For centuries philosophers have addressed human nature, the mind-body dichotomy, perceptions of reality, sources of knowledge, ethics, logic, and social issues ranging from justice to moral responsibility. (See Velasquez [2002] for a complete periodic chronology of important philosophers, their main contributions, and the political, cultural, and scientific events of the period.) Philosophers living before the birth of Christ, such as Buddha and Confucius, began exploring humanity, its place in the universe, and the acquisition of knowledge. According to Velasquez (2002, p. 42) "Western philosophy began with a question the Greek thinker Thales asked around 585 B.C.: What is the ultimate reality of which everything is made?" Socrates' dictum that "The unexamined life is not worth living" was made about 2500 years ago.

Plato and Aristotle, discussed above as the creators of the systemic period of Greek philosophy, synthesized the apparently disparate philosophies of their predecessors and explored language, speech, and hearing. Cicero pondered ethics, morality, good and evil. Saint Thomas Aquinas, a theologist, used reason for his cosmologic arguments for the existence of God, and René Descartes reasoned that a perfect God guarantees accurate knowledge of the world. John Locke, David Hume, and Immanuel Kant addressed the essence of perception and knowledge. John Stuart Mill, Søren Kierkegaard, and James Dewey pursued modern philosophic notions such as inductive reasoning, existentialism and the meaning of life, and pragmatism.

In the early 1900s, Bertrand Russell, a correspondence theorist (belief that truth is an agreement between a proposition and fact) addressed the nature of knowledge. He proposed that truth and falsehoods are simply properties of beliefs, and that the truth of them lies in the relationship between the belief and what is factual and real. In addition, Ludwig Wittgenstein, and others, addressed the role of language in philosophy and sought an ideal language in the pursuit of truth. Jean-Paul Sartre, the premier atheistic existentialist, proposed that one can only obtain truth about thoughts and behavior from examining human consciousness.

Of course, Charles Darwin, with his publication of *The Origin of Species* and *The Descent of Man* in the mid-1800s, proposed the theory of evolution and natural selection, revolutionizing beliefs about the fundamental nature of human thought and behavior. In effect, Darwin removed the idea of "human being" and proposed that human existence is simply a higher form of "animal being." By extension, human thought, and the acquisition of knowledge, are not fundamentally different from what is seen in lower species; they are simply more evolved. As discussed previously, in Darwin's view, the human innate need to communicate is based on a survival imperative and is neither God-given nor the result of reason. Today, some theorists, scholars, and researchers adamantly resist Darwinian views of animalistic human behavior, especially concerning language. Creation science attempts to rebut evolution, and in many schools in the United States, intelligent design of the universe is taught, formally or informally, along with the theory of evolution.

In the mid-1900s, the philosopher Thomas Kuhn addressed how to know real science and distinguish it from pseudoscience and untested belief systems. He noted that in real science, theoretical assumptions should be consistent and agree with the existing body of research. The theory should be simple, yet broad in scope and extend far beyond the particular observation, laws, or other theories it was designed to explain. Finally, ". . . a theory should be fruitful of new research finding; it should, that is, disclose new phenomena or previously unnoted relationships among those already known" (Kuhn, 1977, p. 321).

Modern Epistemology and the Discipline of Communication Sciences and Disorders

Linguistic analysis: "A contemporary form of analytic philosophy claiming that philosophical problems are partially language problems; the purpose of philosophy is to dissolve, not resolve, problems by a rigorous examination of language" (Velasquez, 2002, p. 720).

Epistemology is a branch of philosophy addressing the nature and source of knowledge. According to Velasquez (2002, p. 11), "Among the problems usually discussed as parts of epistemology are the structure, reliability, extent, and kinds of knowledge we have; the meaning of truth (including definitions of truth and validity); logic and a variety of strictly linguistic concerns; and the foundation of all knowledge, including the question of whether real knowledge is even possible." Epistemology is different from metaphysics, which addresses reality and existence. Socrates is generally credited with being the first epistemologist. In epistemology, there are two basic approaches to achieving knowledge: rationalism and empiricism. (A third epistemologic discipline is skepticism, which doubts all assumptions, claims that knowledge is unattainable, and questions the certainty of all facts.)

In rationalism, reason allows making logical inferences and reaching conclusions about the nature of the world. Rationalism is based on reason. "Among the outstanding rationalists is René Descartes, who attempted to demonstrate the validity of a priori knowledge—that is, knowledge independent of sensory perception" (Velasquez, 2002, p. 415). To the rationalist, all knowing and knowledge is based on reason and provides certain universal truths. Rationalism involves logical conversations designed to arrive at universal truths and the attainment of knowledge through reason. The rationalist tries to arrive at intellectual certainty through reason.

"In vigorous reaction to Descartes and the rationalists are the British empiricists: Locke, Berkeley, and Hume. They insist that all knowledge of reality is a posteriori—that is, it follows from experiences" (Velasquez, 2002, p. 415). In empiricism, knowledge must be a direct result of sensory experiences, for example, observation. To the empiricist, all knowledge is based on sensations and knowledge is attained through experience. In empiricism, experience leads to impressions, the formulation of simple ideas, and culminating in complex ideas.

Twenty-first century speech and hearing scientists and clinicians continue to wrestle with issues addressed by the great thinkers of the past. For example, human nature and behavior, whether addressing motivation of people who stutter, the uses of behavior modification in language therapy, or treatment programs for people with aphasia are dealt with by modern speech and hearing scientists and clinicians. The perception of time and the nature of reality are addressed in patients with brain injury. Issues related to God and other supernatural forces surface professionally with alternative treatments for communication disorders, faith healing, and spontaneous recovery. The scientific method is used to explore new diagnostics and treatments for communication disorders, and clinicians use reason and deductive logic for therapies not yet proven to be beneficial (Tanner, Sciacca, & Cotton, 2005). Brain mapping of speech and language centers of the brain delve into the ancient mind-body quandary. Ethics and morality of health care delivery systems are current passionate political issues, and philosophy has explored similar moral dilemmas for centuries. Even some metaphysical issues are relevant and pertinent given new theories of the universe, molecular and cellular functioning in the brain, and linguistic representations of reality. Knowing and believing are put to the test daily by modern scientists and clinicians, and seeking these truths continues to be the foundation of science and philosophy. Science and philosophy have never been more crucial to communication sciences and disorders, and together, they merge knowledge and beliefs systems into modern perspectives.

CHAPTER SUMMARY

Communication sciences and disorders involves both empiricism and rationalism; it uses sensory observation, experimentation, repeated replication of experiments, confirmation, and inductive and deductive reasoning to reach conclusions. In a world of increasing bombardment of "information," many people are inundated with facts often without a greater perspective on them. Philosophy addresses the wisdom that may or may not come from facts and information. Philosophy in general, and epistemology in particular, examine knowledge and beliefs, put facts and information into larger perspectives, and provide a basis with which to know ourselves and the universe.

Study and Discussion Questions

1. Describe some of the recent technologic advances that have occurred in your lifetime.

2. How much information do you get from books, television, newspapers, and the World Wide Web? Do you consider the information equally factual? Why or why not?

3. Compare and contrast information that is "known" to be true from information that is "believed" to be true. Provide a personal example.

4. What are your thoughts about why there are approximately 10,000 languages and dialects in the world today?

5. Do you think the ability to talk is a product of evolution or divinely created? What about communication disorders? Defend your position.

6. Summarize the ancient Egyptians' ideas about communication and its disorders.

7. Summarize the early Greek philosophers' ideas about communication and its disorders.

8. Describe the study of communication and its disorders during the Dark Ages, Middle Ages, and the Renaissance. How were people with communication disorders viewed during those times?

9. What was the Phrenology theory and its basic assumption about mental abilities?

10. What is epistemology? Compare and contrast rationalism and empiricism.

11. Why is communication sciences and disorders epistemology important for modern students, scientists, and clinicians?

12. Describe recent discoveries about communication and its disorders that have occurred since you became a student.

Suggested Reading

Lum, C. (2002). *Scientific thinking in speech and language therapy.* Mahwah, NJ: Lawrence Erlbaum Associates.

Velasquez, M. (2002). *Philosophy* (8th ed.). Belmont, CA: Wadsworth/ Thomson Learning.

CHAPTER 4

Perspectives on Science and Logic in Communication Sciences and Disorders

*"To know that we know what we know,
and that we do not know what we do not know,
that is true knowledge."*

Henry David Thoreau

CHAPTER PREVIEW

This chapter explores the scientific method as it relates to communication and its disorders. It describes the various research methodologies that have contributed to the formulation of *The Unified Model of Communication Sciences and Disorders.* Catalog-epidemiologic and descriptive research methods are discussed as is a detailed review of the experimental design. There is a discussion of the methods and procedures of evaluating nonscientific diagnostic and therapeutic methods and procedures used in communication sciences and disorders. In addition, clinical decision-making is discussed using conflict theory as a basis to understanding the psychology of the process.

"Individuals shall evaluate the effectiveness of services rendered and of products dispensed and shall provide services or dispense products only when benefit can reasonably be expected." (Code of Ethics, American Speech-Language-Hearing Association, 2003)

Science

Research in communication sciences and disorders often uses very large or very small numbers. Scientific notation is a method of writing them. In scientific notation, the numbers are written with one digit before the decimal point and multiplied by a power of 10.

The origin of the word "science" is Latin: *scientia* meaning "know." Science is the systematic study of the universe, including humanity and the natural world, producing theoretical explanations based on experiment and observation. "History tells us that the first signs of science were present around 2500 BC, when humans could predict solar eclipses and the early Egyptian and Babylonian civilizations therefore possessed an understanding of the principles of geometry and arithmetic, which means they were capable engineers and land surveyors" (Lum, 2002, p. 36). A relatively recent addition to the community of sciences is the discipline of communication sciences and disorders. It essentially meets the requirements as a science because it is an organized body of knowledge that is systematically and objectively studied, largely based on verifiable empirical evidence, and employs hypotheses testing and answering of research questions. Lum (2002) notes, that if a discipline is to be a scientific profession, the knowledge would have to be based on scientific principles. In a truly scientific profession, clinicians would use scientific standards in clinical practice and the scientific method to judge the efficacy of intervention. They would also have a common language by which to communicate evidence and evaluate knowledge. Although the discipline of communication sciences and disorders does not consistently meet the above rigorous criteria, it certainly aspires as a science.

Two general scientific research divisions exist within the discipline of communication sciences and disorders: speech, language, and hearing sciences, and speech-language pathology and audiology. Although the titles of the divisions may differ from university to university, region to region, and country to country, in general, speech, language, and hearing scientists address normal aspects of communication and engage in pure research. In pure research, there is no apparent practical or treatment goal to the studies, although these studies often lay the foundation for applied research. In addition, some studies may fortuitously make practical discoveries. According to Powers (2000, pp. 6–7),

Speech, language, and hearing scientists come from a variety of educational backgrounds. Some individuals are primarily speech scientists, others are hearing scientists, and others are language scientists. Because of this diversity, it is difficult, if not impossible, to define the limits of CSD [communication sciences and disorders] scientists. Suffice it to say, however, that the majority have strong backgrounds in the sciences and hold advanced degrees, most often a Ph.D. (Doctor of Philosophy). The degrees may be awarded in areas such as acoustics, anatomy and physiology, biological sciences, communication sciences and disorders, education, linguistics, physics, psychology, or speech communication.

Powers (2000) notes that the speech, language, and hearing scientist engages in basic research to provide a better understanding of human communication processes.

Although not excluded from speech, language, and hearing sciences, speech-language pathologists and audiologists engage in applied research with practical goals involving the etiology, diagnosis, and treatment of communication disorders. According to Lum (2002, pp. 2–3):

> The study of speech and language therapy draws heavily for its theoretical bases from the domains of psychology, medicine, linguistics, and, to a lesser extent, sociology. A traditional view of the speech and language therapy discipline is that it acquires its theoretical perspectives on a particular condition from one or the other domains and applies this knowledge to the treatment of a communication disorder. Speech and language therapy is an applied science in the sense that the study and practice of speech and language therapy is predicated on adopting the relevant theories and methods from other disciplines and applying these to the context of abnormal communication.

Speech, language, and hearing scientists and speech-language pathologists and audiologists use the scientific method as a base for knowledge and adhere to the philosophy of empiricism. Communication sciences and disorders is primarily a social science, and research generated is generally qualitative. In qualitative research, some aspect of communication and its disorders is measured against some other factor or entity and/or the distinctive characteristic of the entity or factor is discovered. Qualitative research is usually conducted in nonlaboratory conditions where complete control of variables is not possible. Communication sciences and disorders, to a lesser extent, also is involved in quantitative research. Quantitative research involves determining a certain amount or number and/or the properties of a factor or entity associated with communication and its disorders. Laboratory conditions are usually used in this type of research where there is exacting control of variables. Qualitative research is associated with the "soft sciences," such as sociology, general psychology, and anthropology; quantitative research is associated with the "hard sciences" such as acoustics, biology, and physiology.

In general, there are three types of empirical research in communication sciences and disorders and they follow a general format: catalog-epidemiologic, descriptive, and experimental. Although the experimental format is often more detailed (see below), all scientific research requires a statement of the issue, topic, or problem to be researched. These statements are usually provided in the form of a description of the goals, research questions, or formal hypotheses. The procedures followed are described, and the results detailed. The procedures detail how subjects are used, the instrumentation and testing, and the gathering of data. The results section involves placing the obtained data in readable, easily interpretable forms, including the statistical analyses. Finally, all scientific research requires an interpretation of the results relating to the initial statement of the issue, topic, or problem. The main purpose of the above format is for replication purposes. This format provides scientists an opportunity to replicate the studies with different subjects to learn whether the results are reliable.

> In the social sciences, statistical association, the relationship between two or more variables, is considered statistically significant if the result would occur fewer than 5 times out of 100 by chance.

Catalog-Epidemiologic Research

Catalog-epidemiologic research is used to learn the number of entities and factors associated with a particular aspect of communication or its disorders. Cataloguing is associated with normal communication, and epidemiologic research addresses communication disorders. A catalog study involves placing entities and factors about communication in the general population or subpopulation in a systematic order. An epidemiologic study involves determining the occurrence and distribution of communication disorders in the general population or subpopulation. Epidemiologic studies usually involve the incidence, the number of new communication disorders, or the period prevalence, the number of occurrences in a specific population during a particular period.

Catalog-epidemiologic studies determine the frequency and magnitude of certain communication functions and the occurrences of disorders regarding gender, age, or other aspect of a population. A profile of some aspect of communication and its disorders is created and a correlation is often drawn. Although some authorities place catalog-epidemiologic studies in the descriptive category of scientific research, these studies usually involve large-scale incidence and prevalence statistics, use surveys to obtain data, and go beyond describing a communication function or disorders. The following types of research questions are answered in catalog-epidemiologic research:

1. What is the unemployment rate for communication-disordered Native Americans on American Indian Reservations?

2. What are the psychological characteristics of mothers of children who stutter?

3. What are the hearing aid use rates for elderly males and females?

4. Where are the dialectic geographic boundaries in the United States?

5. What are the number of lawsuits involving communication disorders, by legal jurisdiction, involving the Individuals with Disabilities Education Act (IDEA) during a particular year?

The Acoustical Society of America was organized in 1929 to increase and disseminate the knowledge of acoustics, including speech acoustics, and to promote its practical applications. *Echoes* is its newsletter.

Descriptive Research

A descriptive scientific study involves the systematic and methodical recording of observable events. Whereas experimental research is objective, descriptive research tends to be subjective. "In a descriptive study the scientist simply observes and records behavioral events and then, in most instances, tries to systematize the relationships among them" (Borden, Harris, & Raphael, 1994, p. 234). This type of study is passive in that the experimenter is not involved actively in manipulation of variables, only the description and correlation of existing phenomena.

Descriptive research in communication sciences and disorders involves single-subject designs or small groups of subjects. (Large group descriptive research is included in the catalog-epidemiologic category discussed above.) In single-subject designs, the researcher obtains a baseline of a particular behavior or other function in a single subject and observes the effects of treatment, teaching, or other variables on the target behavior or function. In single-subject descriptive research, there is no attempt to find the cause and effect by manipulation of variables. Descriptive research is often used in acoustics, anatomy, and physiology to describe speech sound production. Single-subject and small group descriptive research provides information about individual performances and no formal generalization can be made to large groups of subjects. However, single-subject and small group descriptive studies provide foundations for research to determine causal relationships concerning treatments or functions.

The following are types of research questions answered in single-subject or small group descriptive studies:

1. What muscles are involved in the isolated production of the /k/ phoneme?

2. What is the degree of rocking of the arytenoid cartilage during a one-octave pitch change?

3. How does whispering affect the self-correction of an apraxic adult?

4. What effect on an optimism scale does a religious healing ceremony have on an aphasic patient and his family?

5. What is the activity level of the left occipital lobe in a patient with dyslexia?

Experimental Research

In communication sciences and disorders experimental research, variables are manipulated to reach conclusions that can be generalized to larger populations. Scientific research in general, and experimental research in particular, operate on inductive reasoning; explanations of communication and its disorders are drawn from sensory observations. "Science is based on inductive reasoning: from observations made in the past, the scientist draws conclusions about the laws and theories that will operate on in the future" (Velasquez, 2002, p. 405). Experimental research involves a series of formal steps to test hypotheses and answer research questions. Experimental research requires the use of inferential statistics that allow generalizations that go beyond the data obtained in the study.

Although scientific societies, professional associations, and journals may use different terminology, there are several essential components of the experimental research design. The purpose of precisely following the protocol is threefold. First, the steps in the scientific method are followed to provide an empirical base to the study. The foundation of this protocol was initially established by Francis Bacon in the 1600s and improved upon by John Stuart Mill in the 1800s with his "canons" of induction (Velasquez, 2002). Second, as noted above, the protocol is detailed to provide for careful replication of the research. Scientists can repeat the research and support or reject the conclusions based on following the steps in the scientific method and using different subjects. Third, the protocol gives the reader an understanding of the methods and procedures followed, giving him or her an opportunity to judge the competency of the research and decide the veracity of the conclusions. Most, but not all, research in communication sciences and disorders follow publication standards established by the American Psychological Association (see *Publication Manual of the American Psychological Association* [5th ed.] published by the American Psychological Association [2001]).

Essentials of Experimental Research Design and Publication Format

Front Matter

The title of the study, abstract, key terms, and references comprise the front and back matter of the research article and are important aspects of the research design and protocol. The title of the study clearly identifies what the study entails. Key terms, usually fewer than 10 in number, are used by Internet search engines and journals to allow for proper accessibility to the studies. The abstract is a concise summary of the study, methodology, results, and conclusions. Because of space limitations, journals usually have character limitation for titles and word limitations for abstracts.

Review of the Literature and History of the Problem

The topical review of literature and history of the problem being researched is provided for two reasons. First, it requires the author of the study to examine the past research related to the topic and to become knowledgeable of current research being conducted. Second, it gives the reader a synopsis of the topic and relevant previous studies completed on it. The past five years of research conducted on the topic are most important, but the review of the literature also includes important and classic studies done in the distant past. When referring to a specific study, the review of the literature addresses the general research design and summarizes the results and the conclusions drawn by the researchers. The review of the literature and history of the problem address the relevant theoretical bases for the research and include the rationale for the present research.

Definition of Terms

A section on the definition of important terms used in the research is important and this is especially true in communication sciences and disorders. As reported in Chapter 3, the discipline of communication sciences and disorders has been plagued by terminology controversy since Hippocrates and other early Greek philosophers and physicians defined speech disorders, loss of voice, and aphasia. Important terms pivotal to the topic are clearly defined providing the researcher and reader with an understanding of what they encompass and exclude. Especially in research addressing the neurology of communication, anatomic and physiologic terms are defined and described, reducing ambiguity about their location and function. In research involving communication disorders, scientists clearly define each diagnostic label to show what is included and excluded in the category under investigation. Defining pivotal terms is also important because many other academic and clinical disciplines are involved in research related to human communication and its disorders (see Table 2–2). Related disciplines often have unique definitions of terms that reflect their academic and clinical orientation.

Hypotheses and Research Questions

A theoretical construct is something that cannot be observed or verified directly. It is sometimes called a hypothetical construct. The Language Acquisition Device (LAD) is a hypothetical construct of the human brain allowing for the acquisition of language in humans.

In general, there are two forms for asking questions in research: hypotheses and research questions. A *hypothesis* is a speculation that is amenable to rejection or confirmation by the research procedure. It is a definite statement that can be studied and includes a prediction of the outcome. Hypotheses are written in null form, that is, there is no statistically significant difference in the relationship being studied. The researcher attempts to reject the null hypothesis leading to acceptance of the hypothesis. This way of doing research reflects the skepticism philosophy noted in Chapter 3. "The skepticism of scientists is reflected in their use of the null hypothesis that contends, in effect, that nothing exists until proven to exist based on certain statistically defined levels of confidence" (Maxwell & Satake, 1997, p. 67). Although research questions are more often used in catalog-epidemiologic and descriptive research, they also can be used to ask questions in experimental research. Research questions tend to be more general and are used when there is little or contradictory information about a topic from which to draw a hypothesis.

Subjects and Sampling

A subject is the person (or animal) used in research, a selected subset of a population. In communication sciences and disorders, the number of subjects used in research can range from one to thousands. As a rule, the larger the number of subjects used in the research, the greater the power of the study to make generalizations about the population being explored. Two general categories of subjects are used in communication sciences and disorders research. A random sample involves a limited number of subjects from a larger group. The limited number may be representative of the larger group and thus include the characteristics of the large population. The sample may also be nonrandom and nonrepresentative of a larger group. These nonrandom samples are also called samples of convenience. Subjects are also separated into control and experimental groups based on manipulation of variables.

Variables

The control groups are those subjects not subjected to or not experiencing the independent variable. The experimental group is subjected to the independent variable. Dependent variables are the responses or behaviors measured in the experiment to determine changes. In the cause-effect expression, the independent variable relates to the cause and the dependent variable relates to the effect. The researcher manipulates independent variables to determine the effect of the dependent variable on the response or behavior. McReynolds and Kearns (1983, pp. 3-4) emphasize the importance of reducing extraneous variables in communication sciences and disorders research:

> An example of the two variables may be illustrated by a study of the effects of noise on speech discrimination. The dependent variable is the subject's performance on speech discrimination tasks and the independent variable is the introduction of noise during the task. The importance of operational definitions of the dependent and independent variables cannot be overemphasized. That is, the exact nature of the discrimination task must be specified clearly, as must the nature of the noise introduced during performance on the tasks. Needless to say, the purpose for designing an experimental study is to try to isolate the effect of the independent variable from all the other variables that may influence the subject's performance before and during the experiment.

Results and Discussion

The results section of the research includes a description of what was observed. The results are tied to the original hypotheses or research questions. The results section consists of objective descriptive or numerical statements and includes tables, charts, and figures based on the data obtained. In the discussion section, the scientist discusses the implications and generalizations of the research. It is important in the discussion that the researcher extends the conclusions and implications only to what is logically induced from the results. In other words, the conclusions and implications are based solely on the data and results. The scientist summarizes how the results of the study are important and relevant to some aspect of communication sciences and disorders. Drawing from the totality of the study, the researcher also suggests the direction of future research.

The following are types of questions asked in experimental research. The general intent of the research question is provided, followed by the hypothesis in its null form.

1. Does four weeks of voice rest reduce the size of unilateral vocal nodules? There is no statistically significant reduction in the size of vocal nodules as a result of four weeks of voice rest.

2. Does the use of a clinical mirror improve self-correction of apraxic subjects? There is no statistically significant improvement in the number of successful self-correction behaviors between treatment group one (with clinical mirror) and control group two (without clinical mirror).

3. Is there a difference in preschool receptive vocabulary abilities between male and female children? There are no statistically significant differences between the means and variances of the male and female groups on a standardized vocabulary test.

4. Is there a positive relationship between auditory discrimination abilities and articulation acquisition? There is no positive correlation between auditory discrimination test results (group one) and articulation acquisition test results (group two).

5. What effect does antiseizure medication have on traumatic brain injured patients' orientation? There is no statistically significant difference between group one (antiseizure medication) and control group two (no antiseizure medication) performance on a memory and orientation standardized test.

Scientific Aspiration in Communication Sciences and Disorders

As a discipline, communication sciences and disorders is not optimally based on the scientific method, although, as noted above, both the study of normal communication and the diagnosis and treatment of its disorders aspire to scientific empiricism. Communication sciences, the study of normal speech, language, and hearing, is more rigorous in meeting the requirements of a science than is speech-language pathology and audiology. The organized body of progressive knowledge in communication sciences, for the most part, has resulted from cataloguing, descriptive research, hypothesis testing, and the answering of research questions. Although in its relative infancy as a scientific discipline, communication sciences has an empirical foundation. Speech-language pathology and audiology are less grounded in science especially concerning the use of scientific standards in clinical practice. As an applied science drawing from communication sciences, medical, educational, and several related disciplines, speech-language pathology and audiology only partially function from a scientific base.

The practice of medicine provides a comparison for equating the relative strength of the scientific method in speech-language pathology and audiology clinical practice. The practitioner of medicine, an applied science that draws from the knowledge base of medicine, biology, chemistry, anatomy, physiology, and other disciplines, rarely prescribes medicines that have not been scientifically tested. The medical practitioner prescribes medications that have been scientifically tested in several clinical trials and knows their application and side effects. In contrast, speech-language pathologists and audiologists often provide diagnostic procedures, treatments, instructions, and therapies not supported by scientific clinical research. This predicament occurs by necessity because the scope of clinical services for speech-language pathology and audiology has greatly exceeded the availability of applied clinical research. Because the discipline has limited applied clinical research on the diagnosis and treatment of communication disorders, practitioners must frequently rely on scientifically untested procedures. Tanner and Gerstenberger (1996, p. 328) comment on the dearth of clinically relevant aphasia research in *Aphasiology*, an international, interdisciplinary journal.

> This unfortunate void of research extends to all aspects of clinician-patient interaction including the utilization of workbooks, apraxia and dysarthria drills, word recall assist strategies,

techniques for reducing perseveration and bouts of emotional lability, reading and writing rehabilitation, orientation and stimulation and reinforcement techniques. Much of what a practicing clinician must do has not been tested empirically. By necessity, therapy is a combination of borrowed teaching strategies from education, psychology, logical inductive and inductive reasoning, commonsense direction and guidance. The limited body of applied research is certainly not desirable, but the practicing clinician must perform; he/she does not have the academic luxury to close the lecture with the statement that "all the data are not in."

Evaluating Diagnostic and Therapeutic Methods and Procedures in Communication Sciences and Disorders

Because of the disparity between available scientific research and clinical needs in communication sciences and disorders, it is important for clinicians to be able accurately to evaluate scientific research and logically assess nonscientifically-based diagnostic and therapeutic services. Below are factors to consider when evaluating the scientific application of research in communication sciences and disorders and procedures for logically assessing nonscientific clinical procedures.

Research Importance and Statistical Significance

Statistics are the numerical procedures for analyzing and summarizing quantitative data. Statistical analyses are used to determine the significance of research and its power to generalize beyond the sample from which the data were derived. A significant result suggests the probability that the findings are not due to chance. Significance, when used in statistics, does not refer to the importance of the study. Not all statistically significant research is important research.

The power of a study to explain some dimension or aspect of communication sciences and disorders is related to the fundamental importance of the hypothesis (or research question) and the research design. Simply finding a statistically significant correlation or difference between two or more variables or groups does not define the importance of the study. For example, it may be statistically significant that males and females with global aphasia differ in their response time during confrontational naming tasks. The data and inferential statistics may provide a strong confidence level that males with global aphasia respond more slowly during picture-naming tasks than do their female counterparts, no matter the success of naming. In this hypothetical example, although this discovered fact does cast light on the general nature of global aphasic patients' confrontational naming behaviors, and thus contributes to the general body of information in clinical aphasiology, it is of little practical importance. It does not give the clinician meaningful diagnostic or therapeutic information to improve the quality of services provided to patients with treatable aphasia. Conversely, a study addressing the relative success rates of confrontational naming strategies in male and female patients with aphasia has more clinical importance. Although both research studies may yield statistically significant results, the clinical importance of the latter is far greater than the former. Research showing which confrontational naming strategies yield the highest success rates in male and female aphasic patients give clinicians valuable clinical procedures to be used in therapy.

Scientific Law: Differences, relationships, or associations that most scientists accept

No one would argue that pure research, and applied research not yielding important clinical information, contribute to the general body of knowledge in communication sciences and disorders and have inherent value. Research on muscle and nerve functions, respiratory pressure and airflow, tongue trajectories during phoneme productions, differences between males and females on clinical tasks, cultural variations in language usage, and velopharyngeal functioning during nasal speech, to name a few areas of investigation, can provide general information about human communication and its disorders. Current areas of pure research in speech and hearing sciences, such as brain mapping research, can yield exciting information about how the brain and nervous system function during normal and abnormal communication. The human quest for knowledge about speech, voice, language, and hearing requires that pure, nonapplied research be funded, competently conducted, and the results disseminated. However, as the discipline of communication sciences and disorders enters the 21st century, this type of research should be of secondary importance to applied clinical research. This is especially true given recent changes in the scientific demographics in communication sciences and disorders.

Today, as in the past, funding resources for research are limited. There is a finite amount of dollars to be used to advance the knowledge base in communication sciences and disorders.

A valid test measures that which it purports to measure. A reliable measure provides consistent results when administered repeatedly. Face validity is the extent to which a test appears to represent that which it is intended to measure.

Additionally, during the past two decades, the percentage of scientists in communication sciences and disorders has declined dramatically. Some doctoral programs in communication sciences and disorders have been eliminated, and there has been a decline in the number of new doctoral graduates. There are fewer scientists in the discipline, especially as a percentage of clinical providers. Also, during the past two decades, the number of clinicians and their scope of practice in speech-language pathology and audiology has increased dramatically.

There are more practitioners than ever before performing a wider range of services. This has created a situation where the scientific base of important applied clinical research has plummeted while the need for it has soared. Consequently, given this fundamental decline in the scientific base for communication sciences and disorders, pure research in communication sciences and disorders is often done at the expense of crucially needed, high-quality applied research. If communication sciences and disorders, as a discipline, continues to aspire as science, it needs to redirect its research priority to the applied sciences and increase, not only the number, but also the clinical importance of its research base. The discipline is losing its applied scientific base and pure research, at the expense of applied research, a luxury it no longer can afford.

Assessing the Value of Nonscientific Diagnostic and Therapeutic Methods and Procedures

In an ideal clinical world, speech-language pathologists and audiologists would select from several scientifically proven diagnostic and therapeutic methods and procedures for every category and subcategory of communication disorders. Furthermore, each diagnostic and therapeutic method and procedure would have research to support its application to individual patients, and have scientific studies addressing variables such as gender, age, race, intelligence, and other case-by-case factors. In this ideal clinical world, speech-language pathologists and audiologists would have a large body of scientifically proven clinical methods and procedures from which they could select the appropriate tests and therapies. These scientifically based methods and procedures would have been studied in several clinical trials, and their indications and contraindications well documented. Yet we do not live in an ideal world, and the applied research base in communications sciences and disorders is far from the ideal.

Clinical Syllogisms

Given the scope of practice for speech-language pathologists and audiologists, and the limited applied research available, a systematic method for assessing the value of nonscientific diagnostic and therapeutic methods and procedure is required. Lum (2002) addresses science, pseudoscience, arguments, and opinions in the context of speech therapeutics accountability. Formal reasoning, using logical methods of deduction, can provide an optimal method of assessing the value of nonscientific diagnostic and therapeutic methods and procedures. Whereas the scientific method is primarily inductive logic based on probabilities, deductive logic results in either valid or invalid conclusions. Deductive arguments are formally either valid or invalid whereas inductive inferences are probable. Makan and Marty (2001, p. 140) provide examples of inductive and deductive arguments and the conclusion that can be made about formal validity.

Deductive Entailment:	*Inductive Inference:*
All cats like mice.	Most cats like mice.
Zhivago is a cat.	Zhivago is a cat.

Therefore, Zhivago likes mice.

According to Makan and Marty (2001), in the above examples of deductive entailment, it would not be possible for the conclusion to be false if the premise were true. In the example of inductive inference, it is only probable that Zhivago likes mice and therefore the argument would not be considered formally valid.

Logical reasoning provides a basis of thought that goes beyond speculation and provides a reasoned link between the evidence and the conclusion of a statement. According to Velasquez (2002, p. 51), "That is, in a piece of correct reasoning, the conclusion that one wants to prove or establish follows from the evidence or the reasons offered in its support, in this sense: if the evidence or reasons are themselves true statements, then the conclusion also has to be true or probably true."

The foundation of all logic is consistency. If an argument is true, it must always be true; if it is false, it must always be false. If an argument proposes that something exists, then it cannot be true that it does not exist and vice versa. Although some may say that the above is philosophic mumble-jumble, it provides the foundation to all logic and reason. The philosophic concept of consistency states that nothing can be said to be and not be something at the same time and in the same respect (Velasquez,

A paradox is a seemingly absurd statement or proposition, a contradiction, and is derived from Greek: "Contrary to opinion." *"This sentence is false"* is a simple paradox.

2002). As discussed below, a clinical argument for a diagnostic and therapeutic method or procedure cannot be indicated for a particular patient and at the same time not be indicated. If it is inconsistent, the argument for a diagnostic or therapeutic method or procedure is illogical. For reasoning to be logical, it must be consistent.

In formal deductive logic, knowing the distinction between valid and true logical arguments is important. A valid argument is one by which the conclusion logically follows the premise, and is a true argument if the premise is true. For example, if A and B are true, then the conclusion C must also be true. If the structure of the argument does not guarantee the truthfulness of the conclusion, then the argument is considered fallacious. Philosophers call these formal logical statements syllogisms; two premises followed by a conclusion. In communication sciences and disorders, clinical syllogisms can be used to evaluate the robustness of nonscientific diagnostic and therapeutic methods and procedures. When clinicians are confronted with the necessity of diagnosing and treating a disability for which there are few, if any, clinical methods and procedures scientifically demonstrating their efficacy, there are three clinical syllogisms for justifying their clinical utility: intuition, authority, and relative application. Formal deductive reasoning is integral to each of the below strategies (Tanner, Sciacca, & Cotton, 2005).

Clinical Intuition

Intuition is knowing something instinctively, immediately, and without apparent conscious thought; it is natural and largely automatic reasoning. Without scientific proof, a clinician may rely on his or her clinical intuition; the clinician can use a particular procedure because it intuitively seems clinically applicable. Intuition is the least robust method of knowing a procedure's clinical utility. In the intuition clinical syllogism, the argument is as follows:

Premise: Clinical intuition can be applied to methods and procedures.

Premise: My clinical intuition says this method or procedure is indicated.

Conclusion: This method or procedure is indicated.

The premise of the intuitive argument above does have value, but is far from an absolute truth. In valid deductive logic, if the clinical premise is true then the conclusion must be true. However, clinical intuition has no empirical base, and it is implied without qualification. "Having a sense or feeling about something does not make it true, even if the event does happen. The basis of one's intuition or introspection is often unknown, implicit, and frequently not communicable to the public" (Lum, 2002, p. 48). In the above argument, the premise is suspect rendering the conclusion at least partially suspect.

Clinical Authority

A professional authority is someone or a professional organization having official power to enforce obedience and is recognized by their knowledge and expertise. A clinician may select a particular clinical method and procedure because an authority has deemed it clinically applicable to that particular communication disorder. Clinical authorities include authors of textbooks, professors, seminar presenters, and clinical supervisors. Clinical authority can also include national, state, and local professional societies and associations and their position statements on the diagnosis and treatment of the particular disorder. The robustness of this decision is related to the credibility of the authority, the theoretical bases to the position, and the applicability of the clinical procedure to the particular communication disorder.

The logic for application by authority is as follows (Lum, 2002, p. 25):

Dr. X (a popular or respected individual) claims procedure X works or Factor Y causes Z.

Popularity and respect are qualities that represent endorsement of this person by the community.

Dr. X is valued in the community and therefore Dr. X's ideas must be valid.

Dr. X's ideas must be credible or right.

The premise for the argument that a particular diagnostic or therapeutic method or procedure is indicated based on clinical authority is more credible than a personal intuitive premise. Belief in a clinical authority that is based on general professional acceptance and recognition is more valid than belief in purely subjective intuition. However, professional acceptance, popularity, and respect by a professional community is only partially credible because professionals are subjected to fads and popular

Clear and unambiguous words are necessary for sound logical reasoning. A fallacy of ambiguity occurs when the use of unclear or ambiguous words results in flawed reasoning.

trends lacking validity. Sometimes, popular authorities promote methods and procedures for financial gain associated with product endorsements, and demands for training and lectures to promote their methods and procedures. The psychological defense of ego protection also can play a role in a clinical authority's promotion of a particular method or procedure. An example of faddish clinical authority occurred with Phrenology (see Chapter 3). During the early 1800s, Franz Joseph Gall proposed that intellect and personality could be discerned by palpations of the bumps and contours of the human skull. In Europe and the United States, there was widespread practice of Phrenology based primarily on Gall's clinical authority. However, as a rule, a clinical authority who enjoys widespread recognition and acceptance by his or her professional peers has face credibility because of peer review and criticism.

Relative Application

A speech-language pathologist or audiologist can select a particular clinical procedure because its value has been shown with similar cases. He or she borrows it from another clinical situation, profession, or circumstance, although the communication disorder for which it is to be used is dissimilar in one or more aspects. Clinicians working in school settings use educational methods and procedures adapted from the education professions. Educational methods for teaching reading, writing, and other language-based activities, such as following directions, auditory perceptual activities, and arithmetic, are borrowed from education and adapted to children with communication disorders. These educational methods may or may not have been scientifically tested for their efficacy on normal children. The speech-language pathologist and audiologist use them for communication disorders diagnostic and therapeutic methods and procedures because of their apparent success in educating normal children. The clinician may vary their usage based on case-specific factors such as concomitant physical disabilities and levels of mental retardation. These goals, objectives, methods, and procedures borrowed from education are adapted to communication-disordered clientele. In most educational settings, they are formalized as Individualized Educational Program (IEP) goals and methods.

Speech-language pathologists and audiologists working in medical settings also may use nonscientific methods and procedures borrowed from related medical and rehabilitation professions. For example, treatment methods and procedures used by occupational therapists and neuropsychologists for improving orientation in patients with traumatic brain injuries can be applied to patients with neurogenic communication disorders (aphasia, apraxia of speech, and the dysarthrias) who also are disoriented. The reality-orientation exercises may or may not have been tested for their efficacy with traumatic brain injured patients with communication disorders. Similarly, counseling approaches and physical therapies may be borrowed by speech-language pathologists and audiologists for application to patients with communication disorders.

The argument for using nonscientific methods and procedures from other disciplines and adapted to communication disorders is as follows:

Premise: Treatment X works with patients in related disciplines.

Premise: Treatments that work with patients in related disciplines can be applied to similar patients with communication disorders.

Conclusion: Treatment X will work with my communication-disordered patient.

Essential to the truthfulness of the premise is the similarity of the applications. The degree of similarity suggests the validity of application. For example, if the phonics method of teaching reading is used frequently and successfully by educational professionals for normal children, then it has relative application to dyslexic learning-disabled students and stroke survivors with aphasia-related reading difficulties. The more similar the communication-disordered individual to normal students, the more valid is its application. In this case, because of the relative similarity of learning-disabled dyslexic individuals to normal children being taught reading in the classroom, the phonics method of teaching reading would be more applicable to a learning-disabled child than to a stroke survivor.

Analytic Questions to Consider When Evaluating Nonscientific Clinical Methods and Procedures

1. What evidence exists that the premise is based on fact?

2. Is the structure of the argument valid? Does the conclusion logically follow the premise?

3. Does clinical experience with other patients support the truthfulness of the premise?

4. Does the premise appear congruent and consistent with natural and physical laws?

5. Does the structure of the clinical syllogism appear logical?

6. Is there a reasonable cause-effect or correlation hypothesis to the syllogism?

7. Does the premise have empirical evidence to support it? Is it, in itself, a logical statement?

Figure 4-1 shows clinical decision making in communication sciences and disorders.

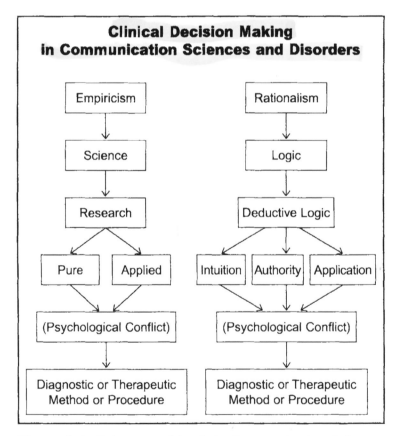

Figure 4-1. Science and Logic in Communication Sciences and Disorders.

The Psychology of Clinical Decision-Making

When a clinician is confronted with selecting diagnostic or therapeutic methods and procedures, his or her certainty about their application to a particular patient, student, or client is not absolute. This is particularly true concerning diagnostic or therapeutic methods with little or no scientific proof as to their efficacy. The clinician is often placed in a conflict situation involving two (or more) diagnostic or therapeutic methods and procedures. In these situations, conflict theory can be applied to the psychological processes involved in clinical decision-making. Conflict theory provides insight into the psychological reactions of the clinical decision-maker in the selection process.

Conflicts occur when a person is prompted simultaneously by incompatible response tendencies. Conflicts are at the core of indecision, and anxiety is generated until they are resolved. There are four basic conflicts applicable to clinical decision-making in communication sciences and disorders: approach-approach, avoidance-avoidance, simple approach-avoidance, and double approach-avoidance (see Table 4–1).

Approach-Approach Conflicts

In the approach-approach conflict, two desirable clinical diagnostic and therapeutic methods or procedures appear equally

Table 4–1. Clinical Decision Conflicts

Conflict	*Approach-Avoidance Tendencies*
Approach-Approach	Two desirable diagnostic or therapeutic alternatives
Avoidance-Avoidance	Two undesirable diagnostic or therapeutic alternatives
Simple Approach-Avoidance	One diagnostic or therapeutic option with desirable and undesirable components
Double Approach-Avoidance	Two diagnostic or therapeutic options each with desirable and undesirable components

applicable to the clinical decision-maker. This conflict is the least distressing, and the easiest resolved, of all the conflicts. In the approach-approach conflict, the clinician ultimately selects the most appropriate and applicable diagnostic and therapeutic method or procedure. During the initial stage of the decision process, the clinical decision-maker is in a state of relative equilibrium. During the analytic process, the clinical decision-maker will be drawn to one diagnostic or therapeutic procedure more than the other(s). This increase in approach may be caused by factors such as a patient's report of his or her preference or testimony from another clinician. The increase in approach may also be a result of increased attention to some aspect of the method or procedure. In the approach-approach conflict, the closer the clinical decision-maker is to the decision goal, the more sense of approach he or she experiences. The decision-related anxiety is eliminated once the method or procedure is decided.

An example from communication sciences and disorders of the approach-approach clinical decision conflict occurs with articulation therapy. Both the traditional sensory-motor approach and the phonologic method of improving articulation have solid research and clinical history to support them. A client with an articulation disorder can benefit from the traditional sensory-motor approach where the clinician works on auditory perception, production, and carryover of correct speech sound production. Similarly, treating the articulation disorders as a language-based phonology disorder and teaching the appropriate phonologic rule, rather than the speech sound error, also produces positive results. Although these two approaches appear dissimilar, there is a strong relationship between phonologic processes discovery and traditional phoneme acquisition (Culbertson & Tanner, 2001a), and a dependency of neuromotor oral maturation on phonologic development (Culbertson & Tanner, 2001b). In this approach-approach conflict, the clinician ultimately selects the one deemed most appropriate to the particular client. Other factors involved in resolving the conflict include the clinician's familiarity with the two procedures, the number of articulatory errors, and time constraints.

Avoidance-Avoidance Conflicts

Whereas the approach-approach conflict involves desirable clinical diagnostic and therapeutic methods and procedures, the avoidance-avoidance conflict involves two (or more) undesirable alternatives. In the avoidance-avoidance conflict, the clinician must choose a clinical diagnostic or therapeutic method or procedure that is unsupported, flawed, unsuited, or inappropriate to a particular patient, student, or client. The dearth of clinically relevant and applied research often necessitates this conflict between two (or more) unsupported, flawed, unsuited, or inappropriate options. When people are confronted only with undesirable alternatives, the tendency is to escape the quandary altogether, to refuse to make any decision. However, clinicians are often in a trap situation where avoidance or escape from the decision is not a professional alternative. Job requirements and conditions of employment dictate that the clinician provide speech and hearing services no matter the proven efficacy of the clinical diagnostic and therapeutic methods available. Most clinicians cannot refuse to provide speech-language pathology and audiology services because the available methods and procedures have not been scientifically proven. In contrast to the approach-approach conflict, when the clinician is closer to the decision and there is a stronger sense of approach, in avoidance-avoidance conflicts, the closer the clinician is to deciding the "lesser of evils" the stronger the avoidance inclination. Ultimately, when the clinician finally makes an avoidance-avoidance decision, the clinical diagnostic or therapeutic method or procedure selected is the one least likely to do harm and most likely to benefit the patient, student, or client.

An example of the avoidance-avoidance conflict in communication sciences and disorders involves stuttering therapy. Tanner and Derrick (1981) found that a majority of Arizona public school clinicians believed they were unprepared to treat stuttering. Public school clinicians reported that they did not receive adequate training in college to prevent or treat stuttering, nor did they keep sufficiently current on new methods and procedures for stuttering once they graduated. Additionally, Arizona public school clinicians did not believe the public schools were the optimal clinical environment to treat children who stutter. They cited large caseloads and time constraints.

The first avoidance tendency in the avoidance-avoidance conflict experienced in the above situation involves the requirement for clinicians to serve children who stutter in an unsatisfactory clinical environment. The clinician avoids employing prevention or treatment methods and procedures that may only exacerbate the children's stuttering disorder. Placing children with developmental stuttering on a caseload, and only providing therapy a few minutes per week, may draw attention to the developing disorder and consequently perpetuate it. This Diagnosogenic Theory of Stuttering is a well-established etiologic principle that was first advanced by Johnson (1938). The second avoidance tendency in the above avoidance-avoidance conflict involves ignoring the developing stuttering disorder and not providing clinical services to a child in need of it. This avoidance tendency occurs because the clinician may know that prevention and early intervention strategies, when properly conducted, are likely to prevent, cure, or significantly minimize the communication disorder. Providing the minimal clinical time in an unsatisfactory clinical environment or ignoring the developing stuttering are avoidance-avoidance conflicts. Both alternatives are clinically undesirable. Today, although the preparation and clinical environment may have changed in Arizona public schools concerning stuttering, the avoidance-avoidance conflict may occur clinically. Public school clinicians still question their knowledge base and treatment strategies especially when confronted with complex communication disorders (Timler, Olswang, & Coggins, 2005).

Simple Approach-Avoidance Conflicts

In a simple approach-avoidance conflict, a single goal has both desirable and undesirable aspects. Professional speech and hearing service providers are occasionally confronted with opposing drives, and the conflict is resolved when one drive weakens or the other becomes stronger. Hearing aid dispensing provides an example of a simple approach-avoidance conflict.

An audiologist may experience an approach tendency to prescribe and sell a hearing aid because of the profit motive. For audiologists, especially those in private practice, hearing aids are profitable, and the profit motive contributes to the approach tendency to prescribe a hearing aid to a particular patient. Profits from hearing aids contribute to the audiologist's private practice, and help ensure that the business will continue to exist. The profit motive drives all businesses in free enterprise and contributes to the system's efficiency. The avoidance drive in the audiologist's simple approach-avoidance conflict may occur when prescribing a hearing aid that may not be used consistently by the patient or will not appreciably improve the wearer's hearing. Knowing this, the audiologist avoids prescribing the hearing aid because of personal morality and professional ethics. In this example of a simple approach-avoidance conflict, the audiologist may oscillate in the decision process as he or she approaches the decision to prescribe the hearing aid because of profit motive, and experiences the moral and ethical avoidance tendencies. The audiologist may vacillate in the decision process as the avoidance tendencies counter the approach tendencies and vice versa. The conflict is resolved when either the approach or avoidance drive becomes stronger or, in non-trap situations, when an alternative is chosen such as providing the patient with a trial period to use the hearing aid.

Double Approach-Avoidance Conflicts

The double approach-avoidance conflict is the most common type of conflict experienced by humans in everyday decision-making. The conflict involves two alternatives both with good and bad implications. These types of conflicts occur in communication-disordered individuals with the drive to speak and the desire to remain silent (Tanner, 1996, 1999). A brief discussion of the double approach-avoidance conflict in communication-disordered persons illustrates the nature of the conflict.

A person with a communication disorder is driven to speak. He or she wants to speak because of all the benefits reaped by verbal communication. The person can obtain goods and services and express thoughts and emotions. Symbolically, speech represents potency and vitality and is psychologically rewarding. Yet for a person with a communication disorder, speaking is fraught with negativity; it is also avoided. There is the negativity of verbal impotence, being disabled and out of control in this, the most basic of human abilities. There is also the embarrassment, shame, and guilt associated with word-finding problems, slurred and stuttered speech, baby-talk, and so forth. Disordered speech violates social norms and creates distress, impatience, anxiety, and pity in listeners. The act of speaking is both approached and avoided.

For the person with a communication disorder, silence is also approached and avoided. Silence is approached because it can be a refuge from negativity. For many speech-disordered persons, the only time they show abnormality is when speaking; in silence, they are as normal as others. Silence is psychologically safe. But silence is avoided, too. Remaining silent when confronted with questions, requests for information, and prompts to participate in a discussion suggests abnormality and negates the safe haven of silence. Additionally, a silent person projects tacit approval of what others have spoken. Silence, like speech, is both approached and avoided. For the communication-disordered person, verbal communication is often a double approach-avoidance conflict.

The double approach-avoidance conflict is the most common type of clinical decision quandary because of the complexity of clinical practice. This is particularly true when clinical decisions require selecting a method or procedure for which there is little scientific information or when nonscientific ones must be used. In the double approach-avoidance conflict, the clinical decision-maker is simultaneously stimulated to approach and to avoid two different diagnostic or therapeutic methods or procedures. In this decision quandary, each option has positive and negative implications. The diagnosis of dysphagia, a swallowing disorder, provides an example of the double approach-avoidance conflict.

When a patient with a suspected swallowing disorder is referred to a clinician, a clinical or bedside evaluation is conducted. Based on that evaluation, review of the patient's chart, and information obtained from the medical and nursing staff, the clinician must decide whether a video swallowing study (VSS) is indicated. In a video swallowing study, the structure and function of the swallowing mechanism is assessed using videofluoroscopy, a real-time motion picture viewing of the patient sucking, chewing, and swallowing a barium liquid or paste (or food substance soaked in barium). The primary purpose of the video swallowing study is to decide whether the patient aspirates. Patient aspiration of food and liquid during the swallow is a serious medical complication that can lead to aspiration pneumonia and congestive heart failure.

In the double approach-avoidance conflict, the clinician approaches the decision to request the video swallowing study because there are one or more clinical bedside indications for performing it. For example, Daniels, McAdams, Brailey, and Foundas (1997) found several factors predicting the severity of dysphagia: Dysphonia, dysarthria, abnormal volitional cough, abnormal gag reflex, abnormal cough reflex, cough after swallow, and voice change had predictive value in determining the severity of dysphagia. The clinician approaches the decision for the VSS recommendation because the patient has one or more clinical bedside indications of severe dysphagia. However, the clinical decision-maker also avoids the recommendation for a video swallow examination because few patients present with all factors suggesting the need for the procedure, and there is the possibility that the procedure is unnecessary.

Not recommending the video swallowing study is also approached and avoided by the clinical decision-maker. Postponing or refusing to recommend the procedure is approached because patients often improve spontaneously and continued observation may be warranted. Additionally, the procedure is invasive, expensive, and often distressing to the patient. Postponing or refusing to recommend the procedure is avoided because physicians, nurses, and other health care professionals may want immediate information about the patient's swallowing function and the clinician is pressured to conduct it. Complicating the decision process is that the clinician knows that oral intake of food and liquid is pleasurable and satisfying for the patient. For some patients, eating may be one of the few pleasurable aspects of life remaining.

For the clinical decision-maker, the recommendation for a video swallowing study is both approached and avoided. The recommendation for the video swallowing study is an important clinical decision that can have serious medical implications for the patient and legal implications for the clinician. Failure to conduct a video swallowing study can be a legal issue in medical malpractice suits (Tanner, 2003a, 2006). Although the clinician recommends the video swallow study, there is no assurance it will yield accurate diagnostic results. There is always the possibility that the video swallowing study will be a false positive, and the patient diagnosed as an aspiration risk when, in fact, he or she can swallow effectively. A false negative shows that the patient is normal concerning the swallow, when in reality, he or she has dysphagia and risks aspiration.

As noted above, when a clinician is confronted with selecting diagnostic and therapeutic methods and procedures, certainty about their application and appropriateness for a particular patient, student, or client is not absolute. The clinical decision-maker is often placed in a conflict situation where both approach and avoidance tendencies are present. Understanding the nature of these conflicts sheds light on the clinical decision process and inevitable anxiety generated by conflicts for the decision-maker.

Anxiety: Worry, angst, fear and apprehension; lacking a sense of well-being, or in the extreme, a feeling of impending doom.

CHAPTER SUMMARY

Catalog-epidemiologic, descriptive, and experimental scientific methods are the empirical foundations to the knowledge base in communication sciences and disorders. In experimental research, a study's statistical significance suggests the confidence and the power of the study, but does not necessarily show its importance. There is a dearth of applied clinical research from which speech-language pathologists and audiologists can base diagnostic and treatment methods and procedures. Clinical decision-making in communication disorders is complex and often generates conflicts and anxiety for the decision-maker. Clinical syllogisms can be used for analyzing the robustness, logic, and truth of nonscientific speech and hearing diagnostic and treatment methods and procedures.

Study and Discussion Questions

1. Describe the two scientific divisions of communication sciences and disorders.

2. Compare and contrast qualitative and quantitative research in communication sciences and disorders.

3. Describe catalog-epidemiologic research in communication sciences and disorders, and provide an example of the type of questions answered by it.

4. Provide an example of descriptive research in communication sciences and disorders.

5. What is the purpose of the literature review in experimental research?

6. What is the null hypothesis, and why is it used in experimental research?

7. Compare and contrast dependent and independent variables in experimental research.

8. What is the relationship between statistical significance and research importance?

9. Write a clinical syllogism.

10. What is a true and valid syllogism?

11. What are the traits that go into making a person or institution a clinical authority?

12. Provide an example of the double approach-avoidance conflict in clinical decision-making.

Suggested Reading

Makan, J., & Marty, D. (2001). *Cooperative argumentation.* Prospect Heights, IL: Waveland Press.

Timler, G., Olswang, L., & Coggins, T. (2005, January). "Do I know what I need to do?" A social communication intervention for children with complex clinical profiles. *Language, Speech, and Hearing Services in Schools, 36,* 73-85.

CHAPTER 5

Consciousness, Language, and Thought

*"In the beginning was the Word
and the Word was with God,
and the Word was God."*

John 1:15

CHAPTER PREVIEW

This chapter examines human consciousness, language, and thought relative to the discipline of communication sciences and disorders. There is a discussion of language and learning in the origin of human consciousness. Human thought is reviewed relative to problem-solving and free-floating thoughts, and the nature of images and symbols used in information processing. The cognitive and association controversy in aphasia is reviewed including differences between adult and childhood cognition. Ego states are discussed relative to mental executive functioning and metacognition. The topics of consciousness, language, and thought discussed in this chapter provide a foundation for understanding *The Unified Model of Communication Sciences and Disorders.*

Human Consciousness and Communication

At the most fundamental level, the study of human communication, and the diagnosis and treatment of its disorders, like all human endeavors, is but one facet of collective human consciousness. Thought and language lie at the heart of a person's consciousness, and it is necessary to examine them scientifically and philosophically to appreciate their roles in *The Unified Model of Communication Sciences and Disorders*. The following provides a framework for understanding consciousness, thought, language, and their disorders. Language plays an important role in people's thought processes. Verbal symbolism and consciousness are fundamentally related in self-awareness, and communication is a conduit for a person's knowledge of the world. Additionally, speech and hearing practitioners diagnose and treat patients with reduced or disordered awareness of self, others, and the environment. From the effects of congenital deafness on a person's perceptions of the world to traumatic brain injury and impairments of mental executive functioning and metacognition, speech and hearing clinicians frequently confront altered consciousness in their patients. As discussed below, communication in general, and language in particular, have played a role in origin of human consciousness, continue to provide it with form and structure, and will influence its future evolution.

Defining Consciousness

"For all organisms—apart from viruses—the basic unit of life is the cell, each of which also possesses the essential characteristics of life, including the potential to move and reproduce." (*Scientific American*, 1999, p. 349).

Consciousness (Latin for "knowing self and others") is self-awareness and having knowledge of surroundings. Yet, to be conscious is more than awareness of self and surroundings. A conscious person actively integrates knowledge of the past and present, realistically appraises the future, and has the levels of wakefulness and arousal to purposefully act on an ever changing environment. Consciousness is sometimes considered a product of the sensorium, a hypothetical part of the brain for the intellect, and the reticular activating system, which regulates wakefulness and arousal. Awareness of one's self and the environment begins at birth and develops and expands with age. Some philosophers suggest that the developing fetus has an unworldly consciousness, and the origin of human life occurs when the fetus is capable of this self-awareness, primitive though it be.

The earliest experiences with communication occur in the womb. Some authorities claim that sound detection and even speech discrimination occur toward the latter part of gestation. The birth cry is usually the newborn's first oral expression announcing his or her willingness to communicate by whatever means possible. Later, cries become differentiated and the infant can use them to express several different needs and wants. The earliest speech sound productions of the infant are perpetuated by his or her awareness of physical and auditory sensations. Through babbling and cooing, the infant gradually discovers the pleasure and power of communication. The developing infant is consumed with self-discovery that his or her immature and developing brain only limits.

Throughout childhood and adolescence, self-discovery occurs for the ever changing physical, psychological, and cognitive human being, and communication serves as a bridge to others' consciousness. For adults, communication is an important conduit for heightening conscious awareness of self, family, occupation, politics, economics, religion, and mortality. Throughout life, communication is a fundamental part of human self-discovery and awareness of the world. It is an integral part of human self-awareness, and speech, language, and hearing provide the primary channels for knowledge and manipulation of the environment.

Defining Language

Human consciousness is the process of abstraction, and this symbolic mental function is inherently tied to language. Language abstraction is the generalization from specific sensations to categorical concepts, which, in turn, are represented by arbitrary symbols. These abstract and arbitrary representations of reality are linguistic symbols with embedded morphemes, their smallest units of meaning. There are many definitions of language and they vary greatly among professionals. The following requirements must be met for any comprehensive definition of language.

First, language, at its core, is dynamic symbolism. Words, whether spoken, written, or gestured, are symbols; they are arbitrary representations of reality. The word is the symbol and that to which it refers is the referent. This symbol-referent relationship, semantics, is the substance of language and the foundation to linguistic meaning. Whether the referent is tangible and concrete such as "chair," or intangible and more abstract such as "honesty," words are arbitrary symbolic representations of reality. The words and their meanings are dynamic because semantics changes over time. Because of changing events, the meaning of each word changes every time it is used. Although the symbol remains the same, the referent, that for which it stands, changes because of the passage of time and the ever changing nature of reality. The Russian linguist Vygotsky (1962) notes that a word does not refer to a single object but rather to a class of objects and this generalization reflects reality differently than does an image (sensation).

Second, language is rule-governed. There are grammatic rules for combining sounds into words and words into sentences. Phonology is the rule-governed way speech sounds are sequenced and organized, and syntax is the sentence organization of language. In contrast to the arbitrary nature of semantics, grammar gives stability, predictability, form, and order to language. Campbell (1982, p. 165) comments on grammatic order:

Language competence and performance can be likened to the board game of chess. Chess players understand the rules of the game (competence), but chess masters are also skilled in the game's strategy (performance).

> Grammar, which is part of [language] competence, acts as a filter, screening out errors and incorrect arrangements of words, showing a speaker which sentence forms are admissible, and whether they are connected with certain other sentence forms by rules of transformation. Language is therefore protected from randomness at the source, giving it great stability and helping to keep it intelligible, even when it is disorderly at the surface level. This, after all, is the basic requirement of any information system, that its messages should vary unpredictably, but vary according to certain specific rules and conditions.

Chomsky (1965, 1971, 1975), and others, distinguish between linguistic performance and competence. Linguistic performance is the use of language in everyday conversations, the speaker's actual use of language. Language competence is the knowledge possessed by native users of a particular language, knowledge of the rules of syntax, grammar, phonology, and semantics. Campbell (1982, p. 163) discusses noise, deep and surface structure, and the role of language in coding messages:

> In Chomsky's linguistics, which is constantly undergoing revision and change, a set of basic rules generates "deep structure," which is the abstract plan of a sentence. Deep structure is closest to the meaning intended by the speaker, and the least affected by distortions and ambiguity. It is the structure to which all other structures can be reduced. Other kinds of rules, known as rules of transformation, change deep structure into surface structure, which, though abstract too, is the final form of the sentence before its conversion into the physical sounds of speech.

Deep structure has less noise and more closely represents reality, and according to Chomsky, is the "mirror of the mind."

Third, language is a social code that a particular community has agreed upon, and is a major part of the culture of the people using it. This arbitrary, rule-governed system is used by a community of like-minded individuals who accept that system as their mode of communication. Language not only expresses a society's culture, but is its foundation and cornerstone.

Finally, there are six primary avenues of language expression and reception: speaking and auditory comprehension (verbal), gesturing (expressive and receptive), and writing and reading (graphic). They are separated into expressive and receptive modalities. The expressive modalities of language are speaking, writing, and using expressive gestures. The receptive modalities are auditory comprehension, reading, and understanding what has been gestured. Mathematical symbolic expression and reception are also modes of language. Mathematics is considered the universal language and is culturally neutral. Based on the above requirements, the following definition of language competence is relevant to the discipline of communication sciences and disorders: *Language—the multimodality ability to encode, decode, and manipulate symbols for the purposes of verbal thought and/or communication.* This definition is used for the following theoretical discussion of the role of language in consciousness and thought (Table 5-1).

Table 5–1. Language Definition Requirements

Dynamic Symbolism	Changing symbolic representations of reality
Rule-Governed	Structured by rules of grammar, syntax, and phonology
Social Code	Code agreed upon by a language society

Modalities of Language	Expressive
	    Speaking
	    Writing
	    Gestures

	Receptive
	    Auditory comprehension
	    Reading
	    Gestures

	Mathematics

The Origin of Consciousness

Human consciousness has been a controversial philosophical and religious concept since humans achieved the level of awareness to question the nature of existence. The origin and nature of human consciousness lies at the core of all major philosophies and religions. Although consciousness has been examined and debated for centuries, contending that, today, the nature of human consciousness is understandable, or even knowable, would be presumptuous. Proposing that the brain-mind dichotomy has been solved by current neuroscientists would also be unreasonable. Although there have been giant leaps in projecting the workings of the brain to what goes on in a particular person's mind, the brain-mind dichotomy remains largely unsolved and controversial. It would be equally unreasonable to assert that the development of language is responsible for the origin of human consciousness, for consciousness is the result of the totality of human evolution. However, exploration of this fundamental aspect of humanity is necessary to understand language and, by extension, language disorders. Consciousness and language are fundamentally intertwined in the human experience, for language not only expresses consciousness, it structures it, and language symbolism certainly played a role in its origin.

Princeton University professor, Julian Jaynes, in *The Origin of Consciousness in the Breakdown of the Bicameral Mind*, postulates that true consciousness did not exist until approximately 4,000 years ago. According to Jaynes (1976), consciousness is a learned process born from evolving brain structures. His "breakdown of the bicameral (two chambered) mind theory" suggests that early humans obeyed voices of gods during a preconscious hallucinatory period, and they had little realistic awareness of themselves or their surrounding. His provocative and controversial theory accounts for supernatural reports made by all religions during this time. In Jaynes' treatise, he also describes several theories for the origin of consciousness including that it is a property of protoplasm, a result of behaviorism, and simply a function of the reticular activating system. He also explores the notion that consciousness is the result of metaphysical imposition and that some supernatural force or deity created it. According to Jaynes, the theory that consciousness is a property of matter is attractive to physicists and is the most extensive explanation for the concept. Consciousness as a property of matter, energy, and a result of learning provides a logical theory for understanding the past, present, and future relationship between consciousness, thought, and language.

Consciousness, Symbolism, and Language

The universe is composed of matter and energy, and on Earth, consciousness has evolved to its existing nature and degree. The Earth is approximately 4.5 billion years old, and given this amount of time, human consciousness emerged from matter and energy. Given the billions of years necessary for it to develop, human consciousness, at the most elemental level, is a property of matter and energy. Of course, there are different levels and types of consciousness unique to each type of animal life. For example, a worm's awareness of self and the environment certainly differs from that of a frog, dog, parrot, or chimpanzee.

Human consciousness appears to be the most eminent and highly evolved on the planet, and it gradually came into existence, at least in part, by the cognitive ability to engage in symbolism. Symbolism is the use of symbols to represent reality, and the symbol is something that stands for something else or represents it in the abstract. Because of symbolism, humans have developed the ability to represent reality, including themselves, in the abstract. Language symbolism permits humans to think about themselves and to go beyond concrete sensations associated with self-perceptions and the environment. Language allows, and in many ways demands, that humans think abstractly about their personal existence. Because of language, a human, unlike a worm, can think about his or her existence in the abstract and ponder mortality, perceptions of the universe, the meaning of life, and question the very nature of his or her existence.

Defining Thought

Defining thought is no simple undertaking. The nature of thought is controversial and often the subject of heated debate. The nature of thought is at the core of understanding dementia, mental retardation, delusions, agnosia, aphasia, and intelligence. Defining thought without defining reason is impossible; thought is the result of thinking, and thinking is the process of reasoning. All philosophers, more or less, address thought, thinking, and reasoning in their philosophies, but it was Plato and Aristotle who considered the human capacity to reason sacrosanct. Plato and Aristotle believed that the ability to reason separated human beings from animals and implicitly tied thought and reason to the human soul. Whether these assumptions are true or false depends on the definition of reason. "Reason [is] the capacity for thinking relatively and making inferences; the process of following relationships from thought to thought and of ultimately drawing conclusions" (Velasquez, 2002, p. 721). Thought, the product of reason, is not exclusive to humans, but the quality and quantity of reasoned information processing are certainly more extensive in the human.

This discussion of consciousness, thought, and language is limited to the human "mind" rather than the "brain." Consciousness, thought, and language, at the brain level, are electrochemical impulses traveling along nerve axons to synaptic junctions, and they constitute brain waves and neurologic reactions that can be read by powerful brain-scanning devices. At the most basic level, consciousness, thought, and language can be reduced to these chemically based electrical impulses and changes in brain chemistry. Changes in consciousness, thought, and language are the result of new neuronal connections and chemical changes occurring in the brain. But describing thoughts as electrical charges and chemical reactions is of little use when trying to understand relationship of consciousness, language, and thought. "After all, when you think, electrical charges and specific chemicals do not come to mind. Thoughts are images of the past, present, and future combined with narratives or self-talk about them" (Tanner, 1999, p. 114).

The cerebral cortex is the site of higher mental functions, comprises an area of 2.5 square feet, and contains as many as fourteen billion neurons (Kirshner, 1995).

British-born neurologist and author Oliver Sacks (1990) notes that one way of understanding the role of language in thought is to examine human beings deprived of language (e.g., in aphasia). However, "If one is to explore the fundamental role of language, one needs to study not its loss after being developed, but its failure to develop" (Sacks, 1990, p. 32). Sacks goes on to postulate the role of multidimensional sign language in inner speech. Sign language, unlike speech, has the three spatial dimensions plus the dimension of time giving it more informational capabilities.

Problem Solving and Free-Floating Thought

Before addressing units of thoughts, the images and verbal symbols used in thinking, describing two general outcomes of information processing is necessary. Generally, thinking is problem solving or free-floating information processing. As the name suggests, problem-solving thoughts are the kinds of information processing used by a person to solve a problem. He or she processes information to find a way around a life obstacle, to answer a problem, to understand a concept, or to discover a new perspective about life and living. "The problem might be minor, such as deciding whether to have a cup of coffee or a bottle of pop, or it might be significant, such as seeking the answer to a major question such as the choice of a career, deciding to have children, or how to answer a tax audit" (Tanner, 1999, p. 113). When a person is engaged in problem-solving thought, he or she has a goal in mind, and cognitive psychologists call this type of thinking "adaptive cognition."

Free-floating thoughts are all other types of thinking that are not problem-solving. Free-floating thought is not goal-directed information processing; there is no desire or need to solve a problem or to reach a goal. "Taking in a beautiful sunrise, appreciating a Mozart waltz, remembering an experience that happened in your youth, or anticipating grandchildren visiting for Thanksgiving are all examples of free-floating thoughts" (Tanner, 1999, p. 113). In free-floating information processing, thoughts come and go. They neither produce answers nor solve problems. People freely and rapidly alternate between problem-solving and free-floating thought. One minute, thoughts may be adaptive and goal-directed, and the next, they are free-floating and incidental. Of course, intellectually disciplined individuals can problem-solve for long periods.

Units of Thought

When thinking, people use images, verbal symbols, and a combination of both as units of thought. Images are iconic representations of reality and verbal symbols (self-narratives, internal monologues, inner speech) are used during problem-solving or free-floating thought. Although the human brain works as a whole, as a rule, visual-spatial-temporal information processing is a product of the right hemisphere, and language is a left-dominate hemisphere function in many people. This left and right brain functional dichotomy is only partially true, although many people erroneously believe it to be a complete, factual, and literal account of brain functioning.

Nearly a century ago, the noted linguist, Edward Sapir, discussed the futility of localizing language to a particular part of the brain. "If language can be said to be definitely 'localized' in the brain, it is only in that general and rather useless sense in which all aspect of consciousness, all human interest and activity, may be said to be 'in the brain'" (Sapir, 1921, p. 10). Sapir contends that language is a fully formed functional system and part of a human's spiritual constitution. According to Sapir (1921, p. 19) "We see therefore at once that language as such is not and cannot be definitely localized, for it consists of a peculiar symbolic relation—physiologically an arbitrary one—between all possible elements of consciousness on the one hand and certain selected elements localized in the auditory, motor, and other cerebral and nervous tracts on the other." According to Brewer (2004, p. 27) "At this time, however, our knowledge of the brain is limited. Some proponents of so-called brain-based learning are making claims that cannot be proven." Claims about the generally accepted belief that the two hemispheres of the brain have vastly different functions are not supported by fact; both hemispheres are involved in almost every processing task (Bruer, 1999).

A good example of bi-hemispheric and holistic brain functioning is prepositional representation. Some proponents of brain-based learning and strict linguistic localization contend that prepositions are exclusively language-based, left hemisphere linguistic concepts. However, with just a moment's thought, it must be acknowledged that prepositions involve visual-spatial and temporal representations. Prepositional concepts such as "in," "beside," "below," "above," and so forth, are as much visual-temporal-spatial concepts as linguistic ones. Attributing prepositions exclusively to the left hemisphere is an overgeneralization and simply an inaccurate conceptualization of brain functioning.

Although an oversimplification, when people process information, whether to solve problems or during free-floating thought, they "show themselves pictures and tell themselves stories." Certainly there is more to cognition than using visual and verbal units to process information, but for the purposes of understanding consciousness, thought, and language, this discussion emphasizes iconic and verbal representations of reality.

Thinking in Images:
Iconic Representations of Reality

Obviously, when visually processing information, a person does not put the objects of the world inside his or her brain and think about them. What is processed through the eyes, or in the mind's eye, are light representations of objects: icons. An icon, Greek for "image," is physically and tangibly related to the object because the light representations are accurate in their depictions of it. It is a visible impression obtained by a person, a direct likeness of the object as a visual sensation. The object seen in the mind or mind's eye is refracted light energy; it is light that the eye's lens deflects. Philosophically, however, because the actual object is not processed in the person's brain, only its icon, thinking visually is always at least one step removed from reality. The visible light spectrum is 400,000 to 800,000 cycles per second, representing the range from red to violet (Goss, 1982). And technically, because of the passage of time, brain processing of information is always in the past because of the time it takes for light and neuronal energy to reach the brain. Campbell (1982, p. 204) comments on the abstraction of imagery:

> Light never stays the same from one moment to the next. It dims or brightens, changes its frequency. The observer, too is never wholly at rest. He moves around things, seeing them from different angles. Cars and people recede into the distance, throwing smaller images into the retina of the eye. Shapes loom up as we walk toward them. Seen through a train window, closer objects appear to move faster than those far away. Yet the viewer imposes a certain stability on all this shrinking and swelling, on these gross distortions and deformations, by paying attention to the stable features of change and ignoring the rest.

In visual processing of information, there are two levels of image processing: image-present and image-stored.

Sight consists of light entering the pupil which is focused by the lens. The image is projected on the retina where light energy is converted to electrical nerve impulses. The optic nerve to the brain carries the impulses, where it is processed as visual images.

Image-Present Icons

Visual processing using images that are present involve real-time sensation, perception, and association through the visual sense. In image-present visual processing, the person sees images of reality and processes the information. For example, to solve the problem of how to get out of a room crowded with people and things, a person can look at all the possible routes and choose the best one. The images necessary to solve the problem are present and do not require language or processing of stored information. This kind of visual processing also occurs when a carpenter decides to change the design of a bookcase or a brick-layer makes a wall level. In image-present free-floating thought, a person appreciates a painting in an art gallery or enjoys the sun setting over the ocean. In free-floating thought, there is no need visually to solve a problem; it is simply the taking in of visual images.

Image-Stored Icons

The ability to store images of reality in the mind, and to process information without being in direct physical contact with it, is a major dimension of human consciousness. Thinking in stored images gives humans the ability to solve problems and to engage in free-floating thought physically removed in time and space from their actual surroundings. Based on previous experiences, they also can conjure hypothetical images not seen or experienced and use them in information processing. People engage in this type of thinking, using stored images, in their "mind's eye."

Washing a car in one's driveway is an example of using image-stored icons. To solve the problem of how to wash the car using stored images, a person can see in his or her mind's eye, the car, driveway, hose, faucet, and soap without being physically home. The person can imagine whether the hose will be long enough to reach the car, speculate on the location of the soap and washcloth, and see in his or her mind's eye the act of washing it. Using images stored in the mind, the person can decide whether to wash the top of the car first or last. The images needed for the problem-solving are stored in the person's brain and can be processed with his or her eyes opened or closed.

Other examples of the kinds of problems solved in the mind's eye include the best route home from work or school, washing dishes in the sink, and how many trips it will take to the laundromat to do the week's laundry. A carpenter can plan a project, determine how much lumber is necessary, and the time necessary to complete it using stored images. Free-floating information processing using stored images include daydreaming about an upcoming vacation, reminiscing about an event in the past, and imagining a romantic stroll through a moon-shadowed footpath. Problem-solving and free-floating thought also can occur using visual symbols such as the American flag, religious artifacts, and actions that are symbolic. Image-stored problem-solving and free-floating thought can also be done while engaged in other activities.

In the eye, rod cells are stimulated for black and white vision while cone cells are stimulated for color vision.

Thinking in Words: Internal Monologues

In the discipline of communication sciences and disorders, the notion of internal monologues or inner speech, and its role in thought and language, have not been widely studied. The concept of internal monologues has not been systematically addressed nor integrated into current theories of cognition, speech, language, and communication disorders. This is remarkable because internal monologues are central to understanding thought, several communication functions, and language disorders. They can help answer several important questions about the nature of communication and its disorders. For example, do globally aphasic persons have intact inner speech? What role does receptive vocabulary have in intelligence? Do people who clutter and stutter do so when engaged in internal monologues? What are the thought processes for congenitally deaf individuals and how do they process verbal information?

Sacks (1990) speculates on the nature of external and internal speech, and the development of a sense of self. According to Sacks (1990, p. 59) "We start with dialogue, with language that is external and social, but then to think, to become ourselves, we have to move to a monologue, to inner speech." At about 24 months, normal children begin internalizing language during regulation and direction of their own behavior. "Dialogue launches language, the mind, but once it is launched we develop a new power, 'inner speech,' and it is this that is indispensable for our further development, our thinking" (Sacks, 1990, p. 58).

Internal monologues, inner speech acts, occur rapidly. Although precisely measuring how fast a person talks silently to himself or herself is impossible, it is estimated that verbal thoughts occur faster than 1,000 words per minute. Internal monologues occur about five times more rapidly than externalized speech which is about 200 words per minute depending on the nature of the conversation and how relaxed is the person. Besides being produced much more rapidly, internal monologues are not like the carefully constructed, detailed utterances spoken to others; they tend to be telegraphic in nature. This is because there is no need for elaborate descriptions of thoughts when engaged in internal monologues. Nevertheless, internal monologues follow the general rules of grammar giving structure to verbal thought.

Internal monologues tend to be more abstract than visual imagery because language itself is more abstract. Abstract thinking involves theoretical concepts, and it is more removed from direct sensation and perception of reality; abstractions exist only as ideas. The nature of language and abstraction may account for the abstract-concrete imbalance seen in aphasic persons first postulated by Kurt Goldstein (1924, 1948, 1952). Goldstein theorized that aphasic patients have specific deficiencies in maintaining an abstract attitude.

According to Sies (1974), John Hughlings Jackson applied the concept of inner speech to the study of aphasia and related disorders. He believed that all forms of speech were similar and that inner speech occurs with the same structure as other propositional utterances. Jackson believed it was artificial to consider the kind of utterance spoken to someone else as basically different from internal monologues. Jackson combined

Cognitive psychology is the psychological specialty addressing thought, perception, memory, and reason. Psycholinguistics is the study of psychological factors associated with language.

thought, language, and the individual's intent in communicating with the study of aphasia and related disorders (Tanner, 2003b).

Little scientific research has been done on brain localization for internalized speech. Neuroscientists have identified general areas of brain activation during various cognitive activities such as reading, concentrating on external objects, talking, listening, meditating, and so forth. It does not appear that there are different language processing centers for internalized and externalized speech. Of course, externalized speech involves motor speech production centers of the brain, but language processing per se during internal monologues does not appear to be neurologically different from what occurs during spoken language acts.

There may be more than one level of internal monologues. Macdonald Critchley postulated the concept of the preverbitum (Sies, 1974). According to Critchley, the preverbitum is the silent thinking process that differs from inner speech and precedes it (Critchley, 1964, 1970). Sacks (1990, p. 60) considers inner speech an expression of self: "Language and thought, for us, are always personal—our utterances express ourselves, as does our inner speech." Brumfitt (1996, p. 352) comments on loss of a sense of self in aphasia: "When this language is taken away it is not clear how this affects the individual's sense of identity. It can be hypothesized that, in order to define ourselves, we need language, and we need to be able to understand other people's definition of us as part of that process."

That thought per se is impaired in aphasia was first postulated by Trousseau (1865) who believed intelligence is always "lamed" in aphasia. The concept of internal monologues is central to the language-thought controversy in aphasiology. The language-thought controversy involves the role of language in thinking and vice versa. Pivotal to this controversy is the definition of language, thought, language disorders, and motor speech impairments. Over the years, two schools of thought have emerged in aphasiology about the language-thought controversy as it pertains to aphasic patients. Adherents to the association school regard intelligence as a function of large areas of the brain working holistically and that the language centers are removed from the sites for intellectual functioning. Conversely, adherents to the cognitive school reject the idea that thought and language centers of the brain are mutually exclusive. The association school of thought assumes that aphasic disorders are limited to disturbances in labeling ideas, objects, and events, and the cognitive school rejects the idea that thought and language are separate entities (Benton, 1981).

The Language-Thought Controversy in Children

The language-thought issues are different for adults and children. In adults, thought processes are mature and developed, while children are in a process of cognitive development. In adults, language facilitates thought, and it is integral to mature reasoning and abstract thinking. However, in children, especially younger ones, language serves the primary function to express thought. Cognitive development in the child is influenced by maturation and experience, and progresses through several stages (Piaget & Inhelder, 1969).

Although the sequence of cognitive development is relatively invariant, the rate is highly variable. "In other words, a child must pass through each stage, but children may pass through the stages at different ages. The transition time between stages is lengthy. Children do not move suddenly from one stage of thinking to another—changes may take months or years, as the child constructs and integrates knowledge. A child may be performing some tasks in ways that indicate preoperational thinking while performing other tasks in very stable operational ways" (Brewer, 2004, pp. 26–27).

In Piagetian terms and stages, language serves only to express thought during the sensorimotor period (birth to 24 months) where the child reflexively responds, more or less, to his or her environment. During the preoperational period, 24 to 72 months, the child gradually develops symbolism. During this lengthy time of cognitive development, thinking becomes progressively more abstract and less egocentric. By the end of this period, in most persons, language moves beyond expressing thought to becoming a fundamental aspect of reasoning. Additionally, according to Bruer (1999), research does not support the widely held belief that learning takes place more readily in young children. There is little scientific evidence that a young person learns more quickly or easily than an adult.

Other Types of Thinking

People also process information using other units of thought. The information coming from the senses of touch, taste, and smell are used as primary representational units for problem solving and during free-floating thought. When a person searches for car keys in his or her pocket or purse, he or she does not need visual imagery or verbal symbols to know when they are

Tactile agnosia, a perceptual disorder, is the inability or impaired ability to recognize objects through the sense of touch.

found. Neither does an individual need visual imagery nor verbal symbols to be repulsed by the taste of sour milk or vacate a room because of the odor of natural gas. Problem solving about finding car keys or ingesting sour milk, and leaving a potentially explosive situation, do not require images or words. Neither are visual images and verbal symbols needed for free-floating information processing; they are not necessary to appreciate the texture of a fine cut of cloth, nor are they needed to enjoy the taste of aged cheese, or to savor the bouquet of a fine wine. Information coming from these senses do not require images or verbal symbols for problem solving or free-floating information processing.

As has been noted repeatedly, no single part of the human brain operates independently of other areas; the brain functions holistically. When processing information coming from the sense of touch, taste, and smell, visual images and verbal symbols are triggered and become part of the total processing. Visual images and verbal symbols not only accompany these sensations, but are often prompted by them. The sense of smell, in particular, is a powerful trigger for association and recall of stored memories. A wisp of a fragrance, odor, or scent can prompt memories of days gone by and subconsciously affect behavior. In addition, pheromones are hormones secreted by an individual and perceived through the sense of smell by another and affecting sexual attraction. This is largely because cranial nerve I, the olfactory nerve, does not go through the filtering and gatekeeping of the thalamus; it directly enters the brain for immediate processing.

Mental Executive Functioning and Metacognition

Professionals in communication sciences and disorders address thought, thinking, and reasoning as cognitive prerequisites in language delay and mental impairment/mental retardation. In adults, thought, thinking, and reasoning disorders are indirectly addressed in aphasia. However, many theoretical and clinical issues related to adult and pediatric traumatic brain injury directly concern thought, thinking, and reasoning. Patients with major traumatic brain injuries often suffer impairments in mental executive functioning. Mental executive functioning is the ability to plan, execute, regulate, and monitor behaviors and actions.

The notion of executive functioning comes from business and industry where the chief executive officer of a company is responsible for planning, directing, and monitoring its business affairs. This corporate officer is ultimately responsible for the actions of the company, and the notion of a person's mental executive functioning is the personification of that business role. According to Gillis (1996), behavioral manifestations of executive functioning include inhibition, deliberation, coordination, and self-regulation. Organically, although the brain operates holistically, the frontal lobes are primarily associated with mental executive functioning. Frontal lobes are the largest lobes of the brain and the most recently evolved in humans. Frontal lobe syndrome is associated with problems controlling and monitoring behaviors, emotional appropriateness, initiating and ceasing responses, and loss of the abstract attitude (see Goldstein above).

A more encompassing term for the concept of mental executive functioning is metacognition: thinking about thinking. Metacognition is the monitoring of one's cognitive operations. It involves knowing how and when to attend to information, and when and what to remember (Gillis, 1996). Metacognition is defining problems and identifying strategies for solving them. Whereas the above discussions of visual and verbal thought concerns units of thought, metacongnition involves directing, controlling, and monitoring cognitive processes. Metacognition not only addresses visual imagery and internal monologues; it encompasses the totality of thought including memory and orientation.

Ego States

Thought, mental executive functioning, and metacognition issues in communication sciences and disorders can be understood by examining the organization of the human personality, in particular, the ego. The ego, a Freudian concept, is broadly defined as the executive of the personality. "The ego is said to be the executive of the personality because it controls the gateway to action, selects the features of the environment to which it will respond, and decides what instincts will be satisfied and in what manner" (Hall & Lindzey, 1970, p. 34). The ego mediates the demands of the id and superego. The id is completely unconscious (subconscious) and contains psychic energy and drives such as thirst and hunger. It houses the libido, one's life force, in particular, his or her sexual and reproductive imperatives. The id operates on the pleasure principle and seeks instant gratification. The superego develops from the ego and is similar to one's conscience. The superego is the moral arm of the personality. The ego separates the id and superego, and mediates the demands of each aspect of the personality. The ego also functions to

Controversial psychoanalyst Carl Jung, a student of Freud, believed in a collective unconscious, a reservoir of memories inherited from a person's ancestral past.

defend and protect the person from external or internal unpleasantness, and these verbal defense mechanisms are unavailable to globally aphasic patients (Tanner, 2003b, 2003c). In the mid-1900s, Transactional Analysis, a cognitive psychology theory and counseling approach, proposed three ego states that incorporate internal monologues as a process of metacognition (Berne, 1961, 1964).

According to Transactional Analysis, there are three ego states: Parent, Adult, and Child. Although there are similarities between the Transactional Analysis concepts of Parent, Adult, and Child and the Freudian ideas of superego, ego, and id, they are not the same. The theory for these ego states is based on brain stimulation studies on conscious subjects. These studies show that when parts of the brain are stimulated with electrodes, single memories from the past and the feelings associated with them become conscious. Actually, the memories were more than recollection; many subjects said they were reliving the past experiences. These good and bad memories, and the emotions associated with them, form and influence a person's thoughts and attitudes. They are manifest in stereotypical and habitual internal monologues, which may or may not be productive, mature, and adaptive. In addition, Transactional Analysis as a counseling approach examines satisfying and unsatisfying communication transactions between people, but for the purposes of exploring internal monologues, in this chapter, only the analyses of intrapsychic ego states, structural analysis, are addressed.

Parent Ego State

According to Transactional Analysis, the Parent ego state consists of regulating and nurturing forces. The Parent consists of thoughts, feelings, and attitudes learned from a person's parents or parent substitutes such as teachers and religious authorities. The Parent tends to be idealistic and regulates other aspects of the personality. The internal monologues associated with this ego state include the "shoulds" and "should nots" taught to children by authority figures and institutions. The Parent ego state causes persons to think and act as their parents or parent substitutes would want them to think and behave. The regulating force in the Parent ego state is the Critical Parent, and the encouraging and accepting component is the Nurturing Parent.

The Critical Parent is developed before five years of age, and at a time when language is not available to put things in a larger context. It consists of controlling, directing aspects of the personality and causes feelings of inadequacy. In the adult person, the Critical Parent continues to produce some thoughts, feelings, and behaviors based on critical comments and directives given to the young child. The Nurturing Parent internal monologues are comforting and help reduce anxiety and feelings of inadequacy in much the same way as do actual parents. The Nurturing Parent provides stability, consolation, and solace. The Nurturing Parent ego state permits the person to expand his or her consciousness and to explore the environment.

Adult Ego State

The Adult ego state is devoid of emotion; it is objective and rational. This ego state can be likened to a computer that gathers and processes information. It operates on facts, statistics, probabilities, and accurate observations, and is in continual contact with and tests reality. The main function of the Adult is to regulate the various influences of the other aspects of the personality. It re-evaluates old information imprinted on a person's brain when he or she was a child. The Adult ego state is fully developed by the early teens and allows a person to make conscious decisions about the validity of early information and its associated internal monologues. Transactional Analysis also identifies a part of the personality that is the emerging adult and is the source of intuition and creativity. When operating in the Adult, it experiences pleasure with success.

Child Ego State

Transactional Analysis identifies two very distinct Child ego states: Natural and Adapted. The part of the personality that seeks love, total freedom, acceptance, and affection is the Natural Child. This part of an individual's personality is curious, happy, and experiences the thrill of discovery. Importantly, the Natural Child strives for total freedom. It is creative, aggressive, spontaneous, and also rebellious. The Natural Child is a reservoir of an individual's memories of the first awesome experiences with life and the emotions associated with them.

A negative aspect of an individual's personality is the Adapted Child, which is influenced by the Critical Parent. It has feelings of guilt, frustration, fear, and anger. The Adapted Child is a duplication of the original reactions of the individual as a child to the reprimands and admonishments of his or her parents.

Transactional analysis contends that when parties relate to each other in parallel transactions, for example, Parent to Parent, Child to Child, Adult to Adult, Parent to Child, communication is satisfying. When crossed transactions occur, for example, Parent to Adult, Child to Adult, Adult to Child, they can be unsatisfying.

A person acting from his or her Adapted Child is passive and inadequate, and he or she feels inferior and clumsy. The Adapted Child is "too much this and too little that." It is a result of the socialization process and these anxieties and feelings of inferiority can permeate an individual's personality in the adult years. Stuttering is born from this part of the personality where the Child expects verbal impotence, rejection, criticism, and shame from the communication disorder (Tanner, 2006). Table 5-2 shows verbal and visual information processing.

Mental Executive Functioning, Metacognition, and Structural Analysis

As previously reported, Transactional Analysis is a result of brain stimulation studies on conscious subject. In these studies, the subjects reported reliving experiences, and the emotions associated with them, when electrodes were placed on various parts of the brain. The conclusions drawn by Transactional Analysis theorists are that these intact preverbal experiences are stored in retrievable form, largely unfiltered, and can be stimulated by an odor, touch, word, or sight. Structural Analysis involves examining a person's ego states, retrievable experiences and emotions, and the way they influence thought and behavior.

Each ego state has internal monologues characteristic of it. Internal monologues are a basic aspect of cognition; they are the verbal thoughts experienced by a person on a day-to-day basis. Parent ego states have both nurturing and critical inner speech statements. Some are nurturing and comforting for the individual. Others are critical and directing and serve a valuable executive function for the personality. The Child ego state, not to be con-

Table 5–2. Verbal and Visual Information Processing

Metacognition	Visual Images	Verbal Symbols
Problem-solving information processing	Image-present icons Image-stored icons	Internal monologues Parent ego state Adult ego state Child ego state
Free-floating information processing	Image-present icons Image-stored icons	Internal monologues Parent ego state Adult ego state Child ego state

fused with childishness, has both natural and adapted inner statements that embody freedom and love as well as frustrations and inferiority. The Adult ego state mediates the demands of the other ego states and provides nonemotional, objective, and reality-based internal monologues. Together, these three ego states are present, to various degrees, in all individuals. Some people are predominantly Parent in their thoughts, emotions, and actions; others are predominantly Child or Adult. Although people have all three ego states, and accompanying internal monologues, some are predominantly Parent, Adult, or Child in their inner speech at any given time in their lives.

CHAPTER SUMMARY

Language and internal monologues are integrally tied to human consciousness especially in adults. Verbal symbols, arbitrary representations of reality, are used to understand self and are conduits to achieving awareness of the environment. The grammar of language gives verbal thought its order, stability, and predictability. Human thought involves free-floating and problem-solving information processing using visual images and verbal symbols as the primary units of thought. Mental executive functioning and metacognition involve ego states and their associated internal monologues.

Study and Discussion Questions

1. Define consciousness. What parts of the brain are associated with it?

2. Define language. What are the rule-governed aspects of any language?

3. Compare language performance and competence.

4. Describe four theories about the origin of human consciousness.

5. Define thought. What are the outcomes of thinking?

6. Describe visual imagery in thinking.

7. Describe the use of verbal symbols in thinking.

8. What is the preverbitum? How does it differ from inner speech?

9. Compare the thought processes in children and adults.

10. Describe mental executive functioning and metacognition.

11. What is structural analysis?

12. List the ego states and provide examples of internal monologues associated with each.

Suggested Reading

Jaynes, J. (1976). *The origin of consciousness in the breakdown of the bicameral mind.* Boston: Houghton Mifflin.

Kirshner, H. (1995). Cerebral cortex: Higher mental functions. In S. Bhatnagar & O. Andy (Eds.), *Neuroscience for the study of communicative disorders* (pp. 302–313). Baltimore: Williams & Wilkins.

Sowa, J. F. (2000). *Knowledge representation: Logical, philosophical, and computational foundations.* Pacific Grove, CA: Brooks/Cole.

Sternberg, R., & Ben-Zeev, T. (2001). *Complex cognition: The psychology of human thought.* New York: Oxford University Press.

CHAPTER 6

Expressive Language and Motor Speech Programming

"For words, like Nature, half reveal
And half conceal the Soul within."

Lord Alfred Tennyson

CHAPTER PREVIEW

This chapter explores expressive language and motor speech programming, the first stages in *The Unified Model of Communication Sciences and Disorders*. There is a discussion of the concept of expressive language in children and adults, and its relationship to motor speech programming. The evolution of the concept of expressive aphasia and apraxia of speech are reviewed including theoretical, diagnostic, and therapeutic considerations. Serially ordered speech production movements dependent on closed-loop feedback are discussed as essential aspects of motor speech production.

The Concept of Expressive Language

During communication, Andrew's thoughts and feelings are placed in linguistic structures for expression, but language also plays an important role in his thought processes. Some verbal thoughts are simply concrete representations of reality, such as "chair," "coffee cup," and "hot." However, others are intangible abstractions; the words are the units of thoughts, ideas, notions, and concepts such as "thoughtful," "honest," "truth," and "sensible." Andrew's thoughts are based on his experiences and drawn from his personal memories and associations. The linguistic structure includes the grammatic forms all languages take. Speech sounds are arranged in an ordered sequence to form words, and there are rules for stringing them into utterances. These language constructs express Andrew's thoughts and feelings, and they convey his experiences and intentions. (Expressive Language Excerpt from *Connections* in Chapter 1)

"A necessary condition for the successful performance of a definite reference in the utterance of an expression is that either the utterance of that expression must communicate to the hearer a description true of, or a fact about, one and only one object, or if the utterance does not communicate such a fact the speaker must be able to substitute an expression, the utterance of which does" (John R. Searle, 1969, p. 80, *Speech Acts*).

Expressive language and motor speech programming are the first stages in *The Unified Model of Communication Sciences and Disorders*. The process of transforming thoughts into linguistic symbols and motorically programming them for speech acts are intricate human functions. Humans begin the transformation of verbal symbols into speech acts when thoughts are motorically programmed. Although the boundaries between expressive verbal symbolism and motor speech acts are vague and ill-defined, they have distinct clinical manifestations. Aphasia, and language delay and disorders, are separate clinical entities from motor speech programming disorders. This clinical distinction is true for both children and adults.

Reviewing the nature of expressive language and motor speech programming provides a foundation for understanding the myriad disorders that can occur at this stage in the communication process. In addition, in the discussion that follows, expressive communication disorders are used to clarify and elucidate the general and specific topics related to expressive language and motor speech programming. Although exclusive theorizing about normal processes may result in basic understanding about communication, comprehensive understanding of normal expressive processes can only be obtained by appreciating their pathologies. For example, a true picture of expressive vocabulary or motor speech production can only be gleaned by observing and examining expressive vocabulary deficits and apraxia of speech in children and adults.

Speech and Hearing Transition to
Speech-Language-Hearing

In the mid-1900s, the discipline of communication sciences and disorders officially assumed language and language disorders as a fundamental aspect of its scientific and clinical responsibilities. The American Speech and Hearing Association changed its name to the American Speech-Language-Hearing Association while keeping the acronym ASHA rather than the technically correct ASLHA. Clinically, to declare the acquired language emphasis, speech pathologists became speech-language pathologists with the new certification acronym CCC-SLP (Certificate of Clinical Competence in Speech-Language Pathology). Although the American Speech-Language-Hearing Association and speech-language pathologists historically addressed language and language disorders, two professional and political factors prompted this official title and name change. First, special educators were increasingly becoming more involved in the evaluation and treatment of language delay and disorders in educational settings. In some schools, they were the primary specialists in language delay and disorders. Second, in aphasiology, scientists and clinicians recognized that aphasia is primarily a language disorder distinct from the motor speech disorders. This theoretical and clinical movement was based on research conducted by Darley, Aronson, and Brown (1975) in their landmark book: *Motor Speech Disorders*. Darley's (1982) equally influential book, *Aphasia*, further clarified the neurogenic language-motor speech disorder dichotomy with the first aphasia-motor speech disorder distinction: "Aphasia is not a speech disorder."

Accompanying the discipline's new theoretical and clinical focus on language and language disorders was the need to define the parameters of language form and content. The division of language into expressive and receptive modalities, and giving equal weight to each division, was an early unfortunate theoretical and clinical trend. Although expressive language constitutes an aspect of language functioning, it is a relatively minor facet of the totality of language form and content. When motor speech planning and execution are rightly excluded from expressive language parameters, phonology, expressive word retrieval, and expressive grammatic construction remain essential aspects of expressive language. This is particularly true when pragmatics, the intent and context for language usage, is independently evaluated and treated as a social-communication function rather than as an aspect of the fabric of language.

The Inviolable Expressive-Receptive
Language Dichotomy Dogma

Although some speech and hearing scientists and practitioners continue to make the absolute expressive-receptive language distinction, this division is an inexact, yet convenient, compartmentalization of language form and content. Language is multimodality and functions holistically for cognitive and communication purposes. There are no clear boundaries for expressive and receptive language, nor are the individual expressive modalities—speaking, writing, gesturing—functionally independent of each other. For example, when an individual constructs a sentence for expression, the process is not substantially removed from receptive vocabulary and grammar. That receptive and expressive communication skills are not mutually exclusive in children is addressed by Zimmerman, Steiner, and Pond (1992, p. 5):

> It is generally assumed that receptive and expressive skills are related, with receptive acquisition of a language skill serving, in most cases, as a precursor to the expressive acquisition of that skill. A child must learn to recognize a word that he or she hears others use for an object. The child must also learn to associate the word with the object before he or she can produce the word for the object. This does not mean that receptive knowledge is perfect before expressive use begins. A child may begin with only a general idea of what "doggie" means; initially he or she applies the word "doggie" to any furry animal. Over time, a child refines that word-object association to refer to a furry animal that wags its tail and barks.

A person's receptive vocabulary is learned first and is much larger. "Clinically, vocabulary understanding precedes expressive usage" (Tanner, 2003d, p. 126). Receptive vocabulary preceding expression is called the *receptive vocabulary precursor principle*. According to Brownell (2000), expressive and receptive vocabularies are similar but expressive vocabulary requires access to the words for production and memory retrieval. There is also an important relationship among vocabulary, reading, and general educational achievement. According to Brownell (2000), testing vocabulary in education is important for two reasons. First, vocabulary tests provide information about an individual's potential for success in intellectual and academic endeavors. Second, they are quick and easy to administer while providing reliable, valid, and objective results. Brownell (2000) reports that expressive one-word vocabulary tests have a high correlation with other broader areas of language development. Expressive one-word vocabulary is obtained from object, action, and concept prompts.

Wiig, Secord, and Semel (1992) list expressive language fundamentals in preschool and school-aged children as including the following: (1) recall and repetition of spoken sentences in context, (2) formulating labels and sentences, and (3) knowledge and use of word structure rules and forms. The precursor principle in language development is also fundamental to other aspects of expressive language in preschool and school-aged children. Knowledge and use of receptive grammar precede expressive usage. Carrow-Woolfolk (1999, p. 13) comments on the common elements of expressive and receptive language in children: "Comprehension and expression draw upon the same stored information about language structure and about the world." In contrast, oral expression and auditory comprehension differ in significant ways. "The comprehension and expression process differ by the sensory and decoding functions required, by the degree of linguistic knowledge required, by the amount of general background knowledge required, and by the motor requirements needed for the execution of oral expression" (Carrow-Woolfolk, 1999, p. 13).

A current diagnostic category encompassing expressive language delay and disorders is "late talkers." These are children who are significantly delayed in language and primarily show it in delayed expressive abilities. "In the research literature, late talkers are typically defined as young children (between approximately 16 and 30 months) whose language skills fall below 90 percent of their age peers" (Plante & Beeson, 2004, p. 177). According to current research, late talkers tend to be at risk for continued language problems, and the earlier the diagnosis of delayed language development is made, the better the outcome; young children fare better than older ones (Plante & Beeson, 2004). Many late talkers remain behind their peers in language development.

As indicated above, one way of determining whether a child is delayed or disordered in expressive language is to compare test scores. Another way of determining the extent of expressive language delay or disorders is to examine the child's use of language and determine whether it affects his or her social, vocational, educational, or psychological well-being (Gillam, Marquardt, & Martin, 2000). According to Gillam et al. (2000), a growing number of clinicians use both test scores and the consequences of the language disorder on the child to make diagnostic and treatment decisions.

Edward Sapir, the noted linguist and philosopher, believed that language and culture are separate from each other. In his 1921 book, *Language*, he took a contrarian belief that language is not an expression of racial or geographic influences and that it is not an inherited skill. He believed that language and cultural boundaries are separate: "Language does not in any way 'reflect' culture."

Multimodality Expressive Abilities and Aphasia

Research confirming that adult neurogenic language disorders are not modality-specific was conducted during the middle 1900s. This multimodality view of aphasia is particularly true today as the ideas of motor speech disorders and agnosia have been clinically clarified. Motor speech programming consists of creating the motor acts necessary to produce speech sounds. Motor speech programming includes all the muscular functions necessary to produce the respiratory support, phonation, velopharyngeal activities, and articulatory movements for voluntary speech utterances. The most important of these programs involves articulation and the articulatory plan for speech. As discussed later, impairment of motor speech programming, although often a component of Broca's aphasia, is different from anomia, the word-retrieval problems seen in this expressive neurogenic communication disorder. However, perceptual disorders, the agnosias, can be specific to a particular sense modality and can occur independent of aphasia.

The agnosias are perceptual disorders in which a person has the inability or impaired ability to attach meaning to sensory information although sensory receptors are unimpaired. Agnosias, unlike central language disorders seen in aphasia, are modality-specific. In agnosia, a person may have one perceptual impairment, for example, auditory agnosia, while the other facets of communication are unimpaired. Aphasia cuts across all modalities, more or less, and is not limited to an impairment in a single avenue of language. According to Darley (1982, pp. 28–29): "The concept most in accord with the facts is that aphasia is a multimodality symbolic disorder resulting from malfunction of a central integrative mechanism not bound to any particular transmission channel—of ingress or egress— but making use of and relating to all of them."

The realization that aphasia is a multimodality language disorder distinct from motor speech disorders and agnosias has emerged from centuries of clinical observation and research. As discussed in Chapter 3, classification and definition controversies have plagued aphasiology since the beginning of the study of neurogenic communication disorders. Sies (1974) notes that historically the nature of aphasia has generated much confusion and heated controversy among professionals. The academic and scientific progress leading to the current understanding of aphasia as a multimodality language disorder, not significantly affecting cognition and distinct from motor speech disorders and agnosias, can be illustrated by examining the history of aphasia classification systems. To fully understand the notion of expressive language and its disorders, tracing the evolution of classifications about language-based neurogenic communication disorders is necessary. Henry Head, in the early 1900s, considered the study of neurogenic communication disorders a chaos of classification.

The Chaos of Classification: The Distinction Between Symbolic and Nonsymbolic Neurogenic Communication Disorders

Today in neurogenic communication disorders, most scientists and practitioners make a clear distinction between symbolic and nonsymbolic disorders. Symbolic communication disorders are language-based and include aphasia, the language of confusion seen in traumatic brain-injured patients, the language characteristics of persons with dementia, and psychotic language. Nonsymbolic communication disorders are the motor speech disorders: apraxia of speech and the dysarthrias. Aphasia is operationally defined as the multimodality inability or impaired ability to encode, decode, or manipulate verbal symbols for the purposes of verbal thought and/or communication. Apraxia of speech is the inability or impaired ability to plan, program, and sequence the motor aspects necessary for voluntary speech production. The dysarthrias are an aggregation of diagnostic categories of motor speech dysfunctions such as occurs in flaccid, spastic, or ataxic paresis or paralysis, or hyperkinetic (excessive) or hypokinetic (insufficient) movement disorders. The majority of dysarthrias are mixed or multiple motor speech disorders and consist of two or more of the above at any given time or progressively evolve from one type to another over time. To further complicate theoretical, diagnostic, and therapeutic issues, a particular patient is likely to have a combination of aphasia, apraxia of speech, and multiple-mixed dysarthrias. Symbolic and nonsymbolic neurogenic communication disorders rarely occur independently of each other.

The distinction between expressive language and motor speech disorders is important clinically. Treatment procedures and therapies differ for patients who require relearning of language form and function from those for patients with motor speech production deficits. For example, a patient with expressive aphasia requires therapies to deblock word retrieval for expression whereas a patient with apraxia of speech may need to relearn the articulatory planning for sound, syllable, and word utterances. An aphasic patient with telegraphic expressive utterances may need to relearn expanded, grammatically correct utterances; one with dysarthria may need to improve range-of-motion of speech musculature.

The differentiation between expressive symbolic and non-symbolic communication disorders historically has been vague. Concerning expression, the symbolic, expressive components of language (word retrieval and grammatic construction) and the motor speech planning (programming and sequencing components) were often combined into one theoretical category, and disorders grouped into one all-inclusive category of aphasia. This combining of diagnostic categories and blurring of clinical boundaries reduced diagnostic precision and compromised treatment and therapeutic efficiency. As noted earlier, the treatments and therapies for expressive language and motor speech disorders are significantly different, involve different goals and objectives, and are theoretically extreme aspects of verbal expression.

Although past boundaries between symbolic and nonsymbolic communication disorders were often vague, some early scientists and clinicians recognized the aphasia-motor speech expressive dichotomy. The distinction between expressive aphasia and motor speech planning was first made during the Renaissance when some physicians began to realize that brain damage could cause nonparalytic types of expressive communication disorders. Johann Schenck von Grafenberg, in the late 1500s, observed that speechlessness could occur even without tongue paralysis (Benton & Joynt, 1960).

The French physician, Pierre Paul Broca, was the first and most prominent aphasiologist to investigate expressive language and motor aspects of aphasia. Broca, in the 1860s, did post-mortem examinations on aphasic patients under his care and discovered that the left hemisphere, specifically the third convolution of the frontal lobe, was the seat for motor speech planning and production. He labeled the motor aspects of expressive neurogenic communication disorders, "aphemia," and suggested it was a breakdown in the ability to plan, program, and sequence voluntary speech. Unfortunately, in his writings, Broca did not clearly indicate whether these patients also suffered from word-finding and/or expressive syntax and grammatic impairments. Figure 6–1 shows Broca's area of the brain.

The German physician, Karl Wernicke, also practicing in the late 1800s and early 1900s, coined the term motor aphasia. According to Eisenson (1984), Wernicke's notion of motor aphasia was the same as Broca's aphemia, and the communication

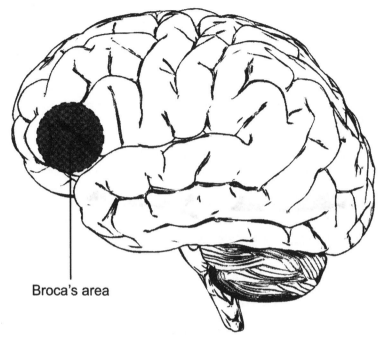

Figure 6–1. Broca's area of the brain.

disorder was the result of damage to the third frontal convolution. Essentially, he described apraxia of speech where the patient's main communicative difficulty is motorically planning, programming, and sequencing motor speech acts. Given the current understanding of the nature of neurogenic communication disorders, Wernicke's "motor aphasia" was the first published diagnostic contradiction in aphasia. Motor aphasia is an oxymoron. Aphasia is a language disorder and, by definition, symbolic and not a motor deficit. Thus, it is a contradiction in terms that a patient can have "motor" "aphasia." Wernicke also coined the diagnostic term "conduction aphasia" as resulting from disruption of the pathways between Broca's area and the center for sound memories.

The neuron is the basic functional unit of the nervous system. It includes a cell body, axon, and dendrites. The synapse occurs when a neural impulse goes from one neuron to another.

Henry Head, an outspoken critic of the brain localization movement, and proponent of aphasia being a multimodality disorder, criticized Wernicke's scientific methods and conclusions. In his 1926 book, *Aphasia and Kindred Disorders of Speech*, Head sarcastically labeled Wernicke and other localizationists as "diagram makers." Henry Head rejected the idea that pure modality-specific aphasias exist owing to isolated brain lesions of the brain. Head identified four categories of aphasia including verbal aphasia, a "predominantly" expressive neurogenic communication disorder.

The Concept of Predominantly Expressive Aphasia

For decades, some aphasia scientists and clinicians recognized that aphasia, when defined as a language disorder, cuts across all expressive and receptive modalities. However, in 1935, a neurologist, Theodore Weisenburg, and Katharine McBride, a psychologist, conducted experimental research on the nature of aphasia and created the diagnostic classification of "predominantly expressive aphasia." They administered verbal and nonverbal tests to aphasic subjects, brain-damaged nonaphasic subjects, and subjects without brain damage. Because of their research, they identified "predominantly expressive aphasia" as one of the four categories of the neurogenic communication disorder.

The concept of predominantly expressive aphasia indicated that the disorder involves all modalities of expression and reception with the main element being expressive functions. According to their classification system, patients with predominantly expressive aphasia have the greatest amount of communication difficulty expressing ideas through speech and writing. They also created a separate category for patients with global, severe language impairments: "expressive-receptive aphasia." In addition, they noted a mental concretism associated with aphasic cognitive processing (see Chapter 5) and set the stage for considering aphasia as a syndrome: "The results of this research demonstrate that aphasia is predominantly a language disorder, but they are equally conclusive proof that it is rarely if ever confined to language processes" (Weisenburg & McBride, 1964, p. 438). Although there were weaknesses in the design of their study, particularly involving how early the subjects were tested post-neurologic insults, their classification system served as the basis for several tests and assessment protocols during the latter part of the 1900s.

The Russian aphasiologist, A.R. Luria (1958, 1974) took an analytic-synthesis view of aphasia and proposed that expressive aphasia can be viewed as a communication synthesis disorder. According to Eisenson (1984), Luria's efferent motor aphasia results in impairments of the ability sequentially to order the articulatory gestures for speech production with accompanying writing disturbances. Semantic aphasia involves grammatic and syntactic impairments in expressive language. Luria also coined the term "dynamic aphasia," a disorder in transforming self-talk into externalized speech.

Luria, and others, took issue with Wepman and Jones' (1961) linguistic regression theory. It proposed that the expressions of aphasic patients can be correlated to childhood speech and language development. According to Wepman and Jones, the speechlessness of an infant corresponds to global, severe aphasia and successive stages of speech and language development in children parallel types of expressive aphasic disturbances. Wepman and Jones (1961) believe that stages of recovery from aphasia should parallel childhood acquisition stages.

Schuell, Jenkins, and Jimenez-Pabon (1964) and Schuell (1965) also rejected the expressive-receptive aphasia dichotomies as artificial. They grouped aphasia into major categories and also addressed sensorimotor involvement and dysarthrias. Regarding expressive language, they noted that aphasic patients typically speak and write at about the same level. According to Schuell and colleagues, the telegraphic expressions of aphasic patients, abbreviated utterances using a reduced number of function words (similar to a telegram), are a result of a reduced attention span and a general lack of vocabulary. In contrast, Jakobson and Halle (1956) considered telegraphic speech, and other problems combining words into complex constructions, essentially a grammatic and syntactic disorder. According to Jakobson and Halle (1956), aphasic word-finding problems are similarity disorders and expressive grammar and syntax deficits are contiguity disorders.

> A paraphasia is a word chosen by an aphasia patient that is close semantically or phonetically to the one he or she wants to speak.

Telegraphic Expressions

Today, the nature of telegraphic speech and other grammatic-syntactic deficits in aphasia remain controversial. One school of thought considers deficits combining words into sentences and expressive language grammatic transformations a result of damaged linguistic grammatic-syntactic processing per se. Because of damage to grammatic-syntactic processors, an aphasic patient loses the ability to construct grammatically correct utterances. Another school of thought considers grammatic-syntactic deficits a direct result of generally reduced vocabulary. Because there are fewer function words compared to content words in a person's expressive vocabulary, the uniform reduction in vocabulary results in telegraphic speech and other grammatic-syntactic deficits. A third school of thought suggests that both damaged linguistic grammatic-syntactic processing and an overall reduction in vocabulary results in telegraphic speech and other grammatic-syntactic deficits. It is likely that telegraphic speech is a result primarily of reduced vocabulary but also impaired grammatic-syntactic processing in patients with co-occurring agrammatisms. "Patients with agrammatic aphasia have maximum difficulty in using (and understanding) grammatical morphemes (connectors and affixes) and lesser degrees of difficulty in the use and understanding of lexical morphemes" (Benson & Ardila, 1996, p. 54).

Anterior-Nonfluent Aphasia

Benson and Ardila (1996), and others, propose evaluating expressive language functioning in aphasic patients by subdividing their output into posterior-fluent or anterior-nonfluent types of aphasia. This division is based on the site of lesion and its proximity to the fissure of Rolando, which separates the frontal lobe from the parietal lobe. Most persons with left hemisphere lesions posterior to the fissure of Rolando have fluent output and concurrent verbal comprehension deficits (see Chapter 10). Nonfluent output is associated with left hemisphere lesions anterior to the fissure of Rolando.

Benson and Ardila (1996) list key features making nonfluent output easily recognized. First, nonfluent aphasic patients have decreased output, often fewer than 10 words per minute. Second, patients with nonfluent expressive aphasia have increased effort and struggle to produce speech. Third, dysarthria is often present in nonfluent aphasia. Fourth, nonfluent aphasia is associated with decreased phrase length and often limited to holophrastic (one word) utterances. The fifth and final feature of nonfluent aphasia output is dysprosody, namely, unmelodic, dysrhythmic, incompetently inflected speech production. "All five of these characteristics need not be present for an aphasia to be considered nonfluent, but some degree of sparse output, short phrase length, and dysprosodic speech are present in almost every nonfluent aphasic patient" (Benson & Ardila, 1996, p. 90).

Agraphia

Agraphia, the writing deficit seen in expressive aphasia, is sometimes considered a less complex aspect of neurogenic communication disorders. In fact, writing is fundamentally as complicated as verbal expression, given the complex brain activity required to perform it, and it is not innate to humans. "Writing is a complex brain activity that demands knowledge of language codes (phonemes, words), ability to convert phonemes into graphemes, knowledge of a graphemic system (alphabet), highly skilled motor ability, and precise spatial ability to distribute and separate letters" (Benson & Ardila, 1996, p. 213). When comparing expressive language delay and disorders seen in children with the expressive communication disorders with adult aphasia, it is important to consider that writing, unlike verbalization, must be taught. Whereas all normal children learn speech without tutoring or teaching, writing must be explained. Humans have the innate ability to attach meaning to verbal symbols without the benefit of education, but attaching meaning to graphic symbols must be taught. Children are born to talk, but writing must be learned.

Broca's Aphasia: Anomia and Apraxia of Speech

Broca's aphasia is the classification term commonly used to describe acquired predominantly expressive speech and language disorders resulting from cerebral insult. It is the preferred term used by physicians, nurses, and therapists and encompasses several clinically technical aspects of aphasia. Similar diagnostic terms and classification categories for aphasic symptoms include motor aphasia, nonfluent aphasia, anterior aphasia, predominantly expressive aphasia, telegraphic speech, and apraxia of speech (Tanner, 2006). Two distinct categories of expressive communication disorders characterize Broca's aphasia: anomia and apraxia of speech. Anomia, the language component, results in high-frequency words being more available for recall than low-frequency words, telegraphic speech, and grammatic-syntactic impairments (agrammatisms). Because the language-based anomia is multimodal, there are concurrent difficulties with writing and using complicated gestures for expression. Mathematical expression is also impaired. Because the word-finding deficits are predominantly, but not exclusively, expressive, receptive modalities are also affected (albeit to a lesser degree) with the patient experiencing verbal comprehension impairments, reading abnormalities, and reduced ability to understand complicated gestural expressions. It often takes detailed testing to quantify these comprehension deficits.

An expressive phenomenon that occurs in normal persons and patients with expressive language communication disorders is the tip-of-the-tongue phenomenon. The tip-of-the-tongue phenomenon is sometimes referred to as a "feeling-of-knowing"

(Nicolosi, Harryman, & Kresheck, 2004). It occurs when an individual has difficulty recalling a particular word and senses that verbalizing it is just beyond realization. In normal speakers, the tip-of-the-tongue phenomenon frequently occurs on proper names such as those of friends and acquaintances. In patients with expressive aphasia and anomia, the tip-of-the-tongue phenomenon can occur on all parts of speech and is widely distributed among them. The tip-of-the-tongue phenomenon suggests that the patient is aware of word-finding difficulties and believes he or she is potentially self-corrective. Verbal trial-and-error is common in individuals experiencing the tip-of-the-tongue phenomenon. Speakers also bide for time by commenting that the recall and expression of the word are just beyond an expressive trigger, and by using fillers such as "ah," "uh," and "You know." To trigger the word, the speaker may utter aloud synonyms and words spelled and sounding similar.

A distinct and separate motor component of Broca's aphasia is apraxia of speech. As discussed above, apraxia of speech, or verbal apraxia, is the inability or impaired ability voluntarily to program the five basic motor speech processes of respiration, phonation, articulation, resonance, and prosody. Primarily affecting articulation, this motor speech aspect of Broca's aphasia is a nonlinguistic, sensorimotor dysfunction affecting voluntary speech planning, sequencing, and execution (see below). Patients with Broca's aphasia can be separated into those whose symptoms are primarily anomia-based and those whose symptoms are primarily apraxia of speech-based. The treatment for anomia-based Broca's aphasia involves relearning and deblocking language in all modalities while the treatment for apraxia of speech involves relearning motor speech planning and execution. Although the above distinction about expressive aphasia provides clinically meaningful information, it also illuminates the core nature of expressive verbal symbolization and motor speech programming in both children and adults.

Limb apraxia is a higher-order motor planning dysfunction affecting the voluntary performance of skilled motor acts of the limbs.

Verbal Symbols and the Motor Speech Plan in Children and Adults

For both children and adults, expressive verbal communication involves two interrelated but distinctly separate cognitive and physical functions: semantics and motor speech. Semantically, each word used for voluntary verbal expression is a symbol selected from a person's memory: verbal and visual associations. As discussed in Chapter 5, the symbol may be concrete such as "chair," "car," and "run," or abstract such as "truth," "thoughtful," and "God." The semantics of an utterance consists of the arbitrary sequence of phonemes, the verbal symbol, and that to which it refers, the referent. A language community has agreed upon the meaning of these words; there is agreement in the arbitrary relationship between the sequence of speech sounds and that to which they refer. This relationship between the symbol and that to which it refers is the essence of semantics. The meaning of every expression, no matter how trite or profound, lies in this symbol-referent relationship.

> *Once the language constructs are formulated, they are routed to the motor speech programming centers of Andrew's brain. The primary motor speech center is in the left hemisphere of his brain, and where most of the movements, timing, and positioning for the act of purposeful speech are programmed. Programmed are the respiratory support, frequency and intensity of vocal fold vibrations, tongue, lip, and soft palate movements, and the rhythm and fluency required for normal speech production. The plan and sequence of speech involve more than one hundred muscles, and are activated and monitored by thousands of neurologic impulses. They are nearly instantaneously programmed in response to Andrew's ongoing language requirements to express himself. Only rarely does Andrew give thought to the complicated neuromuscular plans required for each utterance; for the most part, they are done subconsciously.* (Motor Speech Programming Excerpt from *Connections* in Chapter 1)

Distinct from the symbolic aspect of an utterance is the motor speech plan for its production. There are differences in the mental and neurologic requirements for recalling and constructing grammatically and syntactically correct symbols, and the motor requirements for the physical actions necessary to produce them.

The Development of Motor Speech Programming and Childhood Apraxia of Speech

Motor speech programming develops gradually in children and is generally established by the age of seven when most children can produce consonants and vowels in all three positions of words (Tanner, Culbertson, & Secord, 1997). Certainly, other factors are involved in phoneme production mastery such as auditory perception, but by the age of seven, most children have mastered the motor abilities voluntarily to produce speech sounds in the three positions of words. Phonologic development must also be considered in motor speech programming development. Motor speech development and phonologic rule extinction seem divergent processes. However, as reported in Chapter 4, there is a dependency of neuromotor oral maturation on phonologic development (Culbertson & Tanner, 2001a, 2001b). The extinction of immature phonologic processes is dependent on the child's neuromotor oral maturation; he or she must be physically capable of adopting mature phonologic processes.

Oller (1980) reports that during the transition from pre-speech to speech, infants show a series of phase shifts in motor speech development. They are stages in motor speech development and presumably the foundation for articulatory programming of syllables learned during the first year of life. Children move from simple reactive phonation to comfort sounds during the first two months of life. Gooing, guttural articulations that are precursors to consonants, occur from two to three months, followed by the expansion stage. Expansions occur at four to six months and are vocalizations that are the beginning of syllables such as squeals, growls, yells, and isolated vowel-like sounds. At seven to ten months, canonical, basic motor speech productions include true babbling, vowels, and reduplicated syllables. Finally, variegated, multifaceted babbling emerges during the final months of the first year of life. At this stage, the infant uses combinations of different types of syllables.

Children who are born with apraxia of speech, or acquire it before the age of seven, and individuals who acquire it after motor speech production abilities are developed, share similar symptoms. Regarding the five basic motor speech processes in both children and adults, apraxia of speech is primarily a disorder of prosody. In pure apraxia of speech, where there are no other neurogenic communication disorders, the prosodic impairments are caused by the impaired ability to produce motor speech movements accurately, particularly articulatory gestures. In pure apraxia of speech, patients have normal or near-normal comprehension, are aware of their errors, and consequently self-correct, often with struggle. Because individuals with acquired apraxia of speech, usually adults, have produced correctly programmed utterances in the past, they are more likely to struggle overtly, complicate the speech act, and experience frustration at their verbal impotence and suffer loss of integrity of the self (Tanner, 2003b).

Children born with apraxia, or those who acquire it during the motor speech programming developmental period, also experience frustration and verbal impotence. "Often the affected children are forced to struggle at the single-word level. Even when they can produce multiword sentences, their speech lacks the normal prosody" (Plante & Beeson, 2004, p. 74). However, their frustration and verbal impotence is based on general communication incompetence, and the disorder is less threatening to the integrity of the self. Certainly, because of this communication disorder, the child feels the full psychological effects of the impaired motor speech programming impairments, and the prosodic deficits and struggle reflect their frustration. However, the adult who has naturally, easily, and without difficulty produced phonemes, syllables, words, and multiple words thousands of times in the past, and who is aware of this new impairment to perform such an easy task, feels more the impotence, frustration, and threats to self-esteem than does a child with developmental apraxia of speech.

Three factors must be considered when determining the effects of apraxia of speech in children. First, the age at which the child acquires the expressive communication disorder determines the symptoms. Children born with brain and nervous system injury causing praxic disturbances present with different symptoms than those who acquire it during the motor speech programming development period or those who acquire it after it is presumably developed. Second, the degree of motor speech programming impairment determines the nature and extent of symptoms. Mild apraxia creates different compensation and coping strategies than do moderate and severe ones. For example, organically based stuttering in children likely develops from apraxia of speech. Third, the level of motor speech programming deficits influences the nature of the symptoms. Deficits at the conceptual level result in different compensatory symptoms than do impairments with closed-loop feedback or motor speech execution (see below).

One issue that must also be addressed in childhood apraxia of speech is the existence and location of brain injury. Some authorities have questioned whether childhood apraxia of speech is a result of brain damage. "It is also difficult to accept the disorder in a true apraxic context. Apraxia of adulthood has been unequivocally associated with verified brain lesions, in children, however, this has not been the case" (Love & Webb, 2000, p. 307). Nevertheless, because brain injury has not been demonstrated may reflect more the subtlety of the damage and current limitations of brain scanning devices to detect it. Additionally, childhood apraxia of speech may be a result of undetectable brain irregularities and/or deficiencies and imbalances of neurotransmitters.

Oral, buccofacial apraxia is different from apraxia of speech. However, it also results from sensorimotor cortical damage. In oral, buccofacial apraxia, the patient has problems performing volitional nonspeech movements of the jaw, lip, and/or tongue. Patients with oral apraxia may or may not have apraxia of speech.

Serially Ordered Motor Speech Conceptualization, Planning, Execution, and Closed-Loop Feedback

In the mid-1900s, Karl Lashley proposed that speech production is an intricate process of serially ordered speech movements (Lashley, 1951). He theorized that dynamic speech events are combined into units and programmed prior to their execution. At the same time, the science of cybernetics, which addresses the role of feedback in regulating systems, was being applied to theories of motor speech programming and control. The result was the servosystem model of motor speech production. The servosystem model proposed that speech production is a closed-loop system of feedback where the output is evaluated at its source and modifications made if necessary (Fairbanks, 1954). Together, Lashley's serially ordered speech movements and the servosystem model of feedback theorized that speakers conceptualize speech movements with ideal dynamic targets, program and execute them, evaluate feedback about their production, and make ongoing alteration in the program if necessary.

Together these two theories would provide a credible model for understanding the way humans conceptualize, plan, execute, and adjust ongoing motor speech acts. They also provided a basis for Darley, Aronson, and Brown's (1975) distinct stages of motor speech programming and the levels of neurologic damage causing apraxia of speech. According to Darley et al. (1975), disorders occurring at the conceptual level result from damage to both cortical and subcortical structures. Spatial-temporal planning impairments are likely a result of damage to the supramarginal gyrus in the dominant hemisphere. "The detailed programming of the act presumably occurs in the frontal cortex in front of the origin of the upper motor neuron system" (Darley et al., 1975, p. 63). There are three phases of motor speech programming: conceptual, planning, and execution.

Conceptual Motor Speech and Ideational Apraxia of Speech

The theoretical and clinical separation of symbolic and motor aspects of verbal expression are least definitive at the conceptual phase. At the conceptual phase, the motor aspects of the verbal thought prompting the utterance are planned. Here, the motivation to express oneself, thoughts, words, and their motor speech plans are integrated into a volitional act. The conceptual phase of motor speech production can be viewed as the creation of a verbal proposition. In the 1800s, John Hughlings Jackson proposed that an utterance is more than a "heap" of sounds and words. "The unit of speech is the proposition. A single word is, or is in effect, a proposition, if other words in relation are implied" (Jackson, 1878, p. 311). According to this view, purposeful verbal expression is the act of verbal propositionalizing.

At the conceptual phase of motor speech planning, speech sounds are programmed in the larger context of the idea driving the verbal expression. The motor speech disorder at the conceptual phase, ideational apraxia of speech, results from the speaker being unable to grasp the thought, including the motor plan driving the speech act. In ideational apraxia of speech, there is no clear delineation between symbolic and nonsymbolic processing. This type of apraxia of speech is seen in dementia, traumatic brain injury, and other cognitive-linguistic disorders where the patient has trouble appreciating the thought driving an utterance.

Planning Motor Speech and Apraxia of Speech

The timing, speed, strength, and precision of the motor speech act in general, and the articulatory plan in particular, are generated at the planning phase. At this phase, all the motor speech requirements necessary to produce the utterance is created including the specific muscular movements related to each voluntarily produced speech sound production. Although this process is considered a motor speech process, in fact, auditory, tactile, kinesthetic, and proprioceptive sensory feedback are also important to the plan. A person's memory of the sensory feedback associated with motor speech production is integral to the plan. The memory of each articulatory gesture includes its acoustic qualities, and tactile, kinesthetic, and proprioceptive sensations associated with its production. Consequently, it may be more accurate to label this process motor-sensory speech processes.

At the planning phase, the respiratory support necessary to produce an utterance is determined, and other motor aspects of speech production are based on the respiratory support. The anticipated respiratory support during a speech act serves as the foundation for all other aspects of the speech program; more or less anticipated respiratory support affects all other aspects of the motor speech program. Laryngeal valving parameters are planned including which phonemes are to be voiced, and if they are produced with vocal cord vibration, the frequency (pitch)

The primary motor area of the brain is known as the motor strip. Large areas of it are devoted to motor speech production.

and intensity (loudness) of the vibrations. Velar valving of the airstream and acoustic energy generated from the larynx are also programmed so that the proper amount of nasal resonance occurs during the speech act. The most important and intricate aspect to the motor speech plan involves articulatory valving: the articulatory plan. It is generally accepted that the articulatory plan is created in Broca's area proper in the frontal lobe of the left hemisphere of most right-handed individuals. However, the articulatory plan may be formulated in several areas of the brain including the anterior insula and lateral premotor cortex (Wise, Greene, Büchel, & Scott, 1999).

The timing, speed, strength, and precision of articulatory gestures are planned relative to the individual and collective phoneme requirements to produce intelligible speech. Articulation planning involves coarticulation, the anticipated overlapping articulatory influences of one speech sound on another, and assimilation, the anticipated influences of adjacent phonemes on each other. Coarticulation and assimilation factors increase relative to increases in the rate of speech; the faster one talks the more similar phonemes become. The motor speech planning phase involves hundreds of muscles during dynamic, connected speech. Not only is there a high degree of speech sound production variability depending on the rate of speech, speech sound production also varies from utterance to utterance. Speech sounds are not always produced the same way in connected speech, and this variation in production is called allophonic variation. "Because there is considerable overlap in phonemes during the production of speech, many phoneticians suggest that the smallest unit of speech production is not the allophone or phoneme, but the syllable" (Small, 2005, p. 20).

Motor Speech Activation and Apraxia of Speech

At the activation phase, the propositional utterances, and neural commands for the sequencing, timing, speed, strength, and precision of the motor speech movements are sent to the speech production mechanism. Dynamic speech planning and execution of motor speech movements are impossible to separate theoretically or clinically because motor speech plans and their execution occur nearly instantaneously. In static speech production, where a person deliberately and with forethought plans and then executes a motor speech act, the distinction between the plan and its activation is discernible. However, when patients with apraxia of speech rehearse a motor act mentally before attempting it, there is no improvement in motor speech functioning. Mental rehearsal makes speech acts more volitional, and thus more difficult to produce for most patients with apraxia of speech. A disorder at the planning and execution phase results in the apraxia of speech described by Darley, Aronson, and Brown (1975) where the intent and purpose of the movement are present but with defective planning and execution. Patients with apraxia of speech tend to complicate the motor speech process with additions, substitutions, and interjections during voluntary speech. Motorically, they tend to overshoot and undershoot articulatory targets in connected speech. Plante and Beeson (2004) note that apraxia of speech is primarily a phonetic disorder.

Closed-Loop Feedback

The above conceptual, planning, and execution aspects of motor speech programming are not done in a vacuum devoid of feedback. Programming serially ordered speech movements without the benefit of feedback would be impossible. As Figure 6-2 shows, somesthetic (tactile, kinesthetic, proprioceptive) and auditory feedback about each aspect of respiration, phonation, articulation, resonance, and prosody are evaluated for their proximity to ideal motor speech acts. The feedback is sent to a hypothetical comparator, the self-concept evaluator, a part of the mind that evaluates whether the speech acts are within tolerable accuracy levels. If the acoustic, pressure, force, and precision parameters of the speech act are not within the range of tolerable levels, then an error signal is sent to the programming center, the comparator, and immediate adjustments can be made (Fairbanks, 1954). These self-corrective motor commands are collectively referred to as compensatory neuromuscular effectors. Depending on the severity of the motor speech error, the speaker may self-correct and revise the output to create a new speech act that is within the range of tolerance. In some circumstances, the speaker may receive the error signal but tolerate the imprecision while recognizing that it fell outside the parameters for acceptable speech precision.

Serially ordered speech acts-servosystem feedback plays an important role in the etiology and symptoms of several expressive communication disorders. As noted above, disruptions in programming serially ordered speech acts, and the speaker's reaction to disordered speech, are at the core of apraxia of speech in children and adults. Additionally, any disorder involving

In Darley, Aronson, and Brown's (1975) landmark study on motor speech disorders, they used speech samples collected from a total of 212 patients, each unequivocally diagnosed as representing a given neurologic category. The seven groups studied were pseudobulbar palsy, bulbar palsy, amyotrophic lateral sclerosis, cerebellar lesions, parkinsonism, dystonia, and chorea.

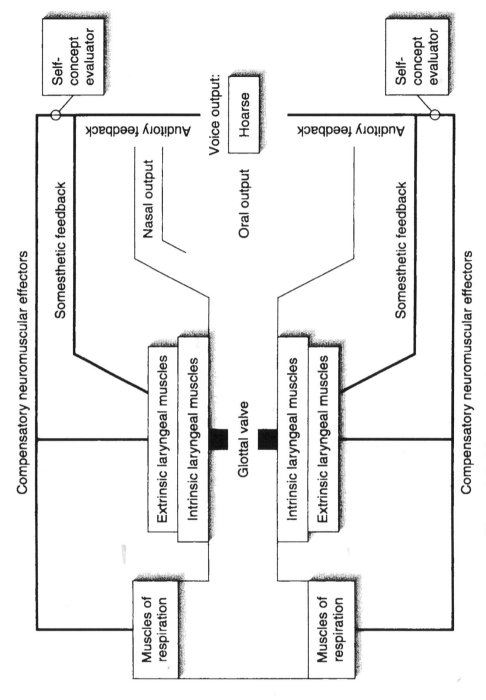

Figure 6–2. Motor speech production and feedback.

prosodic disturbances can be viewed in the serially ordered speech acts-servosystem feedback paradigm. For example, stuttering can be viewed as a combination of motor speech programming impairments leading to the core dysfluencies: repetitions, prolongations, and blocks. The struggle, or secondary symptoms of stuttering, is a result of a person revising articulatory gestures because of the error signal he or she receives about the dysfluencies. "Some stutterers report that they feel as if the motor commands to these speech muscles are out of sync with what they are attempting to say" (Ryalls & Behrens, 2000, p. 131).

Some of the symptoms of aphasia and dysarthria can be attributed to the serially ordered speech acts-servosystem feedback model paradigm. The nonfluent output seen in anterior aphasia is a result of the patient having largely undamaged auditory comprehension so that he or she is aware of expressive motor speech errors and, because of the error signal, attempts to self-correct deficient output. The self-correction may or may not be successful. Some of the speech symptoms seen in ataxic dysarthria, resulting from damage to the cerebellum and causing ill-coordinated utterances, are also attributable to deficient output and the error signals received by the speaker. For example, monopitch and monoloudness are deviant speech dimensions noted in patients with cerebellar lesions (Darley, Aronson, & Brown, 1975). Although excessive pitch and loudness modulation would logically result from cerebellar lesions, the monopitch and monoloudness seen in some patients with ataxic dysarthria are likely a compensatory behavior resulting from their reactions to error signals. They hold pitch and loudness at a relatively steady state to inhibit the ill-coordinated respiratory-laryngeal movements.

CHAPTER SUMMARY

Expressive language and motor speech programming, the first stages in *The Unified Model of Communication Sciences and Disorders*, occurs when thoughts are transformed into verbal symbols There are no clear boundaries between expressive and receptive language, nor are the expressive avenues of communication functionally independent of each other. Today, most speech and hearing scientists and practitioners distinguish between symbolic language functions and their disorders, and nonsymbolic, motor speech functions and their disorders. Because of the holistic nature of thought-communication, expressive disorders in both children and adults are considered predominantly expressive, recognizing that other modes of communication are also impaired. The serially ordered speech acts-servosystem feedback model provides a conceptual schema for understanding motor speech programming and its disorders.

Study and Discussion Questions

1. Why does knowing about communication disorders help theorists understand normal processes?

2. Compare and contrast expressive and receptive vocabulary.

3. What are "late talkers?" How is this diagnostic label determined?

4. Describe the expressive modalities of communication.

5. Compare and contrast symbolic and nonsymbolic neurogenic communication disorders.

6. Define Broca's aphasia as Pierre Paul Broca described it.

7. Why is "motor aphasia" an oxymoron?

8. Write three telegraphic statements and their longer, complete sentences from which they were derived.

9. Describe anterior-nonfluent aphasia.

10. Describe the development of motor speech programming in children.

11. How does apraxia of speech differ in children and adults?

12. List the features associated with conceptual, planning, and execution of motor speech acts.

13. Describe the serially ordered speech acts-servosystem feedback model of motor speech production.

14. Describe how stuttering might fit into the serially ordered speech acts-servosystem feedback model.

Suggested Reading

Campbell, J. (1982). *Grammatical man: Information, entropy, language, and life.* New York: Simon and Schuster.

Fairbanks, G. (1954). Systematic research in experimental phonetics: A theory of the speech mechanism as a servosystem. *Journal of Speech and Hearing Disorders, 19,* 133–139.

Luria, A. R. (1974). Language and brain. *Brain and Language, 1,* 1–14.

Searle, J. (1969). *Speech acts: An essay in the philosophy of language.* London: Cambridge University Press.

Wise, R. J. S., Greene, J., Büchel, C., & Scott, S. K. (1999). Brain regions involved in articulation. *Lancet, 353,* 1057–1061.

CHAPTER 7

Motor Speech Production

*"He draweth out the thread of his
verbosity finer than the staple of his argument."*

Shakespeare: *Love's Labour's Lost*

CHAPTER PREVIEW

This chapter examines the five integrated motor speech processes, respiration, phonation, articulation, resonance, and prosody relative to *The Unified Model of Communication Sciences and Disorders.* Boyle's law and the kinetic theory of gases are discussed including changes in respiratory capacities, volumes, and flow during speech production. Phonation is reviewed as a process of energizing expiration and the myoelastic-aerodynamic principle of vocal fold vibration is detailed. Static and dynamic articulation is described for consonants and vowels. There is a discussion of the sensorimotor and phonologic theories of phoneme acquisition. Fundamentals of resonance and prosody are also reviewed in this chapter.

Muscles and Motor Speech Production

Motor speech production is the neuromuscular activity necessary to create speech. At this stage of *The Unified Model of Communication Sciences and Disorders*, a person's thoughts have been transformed into language constructs and motorically programmed for speech acts. The neural commands for the placement, timing, and sequencing of the physical requirements for speech production have been sent to spinal and cranial nerves and, ultimately, to the muscles that will compress air, produce voice, valve nasality, and make the articulatory adjustments for speech production. The tissues, muscles, cartilages, and bones of the human body synergistically act to modify the medium of air for speech purposes. This synergistic activity involves respiration, phonation, articulation, and speech resonance. The result is fluently integrated speech sound production. Hundreds, if not thousands, of diseases, defects, disorders, and disabilities can disrupt or destroy communication at this stage and several are discussed to clarify aspects of *The Unified Model of Communication Sciences and Disorders*.

Although it is convenient to separate motor speech production into the processes of respiration, phonation, articulation, resonance, and prosody, remembering that speech is an integrated neuromuscular event is important. Speech production requires thousands of neurologic impulses to motorically cause hundreds of muscles alternately to contract and relax. These muscular contractions and relaxations act upon bones, tendons, cartilage, tissues, and other muscles. Additionally, sensory feedback monitors the motor movements. Motor production and sensory feedback produce the respiratory support, phonation, articulation, and proper resonance, and give speech its rhythm, fluency, and melody. Because motor speech processes are essentially neuromuscular events, it is necessary to discuss generally how muscles move body parts.

Contractile Tissue

A muscle is a primary contractile tissue with an origin and attachment (insertion) on a structure of the body. When a neuronal impulse stimulates the muscle, a chemical reaction causes the fibrous tissue to contract, moving the attached structure, and reducing the distance between its origin and insertion. During contraction and bringing the two structures closer together, an opposing muscle must relax to allow this movement. To return the body part to its original position, an opposite muscular process occurs. During movement, muscles are divided into agonist (a state of contraction) and antagonist (opposing or resisting an action) categories. An agonist muscle contracts while the antagonist muscle relaxes. Physiologically, muscles can only forcibly contract to bring two or more structures together; they cannot push with force. When muscles appear to push, such as when protruding the tongue, it is a result of a leverage action and vector force where muscles contract indirectly on an erect or firm structure.

Cytology is the study of cells and histology is the study of tissues.

Respiration: Compressing Air for Speech Production

Respiration is a basic biological process of living creatures. Through the processes of inhalation and exhalation of air, oxygen is used to oxidize organic fuel molecules that provide a source of energy as well as carbon dioxide and water (Dirckx, 2001). Neurologically, the medulla oblongata, a part of the brainstem, is considered the nerve integrating center for respiration. Respiration consists of inspiration (inhalation) where air is drawn into the lungs and expiration (exhalation) where it is expelled. Boyle's law and the kinetic theory of gases account for the human ability to breathe and compress air for speech production (Zemlin, 1998). Boyle's law and the kinetic theory of gases state that a given quantity of gas varies inversely with its pressure, and that gas flows from regions of high pressure to low pressure and vice versa.

Sitting at the coffee shop table, Andrew breathes in and out normally to sustain life; oxygen replaces carbon dioxide to feed the cells of his body. However, when he speaks, the normal breathing ebb and flow of air are interrupted by the respiratory requirements to produce speech. Respiration provides the compressed air from which speech sounds are made. During his speech production, the exhalation phase of breathing is extended to allow for the production of individual speech sounds. Remarkably, when the production of speech sounds results in more airflow resistance in the oral tract, Andrew's respiratory system makes corresponding minor adjustments in muscular force. This subconscious respiratory adjustment occurs on every speech sound. As changes in resistance to airflow occurs in the oral track, Andrew's respiration is correspondingly adjusted so that his ongoing speech has the proper flow, loudness, and emphasis. (Respiration Excerpt from *Connections* in Chapter 1)

When people move from lower elevations such as coastal cities, for example, San Diego and Boston to cities with higher elevations, such as Flagstaff and Denver, there is a period of time required to acclimate to the thinner air. Several sports teams practice in cities of higher elevations to improve stamina and endurance.

To understand human respiration, it is convenient to discuss two ways air can be compressed. One way of compressing air is to pump outside air into a fixed-size container. This is the way an air compressor works; it has a piston that forces outside air into a metal container. When the pressure in the metal air container, measured in pounds per square inch, approaches maximum safety limits, the pump stops. There is also a pressure release valve to prevent explosions. The other way of compressing air is to decrease the size of a closed container. By causing the floor, ceiling, and walls of a closed container to move inward, the air pressure in it increases. Drinker respirators, iron lungs, operate using the former principle, and normal human respiration obeys the latter. Before describing this biological pump and its role in *The Unified Model of Communication Sciences and Disorders*, it is necessary to review respiratory capacities and volumes.

Respiratory Capacities and Volumes

Respiratory capacity is the maximum amount of air the lungs and airways can contain and is measured in cubic units. Whereas respiratory capacity addresses potentials, respiratory volume is the actual amount of space occupied by air in the lungs and airways. Respiratory volume is measured in milliliters, one thousandth of a liter. Both changes in respiratory capacity and volumes are relevant to Boyle's law and the kinetic theory of gases for speech production purposes.

As Figure 7-1 indicates, the total lung capacity (~7.0 liters in adults) is the complete amount of air contained in the lungs and airways at the end of maximum inspiration. Total lung capacity includes residual volume (~2.0 liters), the air in the lungs that cannot be expelled or they would collapse. It also includes inspiratory reserve volume (~2.5 liters), the maximum amount of air that can be inhaled beyond a normal breath, and expiratory reserve volume (~2.0 liters). Expiratory reserve volume is the maximum amount of air that can be expelled beyond a normal exhalation. Normal conversational speech is not produced on inspiration or expiratory reserve. Some patients with oral and laryngeal weakness have audible inhalation and inhalatory stridor (voicing on inhalation) because parts of the oral tract and the vocal folds will not remain completely open during inhalation. Some persons who stutter and individuals with neuromuscular disorders speak abnormally on expiratory reserve due to failure to complete utterances on tidal expiration.

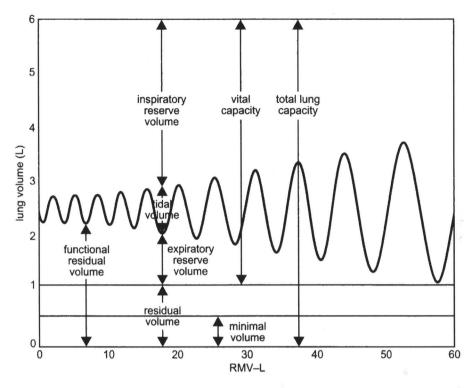

Figure 7–1. Lung volumes and capacities.

Tidal air is the volume of air breathed in and breathed out, excluding inspiratory and expiratory reserves (and residual air). It provides most of the respiratory support, about 0.5 liters or 500 milliliters, for resting speech production purposes. The airflow for resting, conversational speech production relative to the total lung capacity is small, about 10%. As Figure 7–2A shows, when the lungs and airways are expanded, air rushes from a region of high atmospheric pressure to a region of lower lung (alveolar) pressure. This inward flow of air is due to the pressure differences, and when the atmospheric pressure equals the pressure in the lungs and airways, the inward flow stops. During exhalation, muscular activity and the relaxation of distended elastic tissue in the respiratory tract cause the air pressure in the lungs and airways to be greater than that of atmospheric pressure. Consequently, air flows from the region of higher alveolar pressure to the lesser atmospheric pressure. It is during this outflow of air that normal speech is produced (Figure 7–2B).

Robert Boyle (1627–1691) was an Irish chemist and physicist. He published the "Sceptical Chymist" in 1661 that challenged many chemical theories of the day. He formulated Boyle's Law in 1662 (*Scientific American*, 1999).

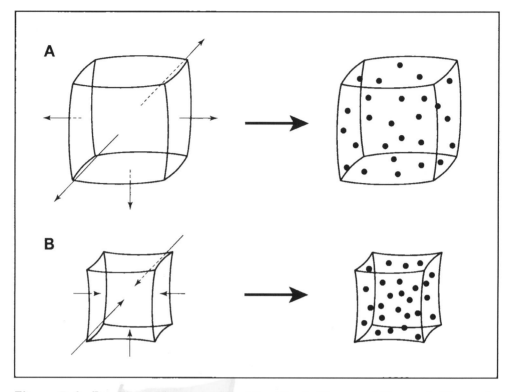

Figure 7–2. The Bernoulli principle and the Kinetic Theory of Gases. **A.** The walls of the box expand and move outward, thus creating low pressure in the box relative to the outside air. In this process, air rushes from the outside to the inside. **B.** Air rushes outward from the box as the pistons cause the walls to move inward, thus creating more pressure inside the box.

The Biological Pump

There is quiet (resting) and forced (active) respiration. Forced or active respiration goes beyond tidal volume changes in airflow when more air is required because of strenuous physical activities and shouting. As noted above, most resting conversational speech is produced using tidal volume changes. Many muscles are involved in respiration, but the diaphragm is the primary inspiratory muscle. The diaphragm is a dome-shaped muscle separating the abdominal cavity from the lungs. When contracting, the diaphragm, the external intercostals (muscles between the ribs), and several other muscles of the chest act together to increase the size (volume capacity) of the lungs. In effect and as described above, they move the walls, floor, and ceiling of the lung air container apart, increasing its size and reducing the alveolar pressure. When the mouth and nose are open, air moves from the higher atmospheric pressure to the lower alveolar (lung) pressure. The movement of air from the atmosphere to the lungs stops when the pressure is equal.

At the conclusion of inspiration, abdominal and respiratory tissues have been stretched and distended, and because of elastic recoil, when permitted to relax, they compress the air in the lungs. Elastic recoil of the abdominal and respiratory tissues combined with contraction of expiratory muscles, such as the internal intercostals, abdominal, and back muscles, cause the lungs to decrease in size. They move the walls, floor, and ceiling of the lung air container closer together, thus decreasing its size and increasing the air pressure within. At this stage of respiration, the pressure is greater in the lungs than the atmosphere, and air moves from the higher lung pressure to the lower atmospheric pressure through the nose and mouth. Air movement ceases when the pressure is equalized.

Respiration and Oral Tract Impedance

Exhalation provides the driving force for motor speech production. Exhalation generates airflow through articulatory constriction such as occurs with the fricatives /s/ and /v/ phonemes, displaces structures, particularly the lips and vocal folds, and creates pressures behind valves in the oral tract. Pressure generation is important for vocal cord vibration and production of plosive phonemes such as /p/ and /g/. Generating airflow through constrictions, displacing structures, and pressure creation in the oral tract depend on ongoing somesthetic (tactile, kinesthetic, proprioceptive) and auditory feedback for proper control of emphasis, loudness, pitch, and fluent phrasing of utterances.

Differing degrees of impedance (resistance) along the speech tract require minute adjustments of respiratory support to produce normal speech. From the increased airflow resistance at the level of the vocal folds when going from unvoiced to voiced phoneme production, to pressure changes associated with bilabial valving to produce /m/, /b/, and /p/, the respiratory system adjusts for varying changes in impedance. The system anticipates and detects significant variations in airflow impedance, and the muscles of respiration increase or decrease respiratory support for proper emphasis, loudness, pitch, and fluent phrasing.

Stage Models of Respiration

Ryalls and Behrens (2000), and others, place expiration into three distinct stages: inspiratory muscles, elastic recoil, and expiratory muscles. The first stage involves the muscles of inspiration working as a braking force to prevent the lungs from collapsing very quickly. The second stage involves the natural recoil of the lungs and other tissue. This stage can be likened to air rushing from a balloon. The final stage involves the muscles of expiration forcing the air from the lungs. This stage prevents reduced airflow velocity from the lungs as they empty and keep it at a constant rate over the entire utterance.

Zemlin (1998, p. 96) describes the respiration during speech as a function of lung volume: "At high lung volumes, the relaxation pressure generated by the thorax may be in excess of the demands of the speech mechanism. In that event, checking action provided by the inspiratory muscles can counteract excessive thoracic-lung rebound in order to regulate alveolar pressure. At mid-volume, just the relaxation pressure may provide the necessary alveolar pressure for speech, and at low lung volumes (below resting level) positive alveolar pressure must be maintained by the muscles of exhalation." Although it is convenient to describe respiration in a stage model, it should be remembered that expiration for speech purposes is a highly integrated neuromuscular process.

Important to this integrated neuromuscular processes is the cerebellum, located at the base of the brain, and known as "The Great Modulator" of muscular movement. Damage to this structure, and the tracts leading to and from it, can cause ataxic dysarthria. Darley, Aronson, and Brown (1975, p. 157), and others, found impaired respiratory control to be part of the clinical symptoms of cerebellar disease: "The smoothly controlled cycling of respiration for speech may be altered irregularly in cerebellar disease." They found the second most deviant speech dimension noted in 30 patients with cerebellar lesions to be excess and equal stress. Duffy (1995) reports abnormal and paradoxic rib cage and abdominal movements, and reduced vital capacity secondary to impaired coordination in patients with ataxic dysarthria.

Normal respiratory rates vary throughout the life span, and by the physical demands and activities of the person. Respiratory rates are most rapid at birth with newborns breathing more times per minute than teenagers. Due to reduced metabolic rates, adults progressively breathe fewer and fewer times per minute as they age. For example, a newborn may respire, on average, more than 50 times per minute whereas a 56-year-old, healthy male may only respire, on average, 15 times per minute. Rest and body position also affect respiration rates. A person having a calm, relaxed conversation is unlikely to change resting respiration rates substantially. That same person engaged in a passionate debate, an animated conversation, or talking while doing something physically strenuous will substantially alter respiratory rates. Some stages of sleep involve increased respiration while others reduce the respiratory rate by as much as 25%.

Phonation: Energizing Compressed Air for Speech Production

With regard to speech production, respiration functionally cannot be separated from other motor speech processes, particularly phonation. Narrowly defined, phonation is the production of sound by the vibration of the vocal folds (Zemlin, 1998). Phonation is broadly defined as any vibratory sound produced at the level of the larynx. A person's voice is even more generally defined; it is a combination of vibratory sound produced at the level of the larynx and the effects of the resonance potentials of the head and neck in modifying the sound source. The human voice is a sound-source resonating system. However, for the purposes of detailing the individual stages of *The Unified Model of Communication Sciences and Disorders*, and addressing each aspect of the five basic motor speech processes proposed by Darley et al. (1975) and others, the narrow definition of phonation is used in this section. Resonance factors and voice quality are addressed in the section Nasal Coupling: Adjusting Nasality.

Some of Andrew's speech sounds are voiced, for example, "uh," "v," and "b," and his vocal folds vibrate during their production. Other speech sounds are voiceless, for example, "s," "sh," and "h," and are produced with no vocal fold vibration. Voicing creates loudness and gives emphasis to Andrew's utterances. Andrew's vocal folds vibrate, on average, 130 times per second, and this itself is a remarkable muscular and aerodynamic event. The respiratory air pressure blows his vocal folds apart, and they are set into vibration because of muscular elasticity, the tendency of muscles to regain their shape, and a suction effect created by air moving through a constricted space. These principles account for his ability to vibrate his vocal folds rapidly. Frequently, Andrew alters the intensity of vocal fold vibration to add meaning, emphasis, and variability to his utterances, and minor adjustments of the cartilages and muscles in his voice box cause resulting pitch changes. (Phonation Excerpt from *Connections* in Chapter 1)

The seat of phonation is the larynx or voice box. It can be viewed as a muscular and cartilaginous (three unpaired and three paired cartilages) valve that opens for air to enter the lungs and closes for liquid and food to enter the stomach. The epiglottis, cricoid, and thyroid are the single or unpaired cartilages, and the arytenoid, corniculate, and cuneiform are the paired cartilages. Figure 7–3 shows the anterior, posterior, and lateral views of the larynx. Although all cartilages contribute directly or indirectly to the protective function of the larynx in keeping food and liquid from the trachea and lungs, the epiglottis snaps over the glottis during the swallow. It is important, but not essential, to a safe swallow. For voiced speech production, the larynx serves as a sound source generator where vibration is superimposed on the compressed air coming from the lungs.

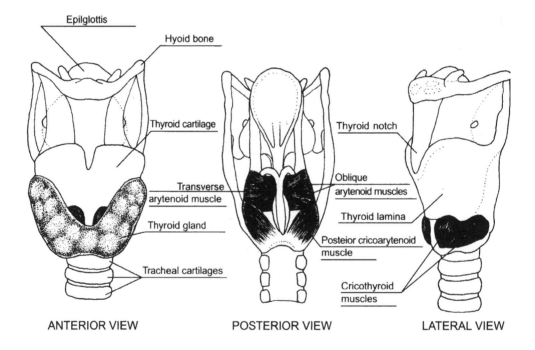

LARNYX

Figure 7–3. Major cartilages of the larynx. (Reproduced with permission from W. R. Culbertson, S. S. Cotton, and D. Tanner, 2006, *Anatomy and Physiology Study Guide for Speech and Hearing*, p. 276. Copyright 2006 by Plural Publishing, Inc.)

Throughout this book, the term vocal "fold" is used rather than vocal "cord." When cord is used, it refers to the vocal ligament that runs along the leading borders of the vocal folds. According to Kent (1997, p. 104) "The term *folds* is used in preference to the term *cord*, because the former is a better description of the anatomic structure. That is, the structure has a folded appearance." A cord more closely resembles a ligament rather than a fold. A ligament is a strong, flexible tissue connecting bone or cartilage in a joint.

The extrinsic laryngeal muscles, sometimes called neck strap muscles, hold the larynx in place and support the structure because it does not rest on a bone. Extrinsic laryngeal muscles have their origin outside the larynx and intrinsic laryngeal muscles have their origin and attachment within it. Extrinsic laryngeal muscles are further divided into suprahyoids, laryngeal elevators, and infrahyoids, laryngeal depressors. These muscles elevate, depress, move the larynx anteriorly, and indirectly help in adjusting the frequency and amplitude of glottal valve vibrations. Cranial nerve X, the vagus nerve, innervates the opening (abduction) and closing (adduction) of the laryngeal valve. Abduction and adduction of the vocal folds are the protective and vibratory actions of the larynx. The vibrations at the level of the larynx serve to energize the expiratory air, and the loudness and pitch of a speaker's voice is a product of that valving.

According to *Scientific American* (1999), the human body consists of more than 650 skeletal muscles, which make up 35 to 45% of a person's body weight.

The Physics of Phonation

Human phonation is a product of aerodynamic principles and the elasticity of muscles, tendons, and tissues of the larynx. These two physical properties are combined into the myoelastic-aerodynamic theory of voice production (van den Berg, 1958). Since the mid-1900s, research has confirmed the basic assumptions of the theory and it is now generally accepted as a principle. There has been no published refutation of its basic premise, and virtually all research supports its tenants. In this text, it is referred to as the myoelastic-aerodynamic principle of voice production.

The laryngeal muscular activity in abduction (opening) is primarily performed by one muscle, the posterior cricoarytenoid. Repeated adduction (closing) of the vocal folds during voicing occurs when the pressure below the glottis (P_{sub}) overcomes the laryngeal tissue resistance and inertia of the column of air in the vocal tract. When this resistance and inertial threshold is achieved, the vocal folds are blown upward and progressively

News reports sometimes attribute the crash of an airplane to a "stall." People sometimes erroneously believe the stall of an airplane is the engine stopping midflight similar to a car's engine stalling. A stall is the failure of an airplane wing to create lift, a disruption in the Bernoulli principle. "An airfoil produces lift most efficiently when the air can adhere closely to its surface. When the air separates from the wing . . . turbulence or 'burbling' destroys some of the wing's lift. As the angle of attack increases, the separation point moves farther forward along the upper wing surface until a stall occurs, because not enough lift is produced to sustain steady flight" (*Cessna Manual of Flight*, 1977, p. 1.19).

apart. They would stay apart if not for the elasticity and resiliency of muscles, tendons, and tissues of the larynx and aerodynamic forces. The primary aerodynamic force is the Bernoulli principle and it describes not only the aerodynamics of adduction (closing), but partially explains the great speeds at which the vocal folds can vibrate. In adult males, the vocal folds vibrate, on average, at approximately 130 cycles per second and in females, the rate of vibration, on average, is approximately 250 cycles per second. These are mean vibratory rates; fundamental frequency (f_0) of vocal fold vibration varies with the phonemes being uttered, age, and other factors. Additionally, there is an optimal mean vocal fold vibratory rate for individuals, a natural fundamental frequency that is less likely to cause laryngeal nodules, polyps, and contact ulcers. This optimal fundamental frequency is the natural mean vibratory rate given the particular person's age, gender, and shape of the larynx. When there is a prolonged and significant gap between the habitual (habit) and the optimal fundamental frequency, some persons may develop voice disorders.

The Bernoulli principle, sometimes referred to as the Bernoulli effect, law, force, and theorem, describes the relationship between air pressure and changes in airflow: "When friction is negligible, the velocity of flow of a gas or fluid through a tube is inversely related to its pressure against the side of the tube: i. e., velocity is greatest and pressure lowest at a point of constriction" (Dirckx, 2001, p. 111). The Bernoulli principle, specifically as it relates to an airfoil, accounts for an airplane wing's lift. This is due to the greater camber or curvature above the wings than below them. "When this kind of airfoil moves forward, even with a zero angle of attack, the air is forced to travel a greater distance above the wing than below. Since equilibrium is re-established at the trailing edge of the wing, the air moving across the top surface increases in velocity, thus reducing the static pressure. This reduction in static pressure across the upper surface is responsible for the generation of lift" (*Cessna Manual of Flight*, 1977, p. 1.16). The pressure-flow relationship of gas through a tube and the lift generated by wings of an airplane appear to be different principles. Nevertheless, they are aspects of the same aerodynamic principle and can be described by a simple experiment (see Figure 7-4).

Describing a person blowing air through two sheets of paper reconciles this apparent disparity and provides an accurate analogy of the aerodynamics of voice production. The two sheets of paper represent the constricted region of the glottis. At the points of constriction, the velocity of airflow is greater.

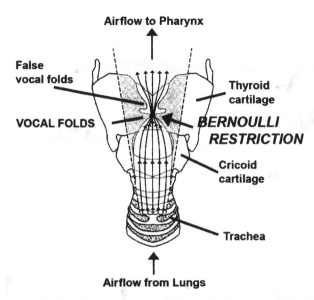

Airflow to Pharynx

False vocal folds

Thyroid cartilage

VOCAL FOLDS

BERNOULLI RESTRICTION

Cricoid cartilage

Trachea

Airflow from Lungs

Figure 7-4. The Bernoulli principle and closure of the glottis. (Reprinted with permission from Nair, G. [2006]. *The Craft of Singing*. San Diego, CA: Plural Publishing, Inc.)

At the points of constriction, the velocity of airflow is greater. According to the Bernoulli principle, as airflow increases, pressure decreases. As the person blows through the two sheets of paper, the air takes two courses. As the darkened arrow shows, some air takes a direct route through the paper constriction, and other air flows along the curvature of the papers, and travels farther. Pressure is reduced as flow increases, and there is a suction effect bringing the vocal folds together. Zemlin (1998, p. 147) describes the process succinctly: "This means that if volume fluid flow is constant, velocity of flow must increase at an area of constriction, but with a corresponding decrease of pressure at the constriction." The suction effect is complemented by the elastic recoil of the laryngeal tissue, the myoelastic aspect of the principle, and the vocal folds completely close. They stay closed until the subglottal pressure again overcomes the laryngeal tissue resistance and inertia of the column of air in the vocal tract. Pulses of air are released during each cycle of vocal fold vibration and expelled through the oral and/or nasal openings. The contact of the vocal folds creates acoustic shock waves that travel through the oral tract at the speed of sound (about 300 meters per second or 1,100 feet per second). The psychological perception of loudness of the voice is proportional to the intensity of vocal fold vibration.

Intensity of Vocal Fold Vibration and Loudness

Variations in the intensity of vocal fold vibration create changes in loudness. Intensity of vocal fold vibration is the measurable force at which they vibrate. Intensity of vocal fold vibration is the physical property of the strength at which they contact each other, the magnitude of the forced contact. When the vocal folds contact each other with greater force, the amplitude of molecular displacement is greater than when they contact each other with less force. More intense vocal fold vibration causes sound waves with greater amplitude of vibration and vice versa. The magnitude of the acoustic shock wave created by the vocal folds is dependent on the strength of vocal fold vibration.

The strength of vocal fold vibration is a result of increased subglottal pressure (P_{sub}) and the force of vocal fold contact during adduction. When the subglottal pressure is greater, the vocal folds are distended farther apart, causing the aerodynamic and myoelastic forces to be greater during adduction. Consequently, the vocal folds contact each other with greater force, creating acoustic shock waves of greater magnitude. Excessive intensity of vocal fold contact is a causal agent in voice disorder related to strain and abuse. For example, screamers' nodes, benign nodules of the vocal folds, result from frequent and excessive hard glottal contacts in some speakers and cheerleaders. Frequent and excessive hard glottal contact can damage the sensitive vocal fold tissue in some persons.

Positively correlated with intensity of vocal fold vibration is the psychological perception of loudness of a person's voice. The greater the intensity of vocal fold vibration, the greater the psychological perception of voice loudness. However, this correlation, although positive, is not linearly proportional; there is not a 1:1 relationship between changes in intensity of vocal fold vibration and the psychological perception of voice loudness. A unit increase in the intensity of vocal fold vibration does not necessarily translate into identical change in the psychological perception of the loudness of a person's voice.

Frequency of Vocal Fold Vibration and Pitch

Variation in the frequency of vocal fold vibration creates fluctuations in the psychological perceptions of a person's pitch. Frequency is the measurable rate at which something occurs over a particular period; the rate per unit of time. When a person's vocal folds vibrate more rapidly, the pitch of his or her voice is perceived as higher. When they vibrate less rapidly, the pitch of the voice is perceived as lower. However, this correlation, like the one between intensity and loudness, is not linearly proportional; there is not a 1:1 relationship between frequency of vocal fold vibration and the psychological perception of pitch. For example, a unit increase in the frequency of vocal fold vibration does not necessarily translate into identical increase in the pitch of a person's voice. Doubling or halving the frequency of vocal fold vibration does not result in the doubling or halving the psychological perception of pitch. Loudness also affects the perception of pitch. For example, when a singer produces a low-frequency tone very loudly, it seems lower in pitch to the listener. Conversely, when a high-pitched tone is produced loudly, it appears higher in pitch.

As Table 7-1 shows (Tanner, 2006), when all physiologic variables are held constant, the pitch-changing mechanism primarily involves an interplay between subglottal air pressure, vocal fold tension, and changes in the mass per unit length of the vocal folds. Certainly, other factors are involved in pitch changing including the function of the vocalis muscle, relative positioning of the thyroid and cricoid cartilages, and medial compression of the vocal folds. Nevertheless, the above are the primary variables that can be addressed independently, and that ultimately function synergistically in alternating pitch.

The speed of the airflow through the glottis, when all other variables are held constant, affects the frequency of vocal fold vibration and the psychological perception of pitch. Increase in subglottal air pressure causes the vocal folds to be blown

Table 7-1. Primary Factors Affecting Pitch

Variable*	Effect on Fundamental Frequency (f_0)
Increase Mass/Unit Length	Lower Pitch
Decrease Mass/Unit Length	Increase Pitch
Increase Vocal Fold Tension	Increase Pitch
Decrease Vocal Fold Tension	Decrease Pitch
Increase Subglottal Air Pressure (P_{sub})	Increase Pitch
Decrease Subglottal Air Pressure (P_{sub})	Decrease Pitch

*When all other variables held constant.

farther apart, generating more negative airflow pressure through the laryngeal constriction, and elevating pitch. Conversely, decreases in subglottal pressure cause the vocal folds to be less distended, generating less suction, and decreasing pitch. Just as the speed of an airplane affects the lift of its wings, the speed of the airflow through the larynx affects the speed at which the vocal folds vibrate.

Cartilage is flexible skeletal tissue giving structure to organs of the body. There are three types of cartilage: hyaline, elastic, and fibrous. Hyaline cartilage forms the skeleton of the larynx and the trachea.

Sitting atop the cricoid cartilage are the triangular-shaped arytenoid cartilages. They are critical in changing vocal fold tension and adjusting the mass per unit length of the vocal folds. Each arytenoid cartilage has an apex (peak), base, and three surfaces. Because of the function of several intrinsic laryngeal muscles, the arytenoid cartilages slide, rock, and rotate. Contraction of these intrinsic laryngeal muscles causes the arytenoid cartilages to rotate outward and inward. Additionally, they also tilt them to tighten and loosen the vocal folds. The movements of the arytenoid cartilages change vocal fold tension, and increases and decreases in their mass per unit length. The muscle fibers that run parallel to the vocal ligament, when contracted, also increase the vocal folds' mass per unit length, making them thicker, and consequently reducing pitch (when all other variables are held constant).

Articulation: Shaping Compressed Air for Speech Production

So far in the motor speech production stages of *The Unified Model of Communication Sciences and Disorders*, the respiratory system has compressed air for speech production. The larynx has energized the compressed air for voiced phonemes, and acoustic energy and air are flowing through the upper airways. At the articulation stage of motor speech production, the energized compressed air is shaped into speech sounds. The oral tract, using the same muscles and structures for mastication (chewing), sucking, and deglutition (swallowing), form phonemes during static and dynamic speech production.

The articulators can be divided into hard and soft, and fixed and mobile structures. The primary hard articulators are the mandible, teeth, hard palate, and alveolar ridge. The soft articulators are the tongue, lips, and velum. The primary fixed structures are the teeth, hard palate, and alveolar ridge, and the mobile articulators are the mandible, tongue, lips, and velum. Figure 7–5 shows the major articulators and their movement capabilities.

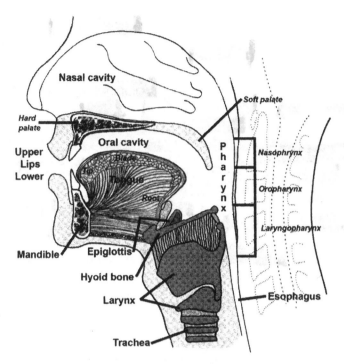

Figure 7–5. The major articulators. (Reproduced with permission from Nair, G. [2006]. *The Craft of Singing*. San Diego, CA: Plural Publishing, Inc.)

The compressed air coming from Andrew's lungs flows through his mouth and nose where it is valved into recognizable speech sounds. Interestingly, Andrew does not produce precise individual speech sounds by making ideal points of contact with his articulators. Because his speech sound production happens rapidly, it becomes a stream of articulatory events. There is overshooting and undershooting of the ideal points of articulatory contact, and the speech sounds preceding and following the one being produced influence its production. Nevertheless, Andrew's tongue, lips, soft palate, and teeth work together to "valve" the compressed air coming from his lungs. (Articulation Excerpt from *Connections* in Chapter 1)

Articulation is the act of shaping the compressed air coming from the lungs into recognizable speech sounds. In English, there are 44 phonemes, each having identifiable acoustic characteristics and distinctive features. Phoneme distinctive features are the perceptual features that distinguish one phoneme from another such as voicing, rounding, stridency (shrillness), nasalization, and

The tongue has four types of taste buds and regions for taste: sweet, sour, salt, and bitter. The sense of taste is closely aligned to the sense of smell. The human sensitivity to taste evolved from a survival imperative. For example, sour and bitter tastes protect one from ingesting rancid and poisonous foods.

so forth. During connected speech, coarticulation (the anticipated overlapping articulatory influences of one speech sound on another) and assimilation (influences of adjacent phonemes on each other) result in sounds having similar acoustic and perceptual qualities (see Chapter 6). Phonemes are separated into two categories: vowels and consonants. Vowels, central aspects of the syllable, are voiced and relatively unrestricted phonemes classified by front to back, and high to low positioning of the tongue. Lip rounding is also a feature of vowels. Consonants may or may not be voiced and produced by some manner of valving using the articulators to modify the airstream.

There are two ways of categorizing consonants: place and manner of production. In the place of articulation category, consonant phonemes are classified by the points in the speech mechanism where they are produced. Beginning anteriorly and moving posteriorly and inferiorly, place of articulation points of contact are bilabial (lips), labiodental (lips and teeth), linguadental (tongue and teeth), lingua-alveolar (tongue and alveolar ridge), linguapalatal (tongue and hard plate), linguavelar (tongue and soft plate), and glottal (vocal folds) sites in the speech mechanism. According to Ladefoged and Maddieson (1988), in the world's languages, there are approximately 16 different places of consonant of production.

Manner of consonant articulation concerns the type of airstream modification. The two major categories of type of airstream modification are continuants and stops. Continuants involve holding the articulators in a fixed position while producing a continuous airstream during production of the particular phoneme. Continuants are separated into nasals (increased nasal resonance), glides (gliding actions of the articulators), and fricatives (constriction of airstream). Stops are produced by completely blocking the airstream briefly and releasing it. Stops are divided into plosives (increased air pressure and abrupt release) and affricates (increased air pressure and release of airstream shaped into continuants).

Some articulation valving sites constrict the air such as during the production of "sh," "v," and "th." During the production of stop consonants, such as "t," "d," and "p," the airstream and acoustic energy completely stop for a brief time. Some speech sounds such as "d" and "t," and "s" and "z" vary only by the presence or absence of voicing. Other speech sounds such as "w," "l," and "r" require a gliding action of his tongue to produce them. The nasality of Andrew's speech is maximized or minimized by his soft palate closing or opening the nasal port. When the nasal port is opened, the speech resonance and energy is pro-

jected through his nasal cavity and nose, and his tongue or lips block the oral cavity. The syllables spoken by Andrew are the basic acoustic and physiologic units of speech, and the vowels are their central components. Andrew's vowels are produced by minor adjustments in the front-to-back position of his tongue, its height in his mouth, and lip rounding. (Articulation and Resonance Excerpt from *Connections* in Chapter 1)

Normal and Delayed Phoneme Acquisition

Although phoneme acquisition rates vary significantly, the sequence of phoneme acquisition is relatively invariant. Consonants, vowels, and their variants (blends and diphthongs) are learned by the age of seven (Culbertson & Tanner, 2001a; Tanner, Culbertson, & Secord, 1997). The ages of phoneme mastery are usually published with articulation tests. Rarely, however, do the tests identify the percent of the children who have mastered the particular phoneme by the age indicated or the contexts in which they can produce them. Two factors are considered when determining age of phoneme acquisition: percent mastery and the positions of words.

The percent mastery is the percentage of children who have acquired the phoneme by the age listed on the test. When these data are listed, some tests give the age at which 51% of the children have acquired the phoneme, while others list 75% or 90% or greater. When comparing the research on phoneme acquisition ages, the 75% figure provides the best comparative milestone for acquisition norms because there are several studies using this percentage. However, it should be recognized that using the 75% norm as a cutoff for diagnosing delayed acquisition is incorrect. Using this percentage as an indication of delay erroneously suggests that 25% of the population are delayed in phoneme acquisition.

The second factor to consider when interpreting phoneme acquisition is the mastery of the particular speech sound relative to its position in words, and this too is rarely published with articulation tests. The context in which a child can produce the phoneme indicates the degree of phoneme mastery and whether the child has emerging competence in producing it. Although producing the phoneme in isolation and in syllables provides information about stimulability (the ability to produce a phoneme with cues and prompts), the child's usage of it in the initial, medial, and final positions of words provides the best indication of his or her functional mastery. While a child who is stimulable has the neurologic and muscular abilities to produce a phoneme, mastery of it in everyday speech is indicated by his or her use of it in words and longer utterances. Use of the phoneme in the initial, medial, and final positions of words shows not only the neurologic and muscular capability to produce the phoneme correctly, but the phonologic and behavioral requisites as well.

Figure 7-6, "The Developmental Articulation and Phonology Profile: Consonants" (Tanner, Culbertson, & Secord, 1997) shows the ages at which 90, 75, and 51% of children acquire English consonants in two and three positions of words (see legend). It also shows the relative frequency of occurrence of each consonant, for example, /n/ is the most frequently occurring consonant and /z/ is the least frequently occurring consonant in English. The darkened vertical bar above each phoneme shows when 75% of children have acquired the consonant in all three positions of words. As noted above, the 75% percentage is optimal for normative comparisons because more than one study supports the phoneme acquisition ages listed and in all three

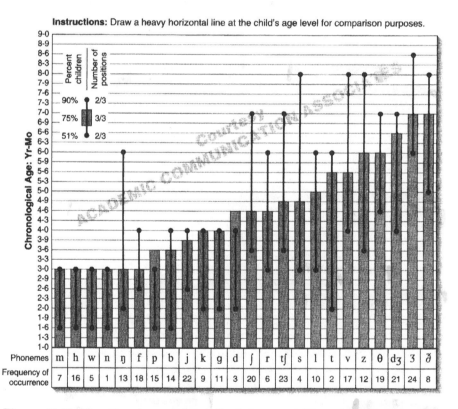

Figure 7–6. The Developmental Articulation and Phonology Profile: Consonants. (Courtesy of and copyright Academic Communication Associates. All rights reserved.)

positions of words. The vertical line superimposed on each phoneme bar suggests emerging mastery from 51% to 90% of the children sampled in two or three positions of words. The most common articulation errors seen by clinicians in schools involved the /r/ and /s/ phonemes. As can be seen in Figure 7-6, 75% of children have mastered these phonemes in the initial, medial, and final positions of words by ages 4.6 and 4.9, respectively. However, 90% of children have mastered these phonemes in two of three positions by 6.0 years.

Vowels and diphthongs are also acquired over a period of several years. Most children have established vowels by the age of 4.0 (Tanner, Culbertson, & Secord, 1997). Vowels, unlike consonants, are rarely produced in error in the absence of childhood apraxia and the dysarthrias. While consonants tend to be misarticulated during speech development, vowels rarely require sensorimotor therapies. Vowels are more likely to be produced correctly in school-aged children for four reasons. First, as noted previously, vowels are the nucleus of the syllable, making them more perceptually, physiologically, and acoustically salient. Second, unlike consonants, all vowels are voiced, giving them more acoustic energy. As a group vowels are louder than consonants. Third, vowels are less complicated in the sensorimotor requirements to produce them. Consonants have more tongue excursion, making them more vulnerable to misarticulation. Finally, vowels occur more frequently than consonants. Children have more exposure to vowels and greater opportunities to produce them. It is likely that all four factors account for fewer isolated vowel errors in children.

Diadochokinesis is the ability to engage in rapid repetitive movements. Digital diadochokinetic rate is the speed at which a person can repetitively move his or her finger. Oral diadochokinetic rate is the speed at which a person can repetitively move his or her articulators such as producing the syllables "puh-duh-kuh" or the word "buttercup."

Phonologic Process Extinction and Phoneme Acquisition

In the discipline of communication sciences and disorders, there have evolved two apparently dissimilar theories concerning the acquisition of phonemes and the treatment of speech disorders in children. One theory, the phonologic approach, suggests that speech sound development is the discovery and fusion of syllable formation principles. Disorders of speech sound production, according to this theory, result from the delayed acquisition of adult phonologic processes, or the rules of language. Phonologic processes are simplified linguistic behaviors used by children when trying to produce adult speech. The other theory of speech sound acquisition and treatment of articulation disorders is the sensorimotor approach. It views the acquisition of speech sounds as a process of sensory and fine-motor maturation. "While recognizing that phonological development follows a predictable sequence for most children, we believe there is wide individual variation in the abandonment of immature syllable formation strategies, and that a major factor underlying this variation is neuromuscular maturation" (Culbertson & Tanner, 2001b, pp. 28–30). The ages of immature phonologic processes abandonment is referred to as the ages of phonologic processes extinction. Clinically, in the phonologic approach, the goal is to help the child discover mature, adult phonologic processes. In the sensorimotor approach, the goal is to develop the sensory and motor abilities to produce each phoneme properly.

Phonologic process extinction is intricately tied to neuromuscular maturation. Culbertson and Tanner (2001a, 2001b) found the ages of phonologic process extinction are closely related in sequence and rate of individual phoneme acquisition. In addition, it is accurate to view a child with a severe phonologic disorder as literally speaking a different language. This idiolect does not have as many phonemes as the standard language, and the child expresses himself or herself by combining phonemes into uniquely different syllables. In many ways, treating a child with a severe phonologically based communication disorder is similar to teaching English as a second language (ESL). Just as the ESL teacher must consider the person's ability to make speech sounds, the speech clinician must be concerned with the sensory and motor aspects of speech sound production. "Phonological diagnosis and treatment emphasize the ontogeny of the linguistic code inherent in a child's speech, but acknowledge that a substrate of this development is sensorimotor maturation. The phonological aspect of the linguistic code may evolve as a child senses the effects of coarticulation when phonemes are juxtaposed and encodes those effects that are linguistically useful. Sensorimotor maturation is required for articulation of the more complicated releasers, nuclei, and arresters of syllables" (Culbertson & Tanner, 2001a, p. 19). Figure 7–7 "The Developmental Articulation and Phonology Profile: Phonological Processes" (Tanner, Culbertson, & Secord, 1997) shows the composite ages of normal phonologic process extinction for syllable structure processes, substitution processes, and harmony processes.

Nasal Coupling and Nasality

When discussing speech resonance, separating the speech tract into three pharynges, laryngeal, oral, and nasal, illustrates its tube and cavity acoustic function. A pharynx is a tubular space impor-

Instructions: Draw a heavy horizontal line at the child's age level for comparison purposes.

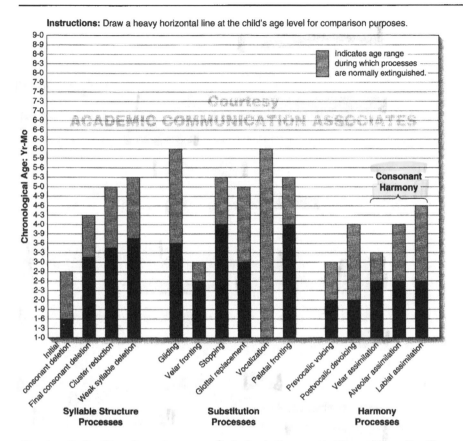

Figure 7–7. The Developmental Articulation and Phonology Profile: Phonological Processes. (Courtesy of and copyright Academic Communication Associates. All rights reserved.)

tant for speech resonance. These pharynges can be viewed as three cavities beginning inferiorly with the larynx. The laryngopharynx is the space between the larynx and the hyoid bone. The oropharynx is the space from the hyoid bone to the velum (soft palate). The nasopharynx is the space above the velum and includes the entire nasal cavity including the nares opening. It is at the junction of the oral and nasal pharyngeal cavities that the speech tract makes an approximately 90-degree angle when measured from the glottis.

Nasal coupling occurs when the velum is lowered, allowing air and acoustic energy to enter and escape the nasal cavity. The levator palatini is the muscle primarily responsible for moving the velum and closing the velopharyngeal port. In the majority of people during most non-nasal phoneme production, the pharyngeal wall also contracts to help velopharyngeal closure. Passavant's pad of the pharyngeal wall likely serves as a cushion for velopharyngeal closure. However, some scientists question its cushion function, whether the point of velar contact closure is above Passavant's pad, and even whether such a structure exists in some people (Zemlin, 1998). It is said that velopharyngeal closure operates on a binary function, that is, zero-one. The velopharyngeal port is functionally either opened or closed although significant assimilated hypernasality occurs in speech pathologies affecting the strength and speed of velar and palatal movements. Of course, unrepaired clefts of the velum and velar insufficiencies affect this nasal valving process. The perceptual features of hypernasality, hyperrhinolalia, is too much nasality on non-nasal phonemes, whereas hyponasality, hyporhinophonia (denasality), is too little perceived nasality on nasal phonemes.

Three phonemes in English are produced with the velum lowered and the oral cavity obstructed by the tongue or lips to redirect the air and energy: /m/, /n/, and /ŋ/. These are the nasal phonemes in the word "mining" (Borden, Harris, & Raphael, 1992). Other languages such as Navajo and French have more nasals. Acoustically, these nasals are produced by lengthening the vocal tract, thus reducing pitch similar to a trombone extending its slide and causing a proportional pitch reduction in the musical note. Nasals also affect the acoustic characteristics of speech by adding another speech resonating cavity. Nasal speech sounds, as a group, tend to be less intense than their non-nasal counterparts.

Reduced overall intensity of nasal phonemes is due to the moist, absorbent nature of the nasal cavities, increased length of the speech tract, and to antiresonances, the canceling and filtering effects of the oral and nasal resonating chambers. According to Borden, Harris, and Raphael (1992, p. 121), "The frequency ranges for the antiresonances associated with [m], [n], and [ŋ] vary with place of articulation (and thus with the size of the oral cavity, which acts like an acoustic cul-de-sac). The labial nasal consonant [m] is characterized by an antiresonance which is lower (in the 500–1500 Hz range) than that for [n] (around 2000–3000 Hz) or for [ŋ] (above 3000 Hz)."

Prosody: Suprasegmental Aspects of Motor Speech Production

Consonants and vowels are the segmental aspects of speech; the segments that make up syllables and words. Overlaid on the segmental aspects of speech are the suprasegmental components: intonation, stress, and duration. Prosody is an all-encompassing term for suprasegmental variations in loudness, pitch, and time in a person's speech. Prosody is highly individualized and there is a wide variety of prosodic aspects to a person's speech. Prosody is also the prime carrier of emotion in an utterance. Generally, prosody includes the rhythm and melody of speech and encompasses fluency disorders. Fluency disorders involve disruptions in the smoothness and flow of speech and are often defined by the number of repetitions, prolongations, blocks, and hesitations during utterances. Although many speech pathologies involve disruptions in a person's ability to produce speech fluently, stuttering, cluttering, and ataxic dysarthria are primarily fluency disorders.

> *As Andrew talks, there is also a rhythm to his speech; it is not choppy or broken. His brain plans and programs speech based on the available respiratory support, and the voicing, nasalization, and articulation are coordinated in a way that produces fluent, effortless utterances. Rarely does Andrew repeat, prolong, or otherwise struggle during speech; all of the neurologic and muscular events are produced with precision and ease. This is noteworthy given that Andrew can produce words very rapidly, more than 500 words per minute, eight to ten per second, and still be understood by Angela.* (Fluency Excerpt from *Connections* in Chapter 1)

In the past, authorities on speech prosody suggested that the right hemisphere is the "seat" of speech prosody. The basis of this belief is because prosody carries emotions, the right hemisphere is the location of this fundamental and integrated aspect of human existence. However, the brain operates holistically, and it is inaccurate to link prosody to a single hemisphere or region of the brain. Certainly, there are areas of the brain important for production and interpretation of the suprasegmental aspects of speech production, but suggesting that one hemisphere, tract, or site is the primary prosodic center is fraught with overgeneralization. Ryalls and Behrens (2000) note that concerning prosody, the two hemispheres work together, and that both integrate suprasegmental information. "It may well be that the two hemispheres of the brain are not working separately, but instead are integrating information, both linguistic and affective" (Ryalls & Behrens, 2000, p. 66).

The intonation of speech is the shifting pattern of pitch (and stress) over several syllables. The intonation of an utterance has specific linguistic implication. For example, change in intonation can reflect an interrogative, where the speaker poses a question by raising pitch at the end of the statement: "You repaid

Speech prosody is integral to the emotion associated with verbal messages. Intonation, in particular, is associated with the emotional aspects of a message.

the money to me?" Phonetic stress is a syllabic comparable phenomenon, the intensity at which one syllable is produced varies relative to others. Generally, these shifting patterns are a result of changes in the intensity and frequency of vocal fold vibration. However, as discussed below, duration of syllables plays an important role in stress. The length of syllables also provides important prosodic factors in an utterance. The relative duration of the syllables, and the pauses between them, are suprasegmental variables.

Speech prosody is integrally tied to rate of speech. Rate of speech is usually measured in words per minute. The average rate of speech is highly variable because it changes with the type of conversation and the speaker. Generally, a relaxed person in a casual conversation speaks at about 150 words per minute. When rate of speech exceeds 500 words per minute, intelligibility, the ability to be understood (in percent), suffers. Most speakers are unintelligible when speaking more than 700 words per minute. Three factors are considered when addressing rate of speech: number and length of pauses, and duration of the syllable.

As would be expected, the number of pauses influences the rate of speech. When an utterance contains more pauses, rate of speech proportionally decreases and vice versa. In addition, longer pauses decrease overall rate of speech, whereas shorter ones increase it. Variations in the duration of the syllable, primarily by increasing or decreasing duration of vowels, also affect rate of speech. Speaker who "draw out" their speech by prolonging vowels and some consonants, and punctuate their utterances with many and longer pauses, produce fewer words per minute than those speaker who have utterances with syllables of reduced duration, and have fewer and shorter pauses.

Many communication disorders affect rate of speech, and several therapies involve reducing how rapidly the patient produces speech to improve articulatory precision. Parents of children who stutter sometime comment that the child "thinks faster than he can talk" attributing stuttering and cluttering to this cognitive-motor speech production gap. Although there may be diseases and disorders causing a pathologic cognitive-motor speech production gap such as dysarthria and apraxia of speech, all normal persons have internal monologues faster than they can motorically produce speech. Additionally, instructing an active child to slow his or her rate of speech is, for the most part, futile because rate of speech reflects a person's overall energy levels. It would be unnatural for an active, excited child to speak slowly. His or her rate of speech will not be in contrast to his or her animated and spirited general physical behaviors.

CHAPTER SUMMARY

In *The Unified Model of Communication Sciences and Disorders*, the motor speech production phase addresses respiration, phonation, articulation, resonance, and prosody. Respiration can be viewed as a biological pump that provides compressed air for speech production. All vowels and the majority of consonants are voiced at the level of the larynx, and the valving actions of the articulators shape this energized compressed air into speech sounds. Although all phonemes have nasal resonance, the nasal phonemes of English are created by obstructing the oral egress of air and acoustic energy by the tongue or lips, and the coupling of the nasal cavity by lowering the velum. The suprasegmental aspects of motor speech production include the intonation, stress, and duration of syllables and words. Combined, the five basic motor speech production processes allow humans rapidly to produce precise, intelligible speech.

Study and Discussion Questions

1. Describe how muscles move body parts.

2. List and describe respiratory capacities and volumes. How do Boyle's law and the kinetic theory of gases change respiratory volumes?

3. How does the biological pump work? How does it respond to various impedances in the oral tract?

4. Describe the myoelastic-aerodynamic principle of voice production. What are the two factors in the physics of phonation?

5. What is the relationship between intensity of vocal fold vibration and loudness?

6. What is the relationship between frequency of vocal fold vibration and pitch?

7. List each consonant relative to manner and place of articulation. What tongue and lip factors are associated with vowel production?

8. What two factors are important to interpreting normal and delayed phoneme acquisition norms?

9. What is the relationship between phonologic process extinction and phoneme acquisition?

10. List the three nasals in English and describe how they are produced. What role does Passavant's pad play in nasal coupling?

11. Compare the three major suprasegmental aspects of motor speech production.

12. List and describe the three variables involved in rate of speech.

Suggested Reading

van den Berg, J. (1958). Myoelastic-aerodynamic theory of voice production. *Journal of Speech and Hearing Research, 1*, 227–244.

Duffy, J. (1995). *Motor speech disorders.* St. Louis, MO: Mosby.

Kent, R. D. (1997). *The speech sciences.* San Diego, CA: Singular Publishing Group.

Plante, E., & Beeson, P. (2004). *Communication and communication disorders: A clinical introduction* (2nd ed.). Boston: Pearson.

CHAPTER 8

The Speech Resonating System and Acoustic Energy Transmission

"As far as the laws of Mathematics refer to reality,
they are not certain,
and as far as they are certain,
they do not refer to reality."

Albert Einstein

CHAPTER PREVIEW

This chapter explores the human resonating system and the processes by which it creates the acoustic aspects of speech. Frictional-stop and glottal sound sources are examined relative to the resonance potential of the speech mechanism. A speech sound spectrogram is detailed showing the time, frequency, and energy parameters of speech. The power of the voice to suggest personality traits and discrete emotions is discussed along with the ability of listeners to identify speakers by their voices. Also in this chapter is a discussion of communication theory and the property of entropy.

Communication Chain of Events: From Electrochemical to Acoustic Energy

So far in *The Unified Model of Communication Sciences and Disorders*, the essential neurologic, anatomic, and physiologic actions necessary for communication have been performed by the speaker. To this point in the communication chain of events, the information to be communicated has been encoded neurologically. This encoding involves cortical and deep structures of both hemispheres of the brain and several cranial and spinal nerves. It is essentially electrochemical energy and the actions of neurons and nerve impulses. The neuron consists of the cell body (soma), axon, dendrite, and the synaptic junction.

To review electrochemical encoding, nerve impulses are the actions of nerve fibers, electrical charges traveling from neuron to neuron, and involving several chemical agents and neurotransmitters. Neurotransmitters are chemical stimulators and inhibitors, which transmit nerve impulses across a synapse. They cross the synaptic junction, stimulating or inhibiting the postsynaptic cells. The neuron propagates ionic changes, action potentials, which travel from dendrites to axons. The synapse is the electrochemical communication from one nerve to another. The nervous system functions by the special conductivity and directionality of its nervous tissue. However, as discussed in the chapter on language and consciousness (Chapter 5), the goings-on in the brain are not easily translated into the workings of the mind. Neuroscientists refer to the difficulty of projecting the neurologic activities of the brain to what occurs in a person's mind as the "brain-mind leap."

The mental encoding and physical chain of events leading to communication consummation between a speaker and listener requires that thoughts are placed into a language code appreciated and understood by both parties. The semantics, grammar, syntax, and phonology of the message are coded linguistically, and the motor speech requirements for voluntary expression are programmed. The speaker's muscles of respiration compress the air necessary for speech production, the vocal folds energize it, and the articulators shape it into phonemes. The final normal speech act is produced rhythmically and fluently. Gestural and graphic communication also provide a bridge for information sharing between speaker and listener, but speech is the primary mode of communication.

The magnitude of the brain-mind leap can be demonstrated by addressing semantic representations in the brain. Neurologically, the meaning of the word "truthfulness," for example, can be found in the atomic particles in neurons, and the chemical interactions of neurotransmitters at their synaptic junctions. The meaning of the word "truthfulness" is likely a composite of these changes to cellular chemistry and continuous action potentials in thousands of neurons and their dendrite-to-axon connections. These electrochemical reactions somehow create the continuous imagery and semantic memory and associations necessary to appreciate the meaning of the word and to use it expressively. Interestingly, the neuronal impulses, their action potentials, and cellular chemical stores have continuity. They are consistent from one semantic retrieval to another, yet the meaning of the word evolves with life experience. Through this ongoing continuous nervous energy and chemical changes at the cellular level, a person is conscious of the meaning of "truthfulness," and, in fact, the semantics of the word becomes part of his or her consciousness.

Speech Sound-Source Resonating System

Notwithstanding the above mental encoding and neurologic substrates in communication, speech production is also an acoustic phenomenon involving the speech tract as a sound source resonating system. In effect, the speaker transmits complex speech sound waves through the medium of air in addition to sending nonverbal messages through facial expressions, gestures, and suprasegmental features as described in Chapter 7. Speech communication form and content are carried by sound waves from speaker to listener. Briefly, the speaker's thoughts, linguistic coding, and motor speech programming and execution are speech sound waves traveling at the speed of sound to the listener.

For an instant, Andrew's utterances are nothing more or less than acoustic energy. His thoughts and feelings are molecular vibrations, sound waves, traveling through time and space, and captured by Angela's ear. Andrew's thoughts, feelings, and experiences, words and their meanings, voicing, and articulatory valving of the compressed air coming from his lungs are reduced to energy transmitted through the medium of air. Through the miracle of speech communication, the depths of Andrew's thoughts, the totality of his experiences, and the joy and sadness expressed by this college student, for a brief time, are informational units encoded on sound waves. The frequency and amplitude of the complex speech sound waves carry information from speaker to listener, and sound energy is the connection between Andrew and Angela. (Acoustics Excerpt from *Connections* in Chapter 1)

Several authorities on speech acoustics have used analogies to describe the speech resonating system. Comparing the speech resonating system to a bottle, pendulum, tube and cavity, a child's swing, or a musical instrument, while illustrative, does not comprehensively describe the mechanism. All analogies are symbolic, and thus they are not literally applicable to the human speech resonating system. A more accurate way of depicting the human resonating system is by describing the individual and collective anatomic structures involved in the process. Acoustically and physiologically, there are two sound sources for speech: frictional-stop and glottal.

Frictional-Stop Sound Sources

Frictional-stop and glottal sound sources both involve resonance, but the unvoiced frictional-stop sound source does not consist of discrete harmonics. "The spectrum of the frictional source is continuous; that is, it does not consist of harmonics discretely spaced but of sinusoidal waves of all frequencies within the speech range, approximately from 60 Hz to 7000 Hz" (Tosi, 1979, p.35). Because of the minimal resonance associated with unvoiced frictional-stops, the amplitude of the continuous sinusoidal wave is relatively uniform (Tosi, 1975, 1979). The above frictional-stop sound sources produce aperiodic sound waves. Aperiodic sound waves are not repetitive; there is no discernable repetition of the sound energy.

Voice-onset time (VOT), measured in milliseconds, is the time it takes for the energy to be released from a stop consonant and for voicing to begin.

The spectral characteristics of the frictional-stop sound source are dependent on the place of constriction. The closer the sound source is to the lip opening, the higher will be the natural resonant frequency of the vocal tract (Minifie, 1973). Voiceless stop consonants, /p/, /t/, /k/, although technically stops, have the frictional sound-source acoustics during the release of their peak air pressure. Figure 8–1 shows the continuous spectrum of the /s/ phoneme. Note that the amplitude of the frictional source is relatively flat across the frequencies until the resonance curve of the vocal tract is applied. The effect of resonance, minimal though it may be for the unvoiced /s/ phoneme, creates higher amplitudes in the mean frequency range of approximately 6000 Hz.

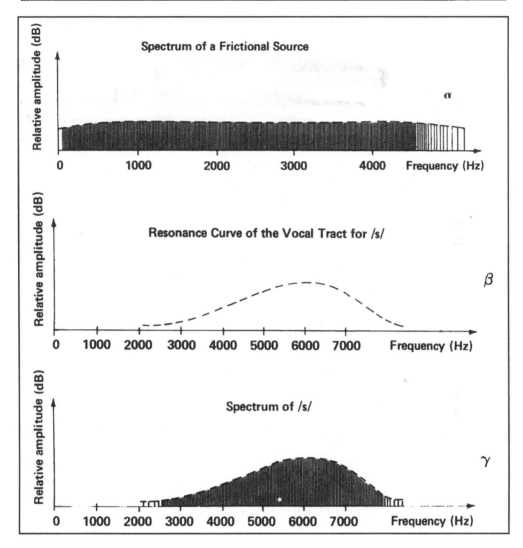

Figure 8–1. Continuous spectrum of the /s/ phoneme. (Courtesy of Oscar I. Tosi, Michigan State University Institute of Voice Identification.)

Glottal Sound Source

The primary sound source for the speech resonating system is the larynx, the buzzing sound produced by the vibrating vocal folds. Acoustic shock waves are created by the vocal folds forcibly contacting each other, and the energy is displaced upwardly through the vocal tract. To illustrate, if the human head and upper neck are removed from the resonating system, the sound produced by the vibrating vocal folds is simply a buzz similar to the sound a person can make by blowing air through his or her mouth and vibrating the lips very rapidly. This sound source produced at the level of the larynx is not a pure tone. Pure tones occur rarely in nature and they have only one frequency with no harmonics or overtones. As Figure 8–2A shows, the buzz produced by the vibrating vocal folds is a biologically produced, periodic complex sound theoretically containing an

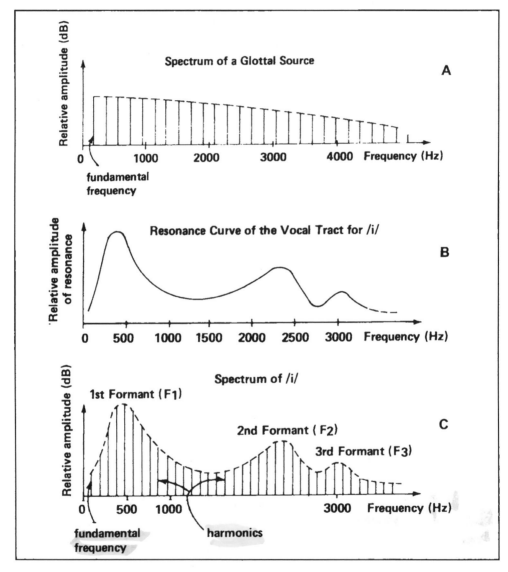

Figure 8–2. **A.** Glottal source spectrum. **B.** Voice tract resonance potential for production of the vowel /i/. **C.** Speech sound spectrum for the vowel /i/. (Courtesy of Oscar I. Tosi, Michigan State University Institute of Voice Identification.)

infinite number of frequencies. Acoustically, this sound is the glottal source for speech resonance before it reaches the resonating chambers of the speech tract. It is from this sound source that certain frequencies within it are amplified and damped by the person's neck and head resonating chambers. Physiologically, the rate of vocal fold vibration is the fundamental frequency. Acoustically, the fundamental frequency is also the lowest frequency in a periodic sound wave.

The glottal sound source is unstable during continuous production. Loudness and pitch are functions of the force and frequency of vocal fold vibration, and shimmer and jitter are the two measures of voice instability. Shimmer is also referred to as amplitude perturbation, the cycle-to-cycle variation in the amplitude of the glottal shock waves during phonation. It is a measure of loudness variation. Shimmer is associated with the voice quality of hoarseness. According to Ryalls and Behrens (2000), shimmer is the way vocal folds vary from one cycle of vibration to the next. Jitter, frequency perturbation, is a measure of vocal fold fundamental frequency variation. "The human larynx is not a perfect machine, and so we would expect some instability in a person's pitch, even when he or she was trying to produce a steady tone. However, extensive research on normal subjects and patients with voice disorders has shown that voices that are heard as normal do not manifest pitch instability, or jitter, that exceed 1% of the person's fundamental frequency" (Dalston, 2000, p. 306).

The optimum pitch, the frequency of vocal cord vibration that is the most natural to produce, is approximately one-quarter of a person's total voice range (including falsetto).

Analyses of glottal source pitch and loudness instability also have forensic application. Voice stress analysis is an evolving technology used to detect and evaluate deception and emotions of speakers. Although not as accurate as the polygraph, voice stress analysis for lie detection can approach the validity and reliability of several physiologic responses measured by the polygraph when the speaker is experiencing significant verbal jeopardy; the procedures used are similar to standard polygraph procedures, and more complex algorithms are used rather than the limited assessment of fundamental frequency instability (Tanner & Tanner, 2004).

Glottal energy, inclusive of the variations of amplitude and frequency discussed above, serves as the primary sound source for the speech resonating system. In addition to frequency and amplitude perturbations, fundamental frequency varies from person to person, and averages have been determined for men, women, and children. Fundamental frequency also varies from phoneme to phoneme. For example, in the production of the vowel /i/, men, women, and children typically have a fundamental frequency of 136 Hz, 235 Hz, and 272 Hz, respectively (Peterson & Barney, 1952). As Figure 8-2A shows, the spectrum of the glottal source is dispersed across the speech frequencies. The spectrum consists of the fundamental frequency and harmonics which are integer or whole number multiples of the fundamental frequency.

The output spectrum of the vowel /i/ shown in Figure 8-2A is a graphic representation of the buzz sound coming from the larynx without the benefit of the potential resonance curve of the vocal tract (Figure 8-2B). Its frequency ranges from approximately 100 Hz to 7000 Hz and each vertical line represents a sinusoidal wave, a whole number multiple of the fundamental frequency (f_0). The spectrum of the glottal source decays in a linear fashion at a rate of about 12 dB per octave, but the overall perception of pitch is primarily due to the fundamental frequency of the glottal source (Tosi, 1975, 1979).

Besides having a higher pitch, women tend to have a more breathy voice quality (Kent, 1997). With increasing age, the laryngeal cartilages tend to ossify more in women contributing to pitch alterations (Zemlin, 1997).

As Figure 8-2B shows, the resonance curve of the vocal tract for the production of the phoneme /i/ has three peaks (~500 Hz, ~2400 Hz, and ~3000 Hz) of potential resonance and two valleys (~1200 Hz and ~2750 Hz) of potential damping with a substantial decrease of energy beyond 4000 Hz. This resonance curve potential is what the resonating chamber of the speech tract will create acoustically when the neck and head resonators of a speaker are placed in the articulatory position to produce the /i/ phoneme. Certainly, individual speakers will vary in the resonance potential based on specific physical and acoustic features of their speech tract and resonating cavities. Nevertheless, the general shape of the speech resonators when positioned to produce the /i/ phoneme will have the potential acoustic qualities to create a discernable /i/ phoneme when the glottal source is applied. To continue the illustration above, if the human head and upper neck are replaced (in the /i/ articulatory position) on the buzzing sound source produced by the vibrating vocal folds, the result will be the acoustic features of the /i/ phoneme.

The output spectrum of the phoneme /i/ is shown in Figure 8-2C. An output spectrum is also referred to as a spectrum envelop and should not be confused with a speech sound spectrogram (Figure 8-3). The spectrum of the phoneme /i/ shows the relative amplitude of the harmonics and formants in decibels (dB) along the vertical axis, and the frequency in hertz (Hz) along the horizontal axis. A formant is a band of harmonics, a region of high relative energy, and the mean frequency of a formant is the peak resonance of a phoneme. Formants are repre-

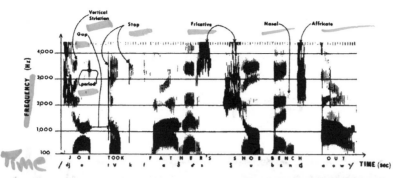

Figure 8–3. Speech sound spectrogram. (Courtesy of Oscar I. Tosi, Michigan State University Institute of Voice Identification.)

sented as F_1, F_2, . . . F_n based on their relative values. Mean frequencies of formants, like the fundamental frequencies on which they are based, vary among and between speakers. As can be seen in Figure 8-2C, the approximate formant mean frequencies for the /i/ phoneme for this particular speaker are 500 Hz, 2400 Hz, and 3000 Hz, respectively. Formant bandwidths and their relative amplitudes provide the basic acoustic features of the respective phonemes.

Fourier analysis is the decomposing of the complex wave into its sinusoidal harmonics. Fourier synthesis is the adding of all the harmonics together to rebuild the complex wave (Tosi, 1979).

Speech Sound Spectrogram

The sound spectrograph was originally developed and marketed by Kay Elemetrics of Pine Brook, New Jersey during the 1940s (Potter, Kopp, & Green, 1947). It provided the first three-dimensional view of dynamic speech.

Before the advent of the spectrograph, analysis of any aural phenomenon could only take place in the time domain, and was limited because of its fleeting presence. Speech analysis was particularly frustrating because of its constant change and by the dependence of its segments upon their sequences, each being influenced by the others, following and leading. Phonetic scientists and others found that the spectrograph could convert an ongoing aural sample of speech to a static visual representation and could examine each instant of the sample in detail. This led to its adoption as a ubiquitous tool for the study of human speech and its disorders (Culbertson & Tanner, 2005, pp. 6-7).

Today, speech sound spectrography has been enhanced by computerized digital technology, and software is now available to allow ordinary personal computers to perform a wide range of dedicated analyses that were not possible with the original analog devices.

The basis to the output spectrum and the speech sound spectrogram is Fourier's law. In the 1800s, Joseph Fourier discovered that any complex periodic sound can be broken down into its simple sound waves. Speech acoustic analysis, based on Fourier's law, is the representation of a complex wave as the sum of a number of simple waves of differing frequencies, amplitudes, and phases. Fourier's law allows speech to be seen as a spectrum. The speech sound spectrogram provides a visual representation of speech by time, frequency, and energy. The spectrogram is a product of a spectrograph or computer program capable of performing repeating Fourier analyses. For forensic purposes, the speech sound spectrogram is referred to as a voiceprint, but this reference is misleading given the dynamic nature of speech production: "A person's fingerprints are static from one sample to the next; they do not vary significantly over time. Acoustic patterns occurring during dynamic (connected) speech change from one speech sample to the next. In dynamic speech, a person may talk faster or slower, with a higher pitch or lower one, and with more or less nasal resonance from one sample to the next" (Tanner & Tanner, 2004, p. 29).

The sound spectrogram represents speech by frequency, time, and energy. Figure 8–3 shows a spectrogram of the utterance of "Joe took father's shoe bench out." On the spectrogram, frequency is represented along the vertical axis: 100 to 4000+ Hz. The lowest horizontal line is the base of the spectrogram and the frequencies are plotted proportionally along the vertical axis. Time is plotted along the horizontal base of the graph; the length of this spectrogram is 2.4 seconds. The relative intensity of speech is portrayed by varying degrees of energy band (formant) darkness. For speech acoustics, there are three primary formants (F_1, F_2, F_3). Formants give phonemes their perceptual qualities. The lowest formant is F_1, and the second formant, F_2, is considered the "hub" formant because it is crucial to the phoneme's perceptual features. The frequency changes in a formant over time is called a formant transition; they are rises or drops in the leading or trailing segments of a formant band. Formant transitions represent changes in the positions of the articulators in connected speech.

Vertical striations show periodic and aperiodic sound energy. The periodic vertical striations have clearly identified

repetitive energy pulses, resonance bars, each corresponding to one opening and closing of the vocal folds. They are visual representations of voiced speech sounds. Unvoiced sounds do not have repetitive resonance bars and appear as random energy bursts. Gaps, areas of a speech spectrogram without energy, are pauses between and within words. In Figure 8–3, the higher frequency of the /s/ phoneme compared to the /ʃ/ phoneme is indicated by the former's midpoint of energy occurring at approximately 4000 Hz and the latter having energy dispersed below 4000 Hz.

Quality and Spectral Characteristics of the Voice

Whereas pitch is the psychological correlate of frequency of vocal fold vibration, and loudness is the psychological correlate of intensity of vibration, a speaker's general voice quality can be attributed to the spectral characteristics of the acoustic signal. General voice quality is a function of the glottal energy applied to the resonating system. In effect, the laryngeal tone is filtered and modified when it passes through the throat and head resonating chambers. Certain frequencies in the glottal tone are either amplified or damped due to forced or sympathetic vibration of the air within the throat and head resonating chambers. When the glottal source vibrations have the same frequency as the natural resonating potentials of the neck and head resonators, they reinforce each other. The harmony or compatibility of the glottal source with the resonance of the speaker's neck and head give the speaker his or her general voice quality. Some speakers have strong, resonant voices and others have weak, frail ones. Just as some musical instruments have better output quality than others due to their construction, some speakers have more pleasing and richer general voice qualities than others due to their anatomy and physiology.

In most songs, the melody and tonal patterns are produced by prolongation of vowels; consonants play a small role in the overall melodic structure.

The overall efficiency of the sound source resonating system also plays a role in a person's unique voice qualities. When the sound source is efficiently amplified by the resonating chambers of the speaker's neck and head, the speaker will have a more resonant voice. When the sound source resonating system has maximum natural amplification across all frequencies, the result is a fuller voice. Oral-nasal resonance balance is also important. Some speakers, by virtue of their neck and head resonance structures, and functional velopharyngeal valving, have more or less habitual nasal resonance. More pleasing voice qualities have a balanced oral-nasal resonance and the entire resonating system is optimally utilized. Many other factors are involved in a person's overall voice quality including melody, pitch range during utterances, duration of syllables, and how efficiently the energy radiates from the person's body. However, a speaker's general voice quality is primarily determined by the strength and power of his or her vocal fold vibration.

The general public uses several terms to describe voice quality. Some common terms for voice quality are strong, weak, feminine, masculine, whiny, metallic, powerful, tinny, hard, raspy, throaty, and sexy. These terms, although clinically nondescript, suggest the power of the voice to communicate the emotional and psychological state of the speaker. The magnitude and complexity of information in a person's voice can be illustrated by describing a conflict between a verbal and nonverbal message.

Suppose a student is chronically late for a class. If the professor says to the tardy student, "It is fine that you come to class late each day," the verbal message is that tardiness is not an issue. However, if the professor says the same words with a lower pitch, harsh voice quality, and with little loudness and pitch variation, the nonverbal message is that it is not acceptable to be habitually tardy to class. When a listener is confronted with conflicting meanings between a verbal message and a nonverbal one, he or she will usually believe the latter; it is not acceptable that he or she is tardy each day to the class. The remarkable fact is not that there are nonverbal messages, it is that so much meaning can be carried by voice quality.

Titze and Story (2002, p. 1) comment on the role of voice quality in verbal and nonverbal multiple messages:

> We send multiple messages when we speak. Some are linguistic and some paralinguistic, meaning that they are independent of the words that we utter. Such paralinguistic messages concern our health, our mood, our genetic makeup, and our upbringing. Many of them are encoded in voice quality, which in the most general sense is everything in the acoustic signal other than overall pitch, loudness, and phonetic contrast (vowels and consonants).

Aronson (1990), in an exhaustive compilation of research spanning several decades, found voice quality related to personality traits and discrete emotions. Breathy voice quality is linked to neurotic tendencies, anxiety, low dominance, and high introversion. Harsh/metallic voice quality is associated with high dominance and emotional instability. Hoarseness is linked to reticence and self-consciousness. Murray and Arnott (1993) found the emotions of anger, happiness, sadness, fear, and disgust are associated with voice quality.

Kent (1997) distinguishes between affective quality, the speaker's emotion, and personal quality, the speaker's identity. Regarding affective quality, the listener, by attending to certain acoustic cues, can discern the speaker's emotions. "Therefore, the listener must 'peel off' the acoustic information pertaining to a speaker's emotional quality" (Kent, 1997, p. 362). Personal quality addresses objective determinations of a speaker's identity. According to Kent, the acoustic signal contains information sufficient to identify a speaker, even if that voice has not been heard for several years. Tanner and Tanner (2004, p. 16) comment on auditory speaker recognition:

> Listeners engage in speaker recognition, the detection of speech patterns, all of the time. Whether it is the matter-of-fact reporting of a nightly news anchor, a relative's message on voice mail, or a friend's voice in a crowd of partygoers, the human ear provides a very reliable way of knowing who is speaking. Pitch, loudness, rate of speech, emphasis, and a host of subtle cues are processed by the listener and judgments made about the speaker's identity. Most of the time, these cues are dealt with subconsciously and the listener is unaware he or she is doing it.

The Breathy-to-Harsh Voice Quality Continuum

There is a continuum of normal voice quality: breathy to harsh. The voice qualities of breathy and harsh result from two inter-related physiologic factors at the sound source. First, the breathy-to-harsh voice quality continuum is related to the duration of vocal fold openings and closings. Breathy voice quality occurs when the period of glottal closure is shorter relative to the period of glottal opening. This allows more air to escape at the sound source during phonation. In contrast, harsh voice quality occurs when the period of glottal closure is longer relative to the period of glottal opening during phonation. The second physiologic factor involved in the breathy-to-harsh voice quality continuum is the force of glottal closure. Breathy voice quality occurs when the force of glottal contact is less than what occurs in harshness. Conversely, harsh voice quality occurs when the attack phase of glottal closure is done with more force than what occurs during the production of the breathy voice quality.

Harsh voice quality is also called strident.

The hoarse voice quality is a combination of harsh and breathy qualities, and results from interference with optimal glottal closure. The hoarse voice is pathologic and may occur as an early indicator of vocal strain and abuse. Often, when there is general laryngitis or a prenodule, nodule, polyp, or ulceration of one or both vocal folds, glottal closure is compromised. This causes more air to escape during phonation and creates the perception of breathiness. The speaker may compensate for this air escape by forcing the vocal folds closed during adduction and contributing to the harsh component of hoarseness. This over-compensation in the form of hyperadduction further irritates the vocal folds. The genesis of some voice disorders related to vocal strain and abuse is the spiral of impaired voice quality and forced glottal closure to compensate for the breathy component of the hoarseness (Tanner, 2003d, 2006). Glottal fry, a low-pitch, pulsating voice quality, although not technically a pathologic mode of vocal fold vibration, may accompany hoarseness.

Complex Speech Sound Waves and Information Duplexing

During verbal communication, the thoughts of the speaker are transformed into acoustic energy by the speech mechanism. The speaker's linguistic constructs, the semantics, grammar, syntax, and phonology are transformed into acoustic energy by the motor speech production mechanism. So too are acoustic characteristics of the phonemes necessary to be perceived and decoded by the listener. The necessary linguistic and acoustic parameters of each phoneme are created by the five basic motor speech processes of respiration, phonation, articulation, resonance, and prosody. As noted above, this transformation also contains the encoding of a plethora of affective and speaker recognition information onto a speech sound wave. It is mind-boggling the amount of information encoded on the complex speech sound wave with the potential for perception and decoding by the listener. All of the thoughts, linguistics, phoneme acoustics, speaker identity, and affect associated with an utterance at the acoustic stage in the communication chain become nothing more or less than progressive high and low pressure transmissions through the medium of air. The molecular movements are graphically represented in a complex speech sound wave.

A common high school physics experiment is to ring a bell in a jar and listen to its sound. When the air is pumped from the jar, sound cannot be heard because sound will not travel in a vacuum.

Complex speech sound waves result from the above valving and resonance actions in the speech tract. As Figure 8–4 shows,

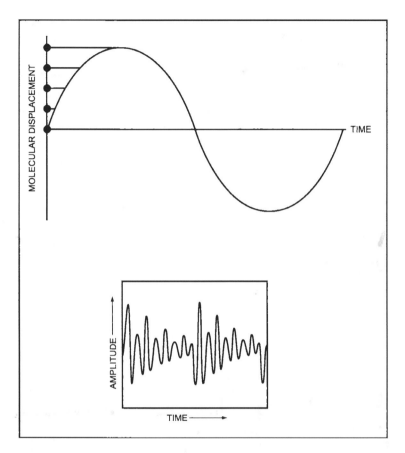

Figure 8–4. Complex speech sound wave.

a complex sound wave is the graphic representation of molecular displacement plotted over amplitude, time, and frequency. Molecules of air are compressed and rarefacted (rarefied) relative to their resting positions. During compression, there is an increase in relative air pressure because the air molecules are more densely compacted, and during rarefaction, there is a reduction of air pressure because the molecules are farther apart. Sound waves are progressive points of compression and rarefaction traveling through the medium of air. The amplitude of the molecular compressions and rarefactions is represented by the degree of displacement on the vertical axis. Time is represented horizontally, and the frequency of the sound wave is the number of waves completed in one second. Vibration can occur whenever there are mass and elasticity, and air is abundant in both. In speech sound waves, molecules (mass) of air are not transmitted from speaker to listener; energy is transmitted.

In all wave motions, it is not the medium that travels from point A to B, it is a pulse of energy moving from A to B.

To better understand energy versus mass transmission, sound waves can be likened to the water waves created by a ship. When a ship passes through calm water, it creates high crests and low troughs in the surrounding water. These peaks and valleys of water are created as the ship displaces the mass of water next to it. The water waves surrounding the ship go up and down, forcing the adjacent water to go up and down, which affects the mass of water next to them, and so forth. This continues until water waves splash on the shore. The mass of water directly in contact with the ship does not reach the shore; it is energy that is transferred through the water to the shore. Information about the size, speed, and shape of the ship can be gleaned by the amplitude, time, and frequency of the water waves lapping on the shore. For the purposes of this analogy, the ship is the speaker, the water is the medium of air, and the shore is the listener's ear. However, this analogy falls far short in explaining the magnitude of the information carried in a speech sound wave.

The movement of the mass of air particles from their maximum positive (compression) to their maximum negative (rarefaction) position, and back to positive position again is called one cycle of oscillation. The wavelength is the distance the wave travels in one cycle of vibration, and the distance between the two crests or troughs, and the distance in space one cycle of vibration occupies. There is an inverse relationship between wavelength and frequency of vibration. Longer waves move slower than shorter waves and vice versa. Wavelength equals the velocity of the sound wave divided by the frequency. The lowest frequency perceived as sound, a 20-Hz sound wave, is about 56 feet. The highest frequency detectable by the normal human ear, a 20,000-Hz sound wave, is much shorter, about 0.06 feet.

Sound wave speed is the rate distance is covered by the sound wave divided by time. Velocity is its speed together with the direction of travel. Acceleration is the rate at which velocity is changing with respect to time.

The number of air particles increases with the distance from the speaker to listener, and this is why sound dissipates the farther away the communicators are from each other. As the speaker moves away from the listener, acoustic energy is spread over an increasingly larger area. The speech sound wave decreases in amplitude the farther the speaker is away from the listener, and his or her loudness varies lawfully relative to distance. The inverse square law states that energy decreases in proportion to the square of the distance from the source. This law also pertains to heat and light; energy decreases in proportion to the square of the distance from the source.

The Property of Entropy and *The Unified Model of Communication Sciences and Disorders*

Modern information theory suggests that any communication system has essentially five parts: source, encoder, channel, decoder, and user (Ihara, 1993). Speech communication is an orderly process of energy transformation involving a source (speaker), encoding (language and motor speech planning and production), channel (the medium of air), decoding (auditory sensation and perception), and receiver (auditory association). Speech communication is an orderly transformation of information.

The first orderly process of energy transformation occurs in a person's brain when electrochemical energy becomes mental representations and it is the least understood process of the communication chain. The human nervous system functions by the conductivity and directionality of neuron-propagated ionic signals, electrochemical impulses, shooting from one neuron to the next, receiving sensations and initiating motor acts, bridging the left and right hemispheres, and associating lobes and specialized centers of the brain. Neurotransmitters stimulate and inhibit these electrochemical reactions at the synaptic level. Through a process of continuous electrochemical impulses, and fundamental changes in brain cellular chemistry, the neuronal impulses provide the energy for mental representations that become thought. The electrochemical reactions in the brain are remarkably transformed into the consciousness of a person. At a fundamental level, the brain-mind leap is the first orderly process of energy transformation. As discussed previously, neuroscientists have just begun to bridge this brain-mind conceptual cavern, and the philosophic and religious implications are profound, but the essence of human consciousness is this electrochemical to mental representation phenomena. Images, sensations, and internal monologues become the mental representations of these electrochemical impulses.

The second orderly process of energy transformation in communication occurs when lanugage structures thought for expression. All-important grammar gives order to essentially random imagery, sensations, and semantics. Structure is provided by the human innate ability to construct words from speech sounds, string words into syntactically ordered utterances, and to make necessary grammatic transformations. Grammar provides the structure for transforming the basic elements of thought into linguistic acts.

The third orderly process of energy transformation occurs when the motor speech production mechanism programs the motor acts necessary for speech production and executes the plan using the five basic motor speech processes of respiration, phonation, articulation, resonance, and prosody. The language constructs are transformed into complex speech sound waves, acoustic energy, by the muscles of the body. This acoustic energy is transformed to mechanical energy at the middle ear. The tympanic membrane (eardrum), which is in contact with the vibrating air molecules, vibrates at a frequency and amplitude that corresponds to the source of the sound waves. The mechanical energy transmission of the information signal continues through the ossicular chain, the bones of the middle ear. The bones of the middle ear amplify the information signal, but its essential mechanical energy state does not change.

As discussed in Chapter 9, the final bone of the ossicular chain, the stapes (stirrup), is in contact with the fluid-filled cochlea. Here, the mechanical energy is transformed to hydraulic energy as the information signal becomes the high and low pressure changes ossicilating in the inner ear. In contact with the fluid in the inner ear is the organ of Corti. At this stage, the hydraulic energy is transformed into electrochemical energy, and the signal travels along cranial nerve VIII to the brain. Finally, the electrochemical energy again is transformed into language construct and mental processes decoded and associated by the receiver.

Order to Disorder

Entropy is a thermodynamic concept addressing a system's thermal energy for conversion into mechanical work. In physics, it is interpreted as the degree of disorder or randomness in the system. Entropy is Greek in origin and means "transformation." Physicists believe the universe is going from an ordered state to one of disorder and that it is spreading and becoming less constrained. Campbell (1982, p. 44) describes entropy and probability of order:

> Another way of looking at the second law of thermodynamics is to say that the higher the entropy, the more numerous are the possible ways in which the various parts of the system may be arranged. In this approach the connection between entropy and probability is plain to see: if there is a large number of possible ways in which the parts of a system may be arranged when the system is in a state of high entropy, then it is improbable that they will be found in any one special arrangements at a particular instant, just as it is unreasonable to expect a pack of cards, while

in the process of being shuffled, to return to its original order, because that single, unique arrangement of the cards is one out of such an astronomically large number of possible arrangements.

Claude Elwood Shannon, in his 1949 paper entitled, "A Mathematical Theory of Communication," tied entropy to randomness in information processing. Shannon, an electrical engineer and mathematician, is considered the father of information theory. According to Sowa (2000), both entropy and information tend to increase, and the rate of the increase is proportional to the increase in the number of bits required to encode their configurations. Entropy and information follow the same mathematical laws. The causality of entropy and information is ultimately connected with time; the degree of disorder occurring in a system is dependent on the passage of time (Sowa, 2000).

Whenever energy freely transforms from one system to another, there is an increase in disorder and a consequent denigration of the signal. The information exchange in communication described above includes transformation from electrochemical, mental, acoustic, mechanical, and hydraulic energy states. According to Shannon (1949), when the information encoded exceeds the channel capacity, then unavoidable errors occur in transmission. Shannon addressed the redundancy of written language and how it improves recognition of signals and efficiency of information communication.

Another way of looking at entropy in information theory is that information is an ordered state and ignorance is its disorder. "Since the early days of statistical thermodynamics the idea has become widely accepted that entropy really signifies nothing more than a lack of human knowledge. The view has been strengthened by the advent of information theory where entropy is specifically equated with an inverse measure of 'information'" (Denbigh & Denbigh, 1985, p. vii). However, this equivalence of information theory to physical properties has been questioned: "As a consequence, those who came to regard statistical mechanics as being a special case of information theory introduced terms such as 'ignorance' and 'surprisal' which implied a very significant epistemological standpoint. No doubt such terms were appropriate to many of the applications of information theory, but they seem entirely alien to the discussion of physical phenomena" (Denbigh & Denbigh, 1985, p. 67).

"Communication theory deals with systems that transmit information or data from one place to another . . . It is significant to note that the actual message is the one selected from a set of possible messages with probabilistic structure" (Ihara, 1993, p. 1).

Disambiguation

Speech communication is redundant and the information carried during communication exceeds the semantics and grammatic structure provided by any language. It is impossible to construct utterances that carry the totality of a person's communicative intent. Acoustically, the perceptual cues necessary to auditorily recognize and decode each phoneme surpass what is required for basic perception. Decades of speech perception research have shown that more than 40% of the acoustic signals of an utterance can be eliminated and still permit speech perception. The redundancy of speech communication combined with the limited transmission capabilities of the oral-auditory channel requires denigration of the message. Anyone who has experienced the frustration of being unable to express a thought, to be unable to communicate the totality of the intended information, has confronted signal denigration despite the redundancy of speech communication.

Two types of speech disorders occur: complication and simplification errors (Darley, Aronson, & Brown, 1975). Complication errors are the result of the speaker adding, substituting, or interjecting unwanted sounds into an utterance. Simplification errors are the result of the speaker failing to produce precise speech sounds such as occurs with articulatory distortions and omissions. Language disorders can also be viewed in the complication-simplification dichotomy. Speakers can provide tangential information which may obscure the deep structure of the message. Speakers can also provide too little information to provide the listener with sufficient information to grasp the underlying concepts embedded in the message. Both complication and simplification errors increase entropy in the system, decreasing the inherent order of the message, and thus contributing to ignorance. Although not all speech or language disorders lead to unintelligibility or semantically meaningless utterances, they decrease the order of the phonemic or semantic associations. This results in denigration of information in the communicative system. Furthermore, this denigration is increased by the presence of noise in the system.

Noise

Noise is defined as any unwanted sound (or information), and the word is derived from Latin for nausea or sickness. Noise cannot be absolutely defined because of the high variability of what individuals consider unwanted. In music, for example, some consider the high-pitched feedback of a guitar to be noise while some rockers consider it music to their ears. The crying of a baby may be noise to passengers on an airplane, but to his or her mother, it is basic communication. Opera, sitar, cello, jazz, rap, and country-Western music all have the potential to be perceived as noise or music.

Although noise is simply unwanted sound (or information), there are also three other variables associated with the concept: loudness, harmony, and distraction. First, sounds that are loud, and thus more intrusive, are more likely to be perceived as noise. Second, sounds that are irregular and lacking harmony are more likely to be considered noise. Tones that are perceived as disharmonious, discordant, and off-key tend to be considered noise. Third, sounds that are distracting and detract from the primary figure are more likely to be regarded as noise. Although the distracting sound (or information) may not be unwanted per se, it is considered noise because of its effect on the listener's ability to attend to and process the primary signal.

CHAPTER SUMMARY

Speech is produced by the motor speech processes of respiration, phonation, articulation, resonance, and prosody affecting the air molecules surrounding speaker and listener. Air serves as the medium by which the thoughts and feelings of the speaker are transmitted to the listener. The human speech production mechanism is a sound-source resonator which uses energy from the vocal folds and amplifies certain frequencies while damping others. A person's voice sounds like him or her because of the unique acoustics of this sound-source resonator. The voice carries not only linguistic meaning, but also personality traits and discrete emotions. The speech signal is a complex speech sound wave traveling through air and impacting the listener's ear. During the orderly transformation of energy, meaning and information are reduced regardless of the redundancy of the encoded system.

Study and Discussion Questions

1. Describe the communication chain of events occurring thus far in *The Unified Model of Communication Sciences and Disorders*.

2. What is the brain-mind leap and what issues related to communication does it involve?

3. What is a frictional-stop sound source? Provide examples. Describe the spectral characteristics of unvoiced frictional-stop sound sources.

4. What is the primary sound source for the speech resonating system? Make the typical buzz created by the vocal folds using your lips.

5. Compare and contrast shimmer and jitter.

6. What is the forensic application of voice analysis in lie detection? Describe it.

7. Draw the output spectrum for the vowel /i/. Note the vertical lines and describe what they indicate.

8. Compare and contrast harmonics and formants.

9. Why is it technically incorrect to label a speech sound spectrogram a voice print?

10. Draw a hypothetical speech sound spectrogram and label the important markers (e.g., the significance of vertical and horizontal axes, formants, gaps, transitions, etc.).

11. List and describe terms used by the general public to characterize a person's voice.

12. Compare and contrast the affective and speaker voice qualities described by Kent.

13. What is the breathy-to-harsh voice quality continuum? What are the physiologic factors involved?

14. What is information duplexing on complex speech sound waves?

15. How is the property of entropy related to *The Unified Model of Communication Sciences and Disorders*?

Suggested Reading

Gillam, R., Marquardt, T., & Martin, F. (Eds.). (2000). *Communication sciences and disorders.* San Diego, CA: Singular Publishing Group.

Kent, R. D. (1997). *The speech sciences.* San Diego, CA: Singular Publishing Group.

Tanner, D., & Tanner, M. (2004). *The forensic aspects of speech patterns: Voice prints, speaker profiling, lie and intoxication detection.* Tucson, AZ: Lawyers and Judges Publishing, Co..

Tosi, O. (1979). *Voice identification: Theory and legal applications.* Baltimore: University Park Press.

CHAPTER 9

The Hearing Mechanism and Accompanying Nonverbal Communication

"Nature has given to men one tongue, but two ears,
that we may hear from others twice as much as we speak."

Epictetus

CHAPTER PREVIEW

In this chapter, the role of hearing in human evolution and survival is reviewed. The hearing mechanism is examined anatomically and physiologically. From the vibrations of the eardrum to the neural impulses that carry sound to the brain, the manner in which this sense organ transforms and transmits information is detailed. Emphasized are the transformations from acoustic energy to mechanical, hydraulic, and the return to electrochemical energy of the communication signal. Facial expressions, gestures, proxemics, and other forms of nonverbal information processing during speech communication are also discussed.

Acoustic to Mechanical Energy Transmission

In Chapter 8, the speech sound-source resonating system and the transformation of the speaker's message into high and low pressure waves traveling through the medium of air were addressed. At this stage in *The Unified Model of Communication Sciences and Disorders*, the speaker's message, the information contained in the form and content of his or her utterances, become acoustic energy. At the tympanic membrane (eardrum) of the ear, the acoustic energy is transformed into mechanical energy. The pressure changes acting on the eardrum are small, but the human ear is very sensitive to these pressure-induced vibrations especially in the primary speech frequency range: 1000 to 2000 Hz. The human ear can detect changes in atmospheric pressure of approximately one part in ten billion. "At this minute pressure variation, the eardrum moves less than one hundred-thousandths the wave-length of light, one tenth the diameter of the smallest atom" (Bell Telephone Laboratories, 1958, p. 2).

The sound waves travel at about 1,100 feet per second and reach Angela in a fraction of a second. (Andrew's visual communications, his facial expressions and gestures, reach Angela much more rapidly because they travel at the speed of light.) In contact with the air molecules vibrating in response to Andrew's speech production is Angela's eardrum, a small, thin, membrane. Because her eardrum is in contact with the air molecules, this extremely sensitive tissue vibrates in concert with them. Consequently, Angela's eardrum vibrates at a frequency and an amplitude corresponding to the source, that is, Andrew's speech production mechanism. Angela's eardrum is so sensitive that it can detect the smallest of molecular displacements. If it were any more sensitive, it could detect the sound of air rushing as people leave the coffee shop or move their hands through the air to swat a fly. Attached to Angela's eardrum are the three smallest bones of the human body, the hammer, anvil, and stirrup collectively known as the ossicles, which vibrate in unison with her eardrum and, in so doing, amplify and transmit energy to her cochlea (External and Middle Ear Excerpt from Connections *in Chapter 1).*

Survival and Human Hearing

The range of human hearing is approximately between 20 Hz and 20,000 Hz. Pressure changes below 20 Hz, those considered infrasonic, are perceived as vibration. Pressure changes above

20,000 Hz, those considered ultrasonic, are above the range of hearing in most people. The primary frequency range for speech is below 4000 Hz with 2000 Hz considered the pivotal frequency. Other animals have different ranges of hearing. For example, the cat can detect sound up to 50,000 Hz and the mouse up to 90,000 Hz (Goss, 1982). The reason for the 20 to 20,000 Hz human frequency range involves the role of hearing in species survival.

As prehistoric humans fought for survival, the sense of hearing, to no small extent, played a role in their ultimate successful adaptation, and eventual supremacy over other animals on the planet. Prehistoric humans evolved the 20 to 20,000 Hz hearing sensitivity because animals threatening to them, or serving as sources of food, typically produced sound in that frequency range. What is most important, evolvement of the 20 to 20,000 Hz frequency range provided the hearing sensitivity for speech communication, which itself provided and continues to provide a powerful survival advantage. Through speech communication, prehistoric humans could plan and cooperate for individual and collective survival.

The sense of hearing also provides a person with a constant reality contact. Unlike vision, where the ability to see is blocked when the eyelids are closed, hearing is always available to warn of danger, ever alert to environmental sounds even during sleep. Whether a nighttime sound is a baby's cry, a pet scratching at a door, or a high-pitched smoke alarm, the sense of hearing is always in contact with reality and vigilant to alarming environmental sounds.

Another important survival benefit for humans, and many other animals, is the ability to localize sound. Prehistoric and present-day hunters and combatants benefit from sound localization. Knowing the directional source of a sound alerts hunters to prey, and provides combatants with warning and avenues to avoid and escape threats to safety. Even for casual conversations, directional hearing is a convenience for the communicators, and contributes to the ease of conversational turn-taking. There are three factors involved in knowing the direction of a sound.

The first and most important factor in sound localization is the relative loudness of the sound in each ear. Environmental sound can be localized because a person has learned the general direction of a sound source; it is perceived louder in one ear compared to the other. Certainly this loudness difference is small, but perceptible. The reason for the loudness difference is that the energy is blocked and consequently damped more in one ear than the other by the head. Second, speech and hearing

Hominids are living and extinct human beings and their near-human ancestors. The oldest known human ancestor lived about 5.8 to 5.2 million years ago. It was about the size of a chimpanzee and may have walked upright (*Time Almanac*, 2005).

A dog's hearing can extend to frequencies of 60,000 Hz or higher and an elephant produces calls with a fundamental frequency as low as 12 Hz (Kent, 1997).

scientists believe that there is a shadow effect. A shadow effect is acoustic energy casting a shadow behind the external ear (pinna). This results in a person being able to sense differences in acoustic energy as a function of the direction from the sound source. The third and possibly negligible reason for sound localization has to do with the speed of sound and differences in its arrival to each ear. Brief in duration though it is, sound reaches the ear closer to the source sooner than when it reaches the distant ear.

The Outer Ear: Channeling Acoustic Energy

Acoustic energy, carrying all the form and content of the speaker's message, is channeled to the eardrum through the outer ear (see Figure 9-1). The cartilaginous pinna (auricle), Latin for "wing," helps capture and direct the energy into the ear canal. It is composed primarily of ridged cartilage, and several muscles that stabilize rather than move it. Although some animals have

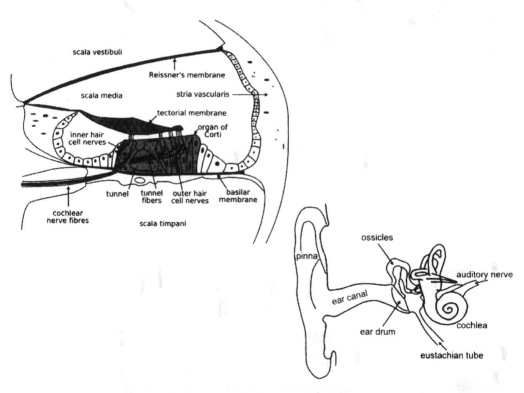

Figure 9–1. The hearing mechanism.

the ability to independently move the pinna to help detect and localize sound sources, the pinna in humans is essentially fixed. (Some people can independently move their pinnae anteriorly and posteriorly.) Another difference between lower animals and humans with regard to hearing is the tragus. The tragus is a small triangular protrusion of the pinna located at the opening to the ear canal. It can be pressed inwardly to block loud sounds and to protect the hearing mechanism from injury. "Although humans cannot voluntarily close off the tragus, as can some animals, vestiges of muscles designed for this purpose remain in the human ear" (Martin & Clark, 2003, p. 222). Large ears in some animals also double as temperature-regulating mechanisms (Zemlin, 1998).

Some authorities in speech and hearing sciences contend that the pinna is useless. "Most authors relegate the human pinna to the position of an earring holder, and little else" (Glattke, 1973, p. 285). Given the larger human evolutionary picture, to say that an evolved structure, especially one as important to survival as hearing, is useless and only cosmetically important is presumptuous. The size, angle, and contour of the pinna, combined with the resonance potential of the external canal, likely contribute to the shadow effect and sound localization ability in humans. However, with regard to hearing sensitivity and auditory acuity, the actual size of the pinna is not a significant variable (Zemlin, 1998).

The first hearing amplification was an ear trumpet, a conical tube that was narrow at the ear and widely opened at the other end, used to help direct the acoustic energy to the ear and to decrease competing sounds. The function of the ear trumpet can be demonstrated by cupping the pinna with the hand. The cupping gesture, common when a person experiences problems understanding the speech of others, helps increase the acoustic energy reaching the ear and reduces competing noise.

The acoustic energy is channeled into the external auditory meatus, the ear canal. The external auditory meatus is essentially an S-shaped tube closed at one end, and in adult males, it is about 2.5 centimeters in length (~ ½ inch) and 1.0 centimeters in diameter. The outer one-third of the ear canal is surrounded by cartilage and the inner two-thirds are supported by the temporal bone (Glattke, 1973). Besides functioning to channel the acoustic energy to the tympanic membrane, the external auditory meatus serves a protective function with the production of wax which is embedded in small hairs and blocks foreign substances from penetrating the canal. Cerumen is a waxy substance which helps maintain the acidic environment of the external auditory meatus. According to Champlin (2000), the skin in the external auditory meatus is more sensitive in the inward portion and stimulation of it may trigger a cough reflex.

Because the external auditory meatus is an air-filled, closed-end tube, it resonates over a wide frequency range with a prominent resonant peak near 4000 Hz (Zemlin, 1998). "Although the boost provided by resonance is not large (maximum effect = 10–15 dB), sounds passing through the outer ear are influenced by its resonance characteristics" (Champlin, 2000, p. 111). Resonance and damping of acoustic energy in the external auditory meatus, along with changes in the dimension of the ear canal during chewing, yawning, and other jaw movements, affect the transmission of energy, and thus the communicative information.

Ambient noise can also disrupt the speaker's message from entering the outer ear. The degree of communicative interference can be viewed as a ratio of desired and wanted information duplexed on the speaker's acoustic signal to the amount of competing and unwanted noise. A high signal-to-noise ratio permits maximal speaker information to be transmitted to the listener, while a low one indicates varying degrees of noise interference. Ambient or surrounding noise competes with the signal and can completely disrupt speech communication.

Obstructing wax and objects, as well as a narrowing (stenosis) of the external canal can prevent acoustic energy from reaching the tympanic membrane. Although cerumen is naturally cleaned from the external canal, in some persons it can become impacted. Objects placed in the ear canal not only impair acoustic transmission of the speaker's signal, but can also create medical complications.

> Audiology got its start as an independent profession after World War II when many solders returned home with hearing loss or deafness.

The Middle Ear: Transforming Acoustic Energy to Mechanical Energy

As Figure 9–1 shows, the cavity of the middle ear is the size of an aspirin located in the temporal bone. It consists of the tympanic membrane and the ossicular chain, the bones of the middle ear. Technically, the outer external surface of the tympanic membrane is part of the external ear and the inner surface is part of the middle ear. The tympanic membrane is an extremely sensitive skinlike sheet of tissue and is only about 9 mm in diameter. The total area of the tympanic membrane is approximately 80 square millimeters (Champlin, 2000). The pressure variations exerted on the tympanic membrane are very slight and measured in small units, microbars. A micobar is one dyne per square centimeter. A dyne is a unit of force exerted on mass; an ounce of sand

Sound pressure = amount of force (dynes) on surface area.

has about 30,000 dynes of gravitational force. Sound pressure is the amount of force (dynes) on a surface area (centimeters). The smallest pressure changes acting on the eardrum necessary to produce an audible sound is 0.0002 dynes per square centimeter^2. When power is measured in energy units, an erg is used. One erg is the amount of work done when one dyne force displaces an object by one centimeter. The power of sound energy is measured in watts per square centimeter. The relative intensity of sound is measured in decibels (dB). (The B is capitalized in deference to Alexander Graham Bell.) The decibel scale is logarithmic, a ratio between two powers. Zero decibel is ten to the minus sixteen watts per square centimeters corresponding to a pressure variation that is less than one-billionth normal atmospheric pressure (Bell Telephone Laboratories, 1958).

Connected to the tympanic membrane is the largest bone of the ossicular chain, the malleus. It resembles a hammer with a large head fixed to a handlelike base. Because of the direct connection to the tympanic membrane, the malleus vibrates in unison to the pressure changes reaching the eardrum. Attached to the malleus is the anvil-shaped incus. Affixed to the incus is the stapes which is shaped like a stirrup. It has a loop appearance with a flat base. The flat base, or footplate, is in direct contact with the oval window of the fluid-filled cochlea and vibrates in response to the sound source pressure changes. "The ossicular chain actually rocks back and forth on an axis, and the action of the stapes in the oval window is not that of a piston but, rather, like a pivot" (Martin & Clark, 2003, p. 243). The area of the tympanic membrane is about 17 times greater than that of the oval window. Consequently, the middle ear has the potential to amplify the energy received at the tympanic membrane by a factor of 17. However, because not all of the tympanic membrane vibrates with equal intensity in response to sound pressure changes, the ratio of tympanic membrane displacement to oval window displacement is about 1.3:1 (Martin & Clark, 2003).

The space from the inner surface of the tympanic membrane to the oval window of the cochlea, the middle ear, would be an air-sealed cavity if not for the eustachian tube, a duct between the middle ear and the nasopharynx. The eustachian tube, also known as the auditory tube, is named after the 16th-century scholar, Bartolommeo Eustachio. Because of the eustachian tube, pressure changes within the middle ear, and drainage of fluids, is possible. The eustachian tube opens to equalize middle ear pressure when people travel from different atmospheric pressures and during chewing, sneezing, yawning, and swallowing. A waking person's eustachian tube opens about once per minute and

The ossicular chain is held in place by muscles and ligaments.

The eustachian tube in an infant remains open until the age of about six months and it is shorter and wider in relation to its length than is an adult's (Martin & Clark, 2003). Some babies cry during airplane flights due to the discomfort caused by changing pressures in their middle ears.

during sleep, about every five minutes (Martin & Clark, 2003). When equalizing pressure, there is often a "popping" effect. It is due to the positive and negative air pressure changes in the middle ear causing the tympanic membrane to be slightly pushed out or sucked in.

People hear speech through air conduction of the sound energy through the external ear. They hear their own speech in the same way that they hear the speech of others. People also hear their own speech through bone conduction, effectively bypassing the external and middle ears. Bone conduction is the stimulation of the cochlea through the vibration of the temporal bone. These two ways of conducting sound energy can be compared to movement in the fluid-filled cochlea with a container of water.

One way of creating movement in the fluid-filled container of water is to use an external source, such as a stirrer, to agitate the fluid. This is analogous to the way the cochlea is stimulated when listening to the speech of others; it is agitated by the movements of the stapes. Another way of agitating the water in the container is to shake the container. This is analogous to the way the cochlea is stimulated when speech sound energy vibrates the skull bone containing the cochlea; energy is transmitted through bone conduction.

The difference in the quality of auditory feedback through air and bone conduction is significant. Bone conduction and air conduction channels create different acoustic qualities in auditory feedback. This difference accounts for the reason many people report that the quality of their speech heard on a recording is unusual, and often, aversive to them. The aversion of hearing one's voice only through air conduction, such as occurs with recordings, is related to the hearer being accustomed to auditory feedback through both air and bone conduction during speech. People comment that the recording "does not sound like them." However, in reality, the recording is the quality others hear and that auditory feedback through both air and bone conduction is only heard by the speaker.

The stapedial reflex reduces the transmission of sound energy by 10 to 30 dB and is also part of a general startle reflex (Kent, 1997).

Several medical conditions can disrupt the energy transmission in the middle ear. A ruptured tympanic membrane, reduced mobility of the ossicular chain, and pressure abnormalities in the middle ear can cause a reduction in the mechanical energy transmission to the cochlea. Disruption of the energy flow at the outer or middle ear is referred to as a conductive hearing loss. An indication that the disruption of energy flow is limited to the outer or middle ear is an air-bone gap. An air-bone gap is where a person can hear tones better when a vibrating oscillator is placed on the mastoid process, thus vibrating the cochlea and bypassing the external and middle ears. Of course, external and middle ear dysfunctions can be diagnosed using other audiologic tests. Acoustic impedance audiometry is used to assess the acoustic reflex. The acoustic reflex, sometimes called the stapedial reflex, is a protective action. The stapedius and tensor tympani muscles contract in response to loud sounds. At about 85 decibels, the acoustic reflex occurs in most people. However, Zemlin (1998) reviewed the literature on the functions of the stapedial and tensor tympani muscles and concluded that the reflex provides little, if any, productive actions.

The Inner Ear: Transforming Mechanical Energy to Hydraulic Energy

The footplate of middle ear bones, the stirrup, is connected to Angela's cochlea and vibrates in response to Andrew's speech. The cochlear fluid also moves back and forth, and embedded in the fluid are nerve fibers, or hair cells, that convert the sound pressure waves into electrochemical energy. The electrochemical energy moves along the VIIIth cranial nerve, also known as the auditory nerve, to the base of Angela's brain where the nerve impulses are routed to a structure of her brain, the thalamus, also known as the "gatekeeper." (Inner Ear Excerpt from *Connections* in Chapter 1).

The inner ear consists of the cochlea and the semicircular canals (see Figure 9-1). The cochlea can be described as a snail-shaped tunnel and it would be about 35 mm in length if unwound. The cochlea is part of a sensory structure in the temporal bone known as the labyrinth. (Labyrinth refers to a maze in Greek mythology.) The labyrinth is a series of tunnels in the temporal bone containing the organs of hearing and balance. The semicircular canals are part of the vestibular mechanism and are important for balance. The vestibular mechanism senses the pull of gravity on its receptors. Through a complex system of interaction, its nerve endings interact with the eyes and the body's skeletal muscles to maintain balance. Vertigo, a sense of spinning and loss of balance, is seen in some diseases that also impair or destroy hearing.

Vertigo, dizziness and spinning, and nystagmus, rapid, rocking movement of the eyes, often occur together. Police officers look for nystagmus as indications of alcohol intoxication.

The cochlea is the end organ of hearing: The eyes are to vision as the cochlea is to hearing. The fluid within the cochlea, endolymph, is set into vibration by the movement of the stapes, which, in turn, sets the organ of Corti into vibration. Attached to the organ of Corti are epithelial hair cells connected to the nerve

Spontaneous otoacoustic emissions are weak sounds produced by the cochlea.

endings of the spiral ganglion. The organ of Corti has three to five parallel rows of 12,000 to 15,000 outer hair cells and one row of 3,000 inner hair cells (Martin & Clark, 2003). Each hair cell movement sets off a subsequent neurologic impulse along cranial nerve VIII, the vestibulocochlear nerve. "The direction in which they are bent during stimulation is of great importance. If the cilia bend in one direction, the nerve cells are stimulated; if they bend the other way, the nerve impulses are inhibited; if they bend to the side, there is no stimulation at all" (Martin & Clark, 2003, p. 280). Here, the hydraulic energy is transformed into electrochemical energy or nerve impulses.

The Inner Ear and Cranial Nerve VIII: Transforming Hydraulic to Electrochemical Energy

There are several theories of audition to explain how the inner ear transforms mechanical energy into loudness and pitch. Although the nature of the sense of hearing is generally understood, exactly how the cochlea functions as a sense organ is far from completely known. There are two general theories of audition: place and frequency.

The first cochlear implant occurred in 1972.

Place and frequency theories of audition address the passage of vibratory energy through the cochlea and disturbances on the basilar membrane (Zemlin, 1998). (Temporal aspects of cochlear functioning are inherent in any discussion of place and frequency.) The basilar membrane extends the entire length of the cochlea and supports the organ of Corti. Based on current research, the sense of hearing appears to be related to place, time, and frequency of disturbances in the cochlea. However, a consensus among speech and hearing scientists on how these disturbances result in the sensation of hearing has yet to be reached. Loudness and pitch are related to the rate and location of nerve firing in some yet-to-be-discovered way. Loudness appears to be related to acoustic nerve firings, spikes in neuron action potential per unit of time, while pitch is associated with the vibratory frequency and the sensitivity of sections of the basilar membrane. The physiology of the cochlea results in the subjective judgment of loudness to vary among different frequencies and intensity levels. Noise exposure can destroy all or part of this sense organ as can a multitude of diseases.

Cranial nerve VIII has its synaptic connection with the brainstem; it is the final common pathway for hearing and balance. Cranial nerves are numbered from the rostral to caudal body positions, meaning cranial nerve VIII is physically below seven other cranial nerves. The brainstem extends from the thalamus to the spinal cord. The brainstem integrates unconscious central nervous system functions including auditory localization, and relays tracts of the spinal cord and the rest of the central nervous system.

There are three sections to the brainstem: midbrain, pons, and medulla. Cranial nerve VIII inserts in the brainstem at the level of the pons. "The auditory nerve extends 17 to 19 mm beyond the internal auditory canal, where it attaches to the brainstem where the cerebellum, medulla oblongata, and pons join to form the cerebello-pontine angle (CPA)" (Martin & Clark, 2003, p. 314). The cell body of cranial nerve VIII is located in the brainstem but technically is part of the peripheral nervous system. "Although the auditory nerve is relatively thick, it contains a surprisingly small number of nerve fibers, about 50,000 in the cat and 30,000 in the human" (Zemlin, 1998, p. 499).

Tumors, and other disease processes affecting cranial nerve VIII can interfere with the neural impulses to the brainstem. Brainstem compressions occurring in traumatic brain injury also impair neural impulse transmission at the brainstem. Although the accuracy of specialized audiologic tests to isolate the site of lesion have improved significantly in the past 30 years, typical conventional testing simply categorizes hearing loss occurring at the level of the cochlea and/or cranial nerve VIII as sensorineural. Table 9–1 shows three general types of hearing loss and their site of lesion.

Table 9–1. General Types of Hearing Loss, Energy Disruption, and Site of Lesion

Type of Hearing Loss	Energy Disruption	Site of Lesion
Conductive	Acoustic and mechanical	Damage or impairment of the external or middle ear.
Sensorineural	Hydraulic and electrochemical	Damage or impairment of the cochlea and/or VIIIth cranial nerve.
Mixed	Acoustic, mechanical, hydraulic, and/or electrochemical	Damage or impairment of conductive and sensorineural components

Accompanying Nonverbal Communication

Thus far in *The Unified Model of Communication Sciences and Disorders*, the speaker's communicative information has been placed into a language code and motorically programmed. The atmosphere surrounding the speaker has been disrupted by his or her motor speech production apparatus, and acoustic energy transmitted to the listener's ear. At the listener's ear, the acoustic energy carrying the speaker's information is transformed into mechanical, hydraulic, and electrochemical energy. But speech communication does not occur in a vacuum; visual communication accompanies the process of hearing, and in many ways, is necessary to the effective transmission of information.

The word "communicate" comes from Latin "communicare," meaning "to make common" or "to share."

The speaker and listener communicate with accompanying facial expressions, gestures, and other forms of communication such as proxemics, clothing, touch, and smell (see Table 9-2). Although no single part of the brain operates independently of other parts, the right hemisphere is important for nonverbal communication; persons with damage to the right hemisphere tend to be impaired in using and appreciating nonverbal communication. The nonverbal communication used by all people can

Table 9–2. Nonverbal and Speech Communication

Accompanying Nonverbal Communication	Nonverbal Dimension	Nonverbal Effect
Facial expression	Eyes, eyebrows, lips	Attention and receptiveness to communicative act
Gestures	Reinforcing Descriptive	Accentuate verbal statements Describe actions and events
Proxemics	Territory Personal Space	Physical zone Movable bubble of space for appropriate communication
Clothing and accessories	Iconic nonverbal representations of self-concept	Sexual attraction Socioeconomic status Credibility
Touch	Tactile stimulation	Pleasure/pain Mental health/survival
Smell	Odor Fragrances Pheromones	Sexual attraction Communicative ambience

be powerful in facilitating the transmission of information or it can contradict and negate the intended meaning. Nonverbal communication is so pervasive and ever present, it has been said, "We cannot not communicate." Even silence can communicate volumes.

Relegating nonverbal communication to "accompanying" speech communication acts may be misleading. Ruthrof (2000, p. vii) contends that nonverbal signs are the deep structure of language:

> The body is present in discourse in the form of nonlinguistic signs: as olfactory, tactile, gustatory, aural, visual, and many other subtle, nonverbal readings of the world. When we learn a language as part of social pedagogy, the community guides us to systemically link the sounds of language expression with nonverbal sign complexes. For language to be meaningful, members of a speech community must be able to share, to a high degree, the way in which language and nonverbal readings are to be associated with one another.

According to Ruthrof, imagery and signs are the bases to all languages, and nonverbal signs are composed of tactile, olfactory, gustatory, aural, visual and other perceptual readings. Addressing the referent in the symbol-referent relationship discussed in Chapter 5, Ruthrof (2000) proposes several axioms related to the body and language. For example, he considers language to be an empty syntactic grid, with no meaning unto itself, and a parasite of nonlinguistic signs. Meaning is an event, and dictionaries only provide verbal substitutions. As discussed in Chapter 5, the meaning of a symbol lies in the relationship of the symbol to its referent, and according to Ruthrof, the body is the foundation of this relationship.

Although authorities disagree on the amount of information communicated visually, no one argues that visual communication carries as much, if not more, information than speech during a communicative act. According to Goss (1982) and others, as much as 70% of information to the brain comes through the visual mode, but the auditory mode of processing information is superior when information is presented rapidly. "When information is presented at a very fast rate (one to two items per second) people remember more items that they hear compared with those that they see" (Goss, 1982, p. 17). Additionally, the sense of hearing is omnidirectional whereas the visual field of input is primarily frontal. Nevertheless, the brain operates holistically; communicators process information auditorially and visually, and their facial expressions are powerful accompanying sources of information.

Facial Expressions

The speaker's and listener's affect are communicated through facial expressions during speech communication. A person's face, particularly his or her eyes and lips, are powerful in communicating the range of human emotion. There are at least eight distinguishable positions of the eyebrows and forehead, ten for the lower face, and eight for the eyes and lids (Adler & Towne, 1978). Scientists have found that a person's face reveals information about how he or she feels and the emotional content of the message, and his or her body gestures reveal the intensity of emotions about the information being imparted. More or less objective information is a function of the segmental speech act, while affect, the emotion associated with the utterance, is largely a nonverbal accompanying phenomenon. (See suprasegmentals of speech production for a discussion of the role of pitch, loudness, emphasis, and melody of speech and their role in nonverbal communication.)

"For language to be meaningful, members of a speech community must be able to share, to a high degree, the way in which language and nonverbal readings are to be associated with one another" (Horst Ruthrof, 2000, p. vii).

Eye contact indicates the degree of attention to the communicative act, and can also suggest whether the listener is open to receiving the message. Eye contact also varies with the degree of authority and submission of the communicative parties. Persons maintain less eye contact with people they feel have more authority than them, and also with strangers and the disabled. Some cultures consider it rude to make lengthy eye contact while others question the sincerity and veracity of people who habitually fail to make eye contact. Although it is often assumed that lack of eye contact signals deception, or that a child cannot lie and maintain eye contact with his or her parents, there is little research to support these claims. However, the pupils may be correlated with truthfulness and deception. The pupils also may suggest the shear degree of interest a listener has in the verbal message; dilation suggests more interest, and constriction less topical engagement. The eyes are best at communicating acceptance, indifference, and rejection. When a person's facial expressions, particularly his or her eyes, show a receptiveness for the information imparted through speech communication, both speakers and listeners are more relaxed and less defensive, thus increasing the likelihood of effective information transmission.

Gestures

Kinetics, the study of body movements, includes the use of gestures during speech communication. Some communicators are more physically demonstrative than others during speech communication, and some topics stimulate more gestures than others. There is a cultural factor associated with the amount and nature of gestures used and understood during speech communication; some cultures naturally use more gestures. Additionally, a nonverbal gesture in one culture may communicate an entirely different message when used in another or have no meaning at all. For example, when indicating direction, some traditional Navajo speakers, rather than pointing with their fingers will gesture with their lips and chin to the general direction of an object or person. There is also a gender difference: women tend to be better at reading nonverbal communication than men. All gestures can be divided into essentially two types: reinforcing and descriptive.

Reinforcing gestures are those a speaker uses, and a listener understands, to stress, accentuate, and emphasize a verbal statement. They can be subtle, such as fidgeting or conspicuous, such as hitting a table with a fist. Reinforcing gestures provide the listener with additional information about the speaker's affect and suggest the intensity of those feelings. Listeners also use gestures to reinforce the degree of their receptiveness to the message. For example, a listener with his or her arms crossed may be communicating a general disapproval of what is being said. Of course, that person may also simply be cold or tired, and the crossed arms gesture unrelated to message receptiveness. Other examples of reinforcing gestures include crossed legs, leaning in or out, touch, pointing, and general body position during speech communication. General body positioning includes the degree to which the speaker and listener are facing each other and the proximity of communicators.

Descriptive gestures, as the name suggests, are used to describe an action or directions to a place. A speaker using descriptive gestures uses his or her face, hands, or general body to help explain an action or provide direction. For example, a person may use his or her finger to point the general direction of a store or restaurant or perform several gestures when giving a lost traveler directions. Frequently, when a speaker uses accompanying descriptive gestures, the listener also performs similar gestures to show understanding, clarify statements, or while repeating what has been said.

Just as sign language has a syntax, a set of rules for combining individual signs into acceptable words and phrases, so too do a person's gestures. The combining of gestures into a series of accompanying physical actions closely follows the verbal syntax of the speaker. The semantics of nonverbal gestures is also tied to the context of the verbal utterances. A gesture may mean one thing in one verbal context and have an entirely different meaning in another. For example, scratching at ones head may mean confusion, curiosity, wonder, or simply an itch, and the verbal context provides cues to the meaning of the gesture.

Other Forms of Nonverbal Communication

Whether the parties are consciously aware of them or not, several other forms of nonverbal communication accompany speech communication. They can profoundly influence the exchange of information. Proxemics, clothing, touch, and smell have the potential to communicate vast amounts of information during speech communication.

Proxemics

Proxemics is the study of spatial relationships on interpersonal communication. It specifically concerns the speaker and listener's relationships to each other in space and time. Proxemics involves both territory and personal space.

Territory is a physical zone a person stakes out as his or her own. Fences, no trespassing signs, reserved parking spaces, and books on a table in a library are examples of territory markings. Students in lecture courses typically sit at the same desks and stake out this territory as their own during the class periods. Although wedding rings are symbolic in many ways, they also are territorial markers. The need to stake out territory is a human need, similar to what is seen with lower animals.

The percent of all students served by federally supported programs for students with disabilities was 13.34% in 2001 to 2002. The percent of students with hearing impairments was 0.15 during the same period (*Time Almanac*, 2005).

Personal space is a zone of area that moves with a person, a bubble of distance reserved for types of communication. Each zone or distance enables certain types of communication, and in fact, the proxemics of speaker and listener communicate limitless amounts of information nonverbally. Authorities recognize four zones of communication: intimate, personal, social, and public.

Intimate space, a zone of communication extending from a person's body to about 18 inches, is reserved for private, very close communicative acts. When parties to communication allow each other to enter their intimate space, and do not feel discomfort, information is imparted that it is a trusting relationship, full of potential to develop further, and that neither party feels threatened. Allowing a person to enter one's intimate space provides opportunities for even closer intimacy through touch and other sensory interaction. What is more important, opening up of intimate zones of communication permit possible repro-duction, which carries individual and evolutionary significance, and the propagation of genetic information.

Beyond intimate distance and extending to about 4 feet, personal space is a zone of communication reserved for public, casual conversations. As with intrusions into intimate distance, when a person feels that his or her personal space is violated, he or she feels discomfort. Adler and Towne (1978) also report that with regard to personal space, people stand closer to friends than enemies, farther away from strangers, authority figures, people from higher status, and individuals from different racial groups. Larger people demand greater amounts of personal space, and women show the least discomfort when the space around them is small. Of course, the physical setting also affects distances in communication; people stand closer in smaller rooms. Violations of intimate and personal space occurring in elevators are the rea-sons people sometimes feel uncomfortable. Interestingly, when trying to verbally reduce the tension in these situations, the small talk only increases it.

Social distance extends from about 4 to 12 feet for commu-nication acts that occur in more formal activities. These are inter-actions requiring little personal contact and intimacy. Public distance is beyond 12 feet, and is the acceptable distance for pro-fessor and students in a classroom setting. The greater the distance from speaker and listener, the less likely the occurrence of dia-logue. Interpersonal communication, speech acts between people, is best when the distances permit free exchange of information.

Clothing

The clothing people wear not only provides protection from the environment, but also communicates a variety of messages nonverbally. For the purposes of this discussion, clothing also includes accessories such as jewelry, cosmetics, ties, tattoos, piercings, religious symbols, and other adornments worn by a person. These accessories, while not clothing per se, are used to express a variety of personal, political, religious, and social state-ments. Clothing not only expresses much about a person's self-concept, but also his or her social-economic status. With regard to self-concept, one of the reasons uniforms are used in the military is to minimize individuality and to promote a collective mentality. Clothing is also used for sexual attraction, and the degree to which it conceals or reveals a person's body sends powerful sexual messages to potential mates.

Ruthrof (2000) emphasizes the importance of icons in nonverbal communication, noting that mental images are essential to meaningful communication. Clothing and other accessories provide cogent iconic representations during the act of communication and they are fundamental to the verbal transmission of meaning. For example, medical information imparted by a person attired in a white coat with a stethoscope draped from his or her neck is given more credibility than medical information imparted from a person wearing a mechanic's coverall while holding a crescent wrench. Although it is possible that both individuals may have credible and substantial medical information to verbally communicate, it is obvious that the latter person's clothing and accessories diminish if not negate the communicative information. Often, the effects of clothing and other accessories on the communicative act are more subtle. However, they have the potential of dramatically affecting, not only the ongoing communication, but also future verbal interactions by creating mental sets based on iconic representations and affecting expectations regarding the person's veracity and credibility.

Touch

Skin, a thin protective covering, is the largest organ of the human body. The epidermis, outer skin, is the primary sense receiver for the tactile sense (touch). Skin is sensitive to stimulation ranging from excruciating pain to euphoric pleasure. Therefore, it is not surprising that it is a powerful organ for nonverbal communication. It is well known that touch and physical contact with others is not only desirable, it is essential to mental health and survival. Studies of touch deprivation in lower animals and infants have shown the importance of physical contact. Infants and lower animals deprived of touch and physical contact with others often fail to thrive. Occupational therapists and speech-language pathologists working with children with multiple disabilities have found that body awareness is important to learning language. Tactile defensiveness is systematically addressed in some children to achieve meaningful progress in activities of daily living and language developments.

Touch, when used as accompanying nonverbal information, can communicate like, dislike, approval, disapproval, affection, repugnance, and a host of other profound or subtle messages. A pat on the back, caress of a cheek, and a hand-push express volumes about a person's emotions. Communication through touch accentuates verbal messages and provides more emotional and affective information. For example, when someone says,

"I like you," the message is accentuated with a touch to an arm or pat on the back. Touch accentuates the verbal message and gives more significance to it. And of course, sexual communication is primarily tactile, and during sexual intercourse, verbal acts are often relegated to accompanying forms of communication.

Smell

The role of smell in communication has not been comprehensively researched, but the olfactory sense plays a nonverbal role in the total process. The olfactory nerve senses chemical changes in the atmosphere, and sends impulses to the insular cortex of the brain. Interestingly, all sensory input, except the sense of smell, have relay centers in the thalamus. Consequently, the sense of smell bypasses the "gatekeeper" and is processed immediately and directly by the brain. Information from the sense of smell is stored in long-term memory, and odors and fragrances readily stimulate past associations. Although the senses of smell and taste are closely related, the sense of smell is far more dynamic.

Pheromones are naturally occurring airborne chemical substances important for a variety of animal behavior, especially reproduction. Pheromones are detectible by the sense of smell. The nature of pheromones is currently being researched, but there is evidence that this type of communication also occurs in humans, albeit to a lesser extent than in lower animals. Studies have linked pheromones to the timing and duration of menstrual cycles in women. Although controversial, there is some evidence that pheromones may have a small attraction effect in some persons; people appear to be sexually attracted to others with different pheromones. Regardless of the effects of pheromones on human behavior, the sense of smell plays an accompanying role in verbal communication. Odors and fragrances can enhance or diminish the pleasantness of the environment, thus stimulating or inhibiting interpersonal communication; they influence the communicative ambience.

Children of a Lesser God is a film about the social implications of deafness. It stars Marlee Matlin who won an academy award for her performance in it.

CHAPTER SUMMARY

At the listener's ear, the speaker's information is transformed from acoustic energy into mechanical, hydraulic, and electrochemical energy. At the outer ear, the acoustic energy is channeled into the external ear canal, and the tympanic membrane vibrates in concert with the pressure changes corresponding to those of the sound source. The ossicles vibrate in unison with the tympanic membrane and transmit it to the cochlea. At the cochlea, the mechanical energy is transformed into hydraulic energy, which in turn, is transformed into neural impulses, and eventually travels along the auditory-vestibular cranial nerve to the listener's brain. Accompanying the auditory energy transmissions are nonverbal messages sent by the speaker, and read by the listener, which provide as much, if not more, information than the spoken words. The listener reads the nonverbal information to learn the speaker's affect, and the intensity of those feelings, about what has been spoken.

Study and Discussion Questions

1. Describe *The Unified Model of Communication Sciences and Disorders* as applied thus far to the hearing mechanism.

2. What survival benefit does the hearing mechanism provide? How does sound localization work?

3. Describe the channeling of acoustic information through the external ear canal to the eardrum.

4. Describe the tympanic membrane and discuss its function.

5. Describe the ossicular chain and discuss its function.

6. What structure is involved in equalizing middle ear pressure? How does it work?

7. Describe bone conduction.

8. Draw the cochlea and identify major landmarks. How does the cochlea work?

9. What is the auditory-vestibular nerve? How does it work?

10. List and discuss the types of injuries that can disrupt the process of hearing.

11. What role does facial expression play during speech communication?

12. What are the two types of gestures and what role do they play during speech communication?

13. How does proxemics affect speech communication?

14. How does clothing affect speech communication?

15. How do touch and smell affect speech communication?

Suggested Reading

Champlin, C. (2000). Hearing science. In R. Gillam, T. Marquardt, & F. Martin (Eds.), *Communication sciences and disorders: From science to clinical practice* (pp. 101–124). San Diego, CA: Singular Publishing Group.

Durrant, J. D., & Lovrinic, J. H. (1995). *Bases of hearing science* (3rd ed.). Baltimore: Williams & Wilkins.

Martin, F., & Clark, J. (2003). *Introduction to audiology* (8th ed.). Boston: Allyn & Bacon.

Zemlin, W. (1998). *Speech and hearing science* (4th ed.). Boston: Allyn & Bacon.

CHAPTER 10

Auditory Perception and Verbal Association

*Understand: verb (past and past part. **understood**)*
1. perceive the intended meaning of (words, a language, or a speaker);
2. perceive the significance, explanation, or cause of;
3. interpret or view a particular way;
4. infer from information received;
5. assume that (something) is present or is the case.

Oxford University Press

CHAPTER PREVIEW

In this chapter, auditory perception and verbal association, the final stage of *The Unified Model of Communication Sciences and Disorders* is detailed. The nature of perception is reviewed including the Sapir-Whorfian hypothesis and the sensory gatekeeping function of the thalamus. Auditory perception in general, and speech perception in particular, are discussed including their functions in decoding the information sent by the speaker. The agnosias are discussed with special emphasis on visual and auditory-acoustic perceptual disorders. The neurologic tracts from the thalamus to the auditory cortex are examined as is receptive language and the process of verbal association. The philosophy of General Semantics is discussed as are the levels of semantic decoding, dynamic symbolism, and discourse semantics.

From Sensation to Perception

In the previous chapter, the acoustic energy created and transmitted by the speaker is channeled into the listener's external ear canal. Because the listener's tympanic membrane is in contact with the atmosphere, it vibrates at a frequency and amplitude corresponding to the very small atmospheric pressure changes caused by the speaker's motor speech production mechanism. The listener's ossicular chain, which is in contact with the tympanic membrane vibrates, and while doing so, transforms the speaker's communicative signal to mechanical energy, and also amplifies it. In contact with the ossicular chain is the listener's fluid-filled cochlea, which is stimulated by the ossicular chain's mechanical movements, thus transforming the mechanical energy into a hydraulic energy state. The nerve endings in the cochlea are resultantly stimulated, setting off electrochemical impulses that travel the auditory-vestibular cranial nerve to the listener's brainstem. From this point in the communication chain, the signal enters the thalamus where it will be routed to higher brain levels.

> There are five senses, each with accompanying perceptual components: visual, auditory, olfactory, gustatory, and tactile-kinesthetic-proprioceptive.

Perception, Latin from *percipere* or awareness, is the mental process of recognizing and being aware of sensory information. Perception allows humans to be aware of events and objects; it is the window to consciousness. Perception is a higher neurologic, mental, and psychologic function than sensation. Sensation is the detection of bodily and environmental information, and perception is the first stage in interpreting them. The attachment of meaning to sense information begins with perception. Although there is no consensus among speech and hearing practitioners regarding the nature of perceptual disorders, the agnosias are generally considered disorders of perception, and are neither sensory impairments nor higher-level association disorders. As will be discussed, aphasiologists typically combine auditory-acoustic agnosia into the receptive aphasia categories.

Acting as a gate, the thalamus allows some sensory information to reach consciousness while denying it to others. In this coffee shop, there is the ever present clanging of cups and saucers, high-pitched scream of boiled water being released, mumbled conversations, and the shuffling of patrons as they pass by Angela and Andrew's table. Through it all, Angela attends primarily to Andrew's utterances and automatically blocks competing sounds from reaching awareness. Although she is aware of the background noise at some level, it does not reach the conscious level to be processed as salient and mean-

ingful information. Also thanks to Angela's thalamus, other sensory stimulation such as the sights of students entering and exiting the union, taste of the expensive Italian coffee, and the way her new shoes pinch her toes are similarly reduced to background stimuli, and not the focus of her perceptions. (The only sense not routed through the thalamus is smell.) What does reach Angela's awareness are the speech sounds, words, and language constructs being rapidly uttered by Andrew. (Perception Excerpt from *Connections* in Chapter 1)

Perception, more than any other brain function, involves the entire peripheral and central nervous system. Nevertheless, brain localizationists, using advanced brain scanning devices, try to localize parts of the brain responsible for perception. "These clinicians, researchers and theorists focus on pinpointing a part of the brain responsible for this, that or the other psychological phenomenon. They engage in brain mapping studies and explore the brain rather than the mind" (Tanner, 2003b, p. 4). These attempts to localize human perception, however well intentioned, are fraught with inordinate complexity, and possibly, futility. For human perception not only enables awareness of the world, it determines what is to be conscious.

That which is perceived is a percept.

"The organism is linked to the world directly, and evolution has designed this linkage to be a snug fit, the brain being tuned to acquire accurate knowledge of the particular environment the organism inhabits" (Campbell, 1982, p. 210). Perception is an ongoing gestalt of sensory detection, appreciation of salient environment information, and the cortical and mental processes of gating and interpreting the meaning of the world. A person not only perceives what is sensed, he or she determines consciously and subconsciously what will be allowed to be perceived. Perception is learned, and throughout a person's life span, he or she constantly adjusts, monitors, and evaluates what is gated to consciousness. As Campbell (1982, p. 212) notes: "An act of perception is personal and unique." The perceiver self-directs the process of perception. The process of perception begins at the thalamus, a brain structure sometimes referred to as the "gatekeeper."

The Thalamus

Although frustrated in determining the site of the brain that is exclusively responsible for perception, neuroscientists know that the thalamus is important to the total process. "The thala-

The gatekeeper function of the thalamus can be illustrated by the reader being unaware of how his or her tongue feels in the mouth before reading this sentence. After reading it, the gate to conscious awareness is opened and the reader becomes aware of the tongue sensation in the mouth. This example of sensory information going from unconscious (subconscious) to conscious awareness shows the all-important gatekeeping function of the thalamus.

mus is very important because it receives all neural impulses, either directly or indirectly, from all parts of the body, except for olfaction" (Zemlin, 1998, p. 342). Some aphasiologists have postulated the clinical category of subcortical aphasia often identifying the basal ganglia and thalamus as the sites of lesions responsible for this language disorder. However, it is likely that subcortical aphasias are modality-specific, predominantly perceptual or motor disorders, and the diagnostic label more accurately describes agnosia or apraxia rather than aphasia. (See Chapter 6 and the section addressing the chaos of aphasia classification terminology.)

The thalamus, about the size of a golf ball, is made up of two halves and located at the rostral end of the brainstem. It consists of gray matter and is part of the diencephalon. The thalamus can be viewed as relay center where sensory information is routed. It consists of three tiers of nuclei each with dedicated functions. The medial geniculate nucleus receives information from the ear and routes it to the cortex. According to Zemlin (1998), the thalamus also processes the perception of crude aspects of pain and temperature, and influences arousal, attention, and sleep-wake cycles. Figure 10–1 shows the brainstem, basal ganglia, and thalamus.

Perception and Intuition

Intuition, the ability to subconsciously (or partially consciously) sense the answer to a question or to know a relationship between two or more variables, begins at the level of the thalamus. The mental representations of intuition usually take the forms of hunches, suspicions, or feelings of insight. Intuition is considered an instinctive response and some persons are more adept at this process than others; they readily intuit answers to questions and understand relationships. Intuition is usually associated with emotional responses, some of which are also routed through the thalamus.

Intuition is an estimation, usually accompanied by an emotional response, about a situation or a predicament. The emotions associated with intuition can range from a sense of euphoria to impending doom. Interestingly, many people when confronted with intuitive and reasoned quandaries will select the intuitive response rather than a consciously logical and rational one. People who appear to operate intuitively in certain vocations such as stock selection, aviation, combat, and so forth are said to have

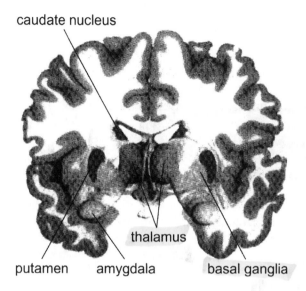

Figure 10–1. The basal ganglia and thalamus.

a sixth sense and the ability to discern the essence of a problem or situation clearly and instinctively. The complete role of the thalamus in intuition has yet to be discovered, but its function as an integrator and coordinator of incoming multisensory information certainly plays a role in this subconscious or partially conscious function.

The Sapir-Whorfian Hypothesis

No discussion of perception would be complete without reviewing its role in thought. (See Chapter 5 for a general review of language, thought, human consciousness, and the role of language in cognition.) Linguists Edwin Sapir and Benjamin Lee Whorf addressed cross-cultural perception in the Sapir-Whorfian hypothesis. According to this hypothesis, the words of a language, be they general or specific, constrain a person's thoughts, and in fact, structure his or her sense of reality. Therefore, because people who speak different languages have different words with dissimilar perceptual and semantic boundaries, people essentially have different realities.

The Sapir-Whorfian hypothesis is based on observations of several Native American languages including Apache, Hopi, and Navajo (Whorf, 1956). A common example given of the Sapir-Whorfian hypothesis involves Eskimos. Because Eskimo languages have many more words for snow, they perceive the reality of snow differently than do people living in Phoenix, Arizona. The Sapir-Whorfian hypothesis is part of a greater philosophic movement advanced by Immanuel Kant, and others, who postulated that reality is largely an individual construct. The Sapir-Whorfian hypothesis places language as the foundation of individual and cultural realities.

Although philosophers and scientists have discounted the formal Sapir-Whorfian hypothesis, many in academia ascribe to the idea that language determines sensation and, by extension, cultural reality. However, rigid adherence to it has been widely criticized by scientists. "The Whorfian hypothesis in its strongest version—that language determines thinking—is not generally accepted today. It was based on comparative linguistic data that show that languages differ in the number of terms for such things as 'color' or 'snow.' The reasoning was that people with many words for 'snow' actually perceive distinctions that people with one word failed to perceive. Language determined their experiences and their thinking" (Borden, Harris, & Raphael, 1994, p. 4). According to Ryalls and Behrens (2000, p. 112) "Criticism, however, soon rained down on the Sapir-Whorf hypothesis, with good reason." The reasons included vague translations from non-English to English and the fact that the hypothesis focuses more on grammar rather than the semantics in its postulates. However, the primary weakness of the Sapir-Whorfian hypothesis involves some academics' overindulgence in radical multiculturalism.

Common sense and logic suggest that the senses—visual, auditory, olfactory, gustatory, and tactile-kinesthetic-proprioceptive—are direct links to the environment, and all normal humans have basically the same sensory mechanisms, regardless of their languages and cultures. All normal humans, irrespective of their race, ethnicity, culture, religion, primary language, and other diversity factors, have essentially the same sensory capabilities. Native Eskimos and Phoenicians are all members of the human species, share the same time-space reality, and therefore sense it in essentially the same way. To prove this point, Sternberg and Ben-Zeev (2001, p. 220) examined color identification and found that speakers of different languages do not arbitrarily sense the color spectrum: "It turns out that different languages name colors quite differently, but in the languages, the color spectrum is not divided up arbitrarily. A systematic pattern seems universally to govern color naming across language."

The Sapir-Whorfian hypothesis, in its extreme, cannot be scientifically supported; all humans sense reality essentially the same. However, the role of perception in thought cannot be discounted, especially with regard to abstract, verbal thought. Whereas the perception of visual, olfactory, gustatory, and tactile-kinesthetic-proprioceptive information involves detection of concrete stimuli, auditory perception, especially of abstract verbal thoughts, is not exclusively based on physical stimuli. For example, the perception of the color red or snow with a powder texture involves sensations of specific, referential stimuli. In the physical world, the color red does not exist independently, that is, there is no entity existing independently as red; only physical referents in the environment may be red in color. Similarly, powder refers to fine, dry, pulverized particles, and when referring to snow, the sight of powder snow to skiers is based on its physical properties. Certainly, for impressionistic artists who manipulate color and light to capture emotions in their paintings, and to downhill skiers who adjust their racing strategy to the texture of snow, these concepts, and the words used to represent them, are more salient, refined, and clarified. Impressionistic artists and downhill racers are more likely to perceive, but not sense, fine distinctions in paintings and snow than inexperienced painters and novice skiers.

Although the sensation of the physical properties of color and snow do not change, the perception of their salient features is affected by language, and this is particularly true with regard to abstract language. It is true that perception is personal and unique, but only with regard to interpretation of environmental stimuli, and not in their physical detection. Nevertheless, universally discounting the Sapir-Whorfian hypothesis as irrelevant is assuming and presumptuous, for the relationship between perception and abstract language is far more complex than the perception of color and snow. Abstract language neither is a direct product of sensory stimuli nor absolutely dependent on them.

The Sapir-Whorfian hypothesis has philosophic and scientific application to the perception of abstract words and their meanings. Words such as "truthfulness," "honesty," and "God" do not have clearly identifiably visual or other sensory detectible referents; their meaning lies in the perceiver's personal and unique associations. When perceiving them, their perceptual boundaries may be different and unique based on the meaning

Edward Sapir advanced the linguistic determinism philosophy about the role of language in thought. His student, Benjamin Lee Whorf, furthered it. Today, the idea that language not only carries thought, but also structures it, is known as the Sapir-Whorfian hypothesis.

of the words in different language. The words may encompass more or less meaning to some individuals than others. Especially for individuals speaking different languages, perception of abstract words and appreciation of their meanings do affect the perceiver's reality of these concepts. One person's reality of "truthfulness," "honesty," and "God" is influenced by the perceptual features of the words and that which he or she considers salient.

To summarize the Sapir-Whorfian hypothesis and the role of perception in thought, it is apparent that language, to a limited extent, affects thought and thus a person's interpretation of reality, but not his or her sensation of it. Linguistic determinism, that language determines all thought, has little scientific support although it is widely believed in some circles. Linguistic relativity, that language influences thought, has scientific support and is a logical and commonsense understanding of cognition. Language affects the coding of sensory information for perception, association, and memory, but does not determine the physical parameters of sensory stimulation. The important role of perception in information coding is illustrated in the concept of saliency.

Perception and the Concept of Saliency

Regardless of its scientific merits, the Sapir-Whorfian hypothesis suggests the importance of perception in human existence. Although the physical reality of what is sensed is not determined by language, the sensations that reach conscious awareness certainly play an important role in cognition. Perception, and particularly the concept of figure-ground, is pivotal in the appreciation of reality, and previous learning is a fundamental aspect of perception.

People learn to perceive those aspects of the world that are important and to filter out the rest. Every normal person is born with this ability to sense the important things and disregard those things that get in the way. A lifetime of learning refines perception. For example, if you have learned to play a band instrument, you are much better at hearing and appreciating it when you hear a band play. The trombone, trumpet and tuba are perceived with more clarity and sophistication by people who play these instruments. When a carpenter, bricklayer and landscaper drive through a neighborhood, each perceives the homes a little differently. The carpenter is attuned to the quality of the framing, the bricklayer notices the masonry, and the landscaper focuses more closely on the placement of the shrubs. This is because each has learned the intricacies of working in these occupations; their perceptions have been heightened and refined (Tanner, 1999, p. 87).

Saliency is the degree to which aspects of sensory stimulation are considered important and noticeable. Aspects of sensation that are important to the perceiver are allowed to reach consciousness because they have more learned meaning. In the above examples, the carpenter, bricklayer, and landscaper have learned to perceive what is important to the quality of their trades and to ignore the irrelevant. The carpenter, bricklayer, and landscaper do not sense reality differently because of their learning, they simply perceive aspects of their trades that are important and usually not perceived as salient by laypersons. Contrasts in saliency are easier to perceive when the differences are great rather than minor. For example, laypersons can distinguish between extremely poor carpentry, masonry, and landscaping, but subtle differences in the quality of those trades are detectible only by people experienced in those trades. Perhaps the best illustration of finely tuned perception is the fictional sleuth Sherlock Holmes and his less perceptive colleague Dr. Watson.

Sherlock Holmes' abilities to perceive important clues associated with a criminal suspect's voice and appearance set the tone for Sir Arthur Conan Doyle's famous detective's powers of deduction. To show the contrast in perceptual skills, while both Sherlock Holmes and Dr. Watson would be present when questioning a suspect in a crime, Sherlock Holmes would perceive much more during the meeting than Dr. Watson. The suspect's suntan, accent, aftershave, and soil on his shoes would be more salient to Holmes, and spark meaning in the investigator's mind. Sherlock Holmes, largely due to his highly developed perceptual abilities, would know where the person was born, preferred mode of transportation, marriage status, vocation and salary, and where he or she vacationed. It was "elementary" that Sherlock Holmes' perceptions were superior to Dr. Watson's observations. Individual differences in a person's perceptual abilities are largely a function of what he or she relegates to perceptual "ground" status and that which he or she considers a perceptual "figure."

Perception and the Concept of Figure-Ground

The concepts of saliency and figure-ground are related theoretically and practically. In perception, the figure is that to which attention is directed; it is the learned salient aspect of environmental stimuli. The ground, on the other hand, is the ambient, background environmental information. In this dichotomy, it would be inaccurate to consider the figure the important aspect of the environment and the ground irrelevant and superficial. The figure, the important aspects of auditory, visual, or other

[Handwritten margin notes: Perceptual figure = that to which attention is directed. perceptual ground = ambient, background information]

[Handwritten/printed margin note: Aphasia cuts across all modalities of communication; agnosia is limited to one.]

sensation,, is intricately tied to the ground, which gives the figure a framework for the perceptual gestalt.

An example of visual figure-ground is a driver attending to the highway and traffic while ignoring the spots on his or her windshield. Although the spots on the windshield are visually sensed, they are not perceived until the driver consciously attends to them. Tactile figure-ground distinctions occur when Braille readers attend to meaningful raised dots and ignore the feel of other surface textures. The same tactile distinction occurs when a person puts his or her hand in a pocket, senses all the objects, but perceives those that are meaningful such as keys or coins. Olfactory figure-ground distinctions occur when the odor of natural gas is perceived as salient while other odors and fragrances are ignored. Wine connoisseurs learn to perceive salient taste aspects of wine, assign meaning to them, and ignore other aspects of the taste of a particular wine. Based on previous experiences and learning, some wine connoisseurs can determine the vintage of a particular wine based on perception of taste-salient features. An example of figure-ground distinctions in the auditory mode involves the cocktail party phenomenon.

The cocktail party phenomenon is aptly labeled; it is the ability of a person to perceive various conversations at a group gathering. It involves selective attention of auditory stimuli. The person experiencing the cocktail party phenomenon can attend to and understand one conversation and, while keeping his or her head stationary and thus not moving the ears, attend to another conversation. This perceptual act is the result of psychologically relegating the previous conversation to background information and the new one to figure status. The cocktail party phenomenon permits a person to sequentially attend to several conversations. Although conversations closest to the perceiver are easier to attend, even distant ones can be selectively perceived while ignoring those occurring in closer proximity. To further show the unconscious (subconscious) nature of selective auditory perception, a person will immediately tune out all conversations when his or her name is spoken in the group gathering.

The Agnosias

The agnosias, a term first coined by Sigmund Freud, are disorders of perception. As noted above, the agnosias are usually limited to one sense and are not mulitmodal communication disorders such as occur in aphasia. Each sense mode, for example, visual, tactile-kinesthetic-proprioceptive, olfactory, gustatory, and auditory have a corresponding agnosia. Tests for agnosias usually have the patient match to sample in a single modality. With regard to *The Unified Model of Communication Sciences and Disorders*, visual and auditory-acoustic agnosias have the most relevance to the disruption of the communication chain at the auditory perceptual stage.

Visual agnosia can be part or the total reading deficit seen in dyslexia. Although there are several varieties of visual agnosia such as color, shape, and visual-spatial, all types of visual agnosia involve the patient being able to visually sense information but not appreciate the significance of it. Visual agnosia may contribute to the dyslexia seen in children with reading difficulties and to adults suffering from aphasia. The reading deficits typically seen in school-aged children is referred to as "dyslexia"; the ones often accompanying aphasia are referred to as "alexia." Perceptual reading problems result from the inability or impaired ability of the patient to recognize letters, or sequences of letters, and are not attributable to problems knowing the meanings of written words. Of course, agnosias are not a result of visual field sensation deficits such as homonymous hemianopsia (blindness in the same one-half fields of both eyes), shortsightedness, tunnel vision, and so forth.

Technically, auditory agnosia is a perceptual disturbance involving all auditory input whereas acoustic agnosia is limited to deficits in the perception of speech. Patients with auditory agnosia have problems attaching meaning and recognizing the significance of environmental sounds such as music, fire alarms, telephones, birds chirping, and so forth. Acoustic agnosia is limited to problems detecting, discriminating, and appreciating the significance of speech sounds. Although these two agnosias can occur independently, they usually occur together and are referred to as auditory-acoustic agnosia.

Anosognosia is the ignorance, lack of awareness, or denial of disability.

Psychological Defense Mechanisms and Anosognosia

From the above discussion, it is apparent that perception is not only a physiologic function of gating and routing sensory information, it is also a psychological process. The utilization of some psychological defense mechanisms is intricately related to human information processing. Psychological defense mechanisms, coping styles, are used by persons for psychological protection, primarily the prevention of anxiety. Anosognosia, the lack of awareness, denial, or ignorance of a disease or disorder is associated

Prosopagnosia is a rare type of agnosia. In this perceptual disorder, the patient's deficits are for faces and not colors, shapes, and objects. One patient could recognize her children by their voices, but not by seeing their faces.

with damage to the parietal lobe of the nondominant hemisphere of the brain. It is also seen in some jargon-aphasic patients and is partially a psychological reaction.

Jargon-aphasic patients often present with fluent, but meaningless, output due to the breakdown of the phonologic, grammatic, and semantic aspects of language resulting from the cerebral insult. Some of these patients appear completely unaware of their disordered speech and engage in projection, the attributing of one's own disturbing thoughts and feelings to another person. They act as if they are speaking perfectly normally and feel that, if listeners would simply try harder, they could understand their utterances.

Tanner (2003b, 2003c) notes that some aphasic patients may lose the ability to use language-based defense mechanisms, such as rationalization and intellectualization, due to loss of language. However, the perceptual defense of denial remains available to patients with aphasia, regardless of the language loss. Anosognosia is sometimes seen in jargon-aphasic patients. Although several physiologic factors may account for the anosognosia seen in some patients with jargon aphasia in regard to awareness of their communication disorder, the perceptual psychological defense of denial may also play a role. The denial and meaning in jargon aphasia were initially addressed by Weinstein, Lyerly, Cole, and Ozer (1966) in their provocative article: "Meaning in Jargon Aphasia" and by Weinstein and Puig-Antich (1974) in "Jargon Aphasia and Its Analogues" both published in the journal *Cortex*.

Auditory Perception and Articulation Acquisition

It takes several years for children to acquire speech sounds, and auditory perception of each phoneme's unique acoustic characteristics is fundamental to the process. Tanner, Culbertson, and Secord (1997) note that 75% of children learn to produce the phonemes of English in the initial, medial, and final positions of words between 3 and 7 years of age. During the phoneme acquisition period, children substitute, omit, and distort speech sounds as they learn to talk correctly. And, of course, some children do not acquire normal speech sound production without professional intervention. The types of speech errors made by children, particularly substitutions, show the importance of auditory perception in the process of speech sound acquisition.

Although several sensorimotor and phonologic factors can account for the types of substitutions seen in normal children and children with speech disorders, inaccurate auditory perception accounts for in-class substitutions. An in-class substitution is the replacement of one sound for another in the same place or manner production category. In-class substitutions, the most common type of substitution errors in children, include the substitution of fricatives for fricatives, glides for glides, plosives for plosives, bilabials for bilabials, affricates for affricates, and so forth. In-class substitutions are the typical speech errors made by many children such as w/r (wabbit for rabbit), θ/s (thee for see), w/l (wamp for lamp), d/g (dun for gun), and so forth.

As noted above, perception of salient features of environmental stimuli is easier when the contrasts in their features are great rather than small. This is especially true for acoustic features. That children often make in-class substitutions shows that their speech production errors, rather than an exclusive motor or phonology problem, are based in their misperceiving the salient acoustic characteristics of similar phonemes. For example, glides have similar acoustic qualities, and when a child substitutes one glide for another, w/r for example, his or her inaccurate perception lies at the core of error. Although some children do substitute phonemes with vastly dissimilar acoustic properties, such as nasals for glides, most children make in-class substitutions. Additionally, virtually all therapies for developmental articulation disorders recognize the importance of perception and incorporate formal or informal auditory training, auditory bombardment, and/or speech discrimination exercises as fundamental aspects of the treatment programs.

Psychoacoustics

The above discussions show the neurologic, mental, and psychologic intricacies of transforming sensory stimuli to perceptual information. Speech perception encompasses all the above complexities of general perception, but also has special unique features. Speech perception is the ability to identify individual or connected phonemes of a language, vowels and consonants, from their acoustic cues. It is a complex process of transforming intangible, acoustic energy into meaningful units of a language. Speech perception is part of a larger science, psychoacoustics, which addresses the relationship between acoustics and the human auditory system, a combined discipline involving psychology and physics.

Tone deafness, a type of agnosia, is when the patient cannot discriminate tones on a scale or perceive a tempo or melody. "Deafness" is a misnomer when used to describe a perceptual disorder.

There are five general auditory perceptual abilities that precede, and are requisites, for effective and efficient speech perception (Table 10-1). First, a listener must be able to detect sound from the environmental information coming from the

Table 10–1. General Auditory Perceptual Requisites

Sound Detection	Sense of Hearing
Selective attention	Focus on salient auditory features
Separation of environmental sounds into categories	Speech detection
Sound localization	Speech localization in time and space
Identification and gross discrimination of speech sounds	Attempt to determine language spoken; gross vowel and consonant perception

other senses. The status of the hearing mechanism, its ability to sense the frequency, amplitude, and quality of sound determines the acoustic features available for perception. Second, the listener must be able to attend to environmental sounds and ignore competing sensory information. Although multisensory information can be perceived more or less simultaneously, competing olfactory, visual, gustatory, and tactile-kinesthetic-proprioceptive sensory information can distract the listener.

The third general auditory perceptual ability involves separating environmental sounds into categories. The listener must be able to distinguish various environmental sounds and separate speech sounds from other sounds. "Apparently, the human ear gives special weight to the onset of sounds, even if they are very brief. The ecological advantage of this strategy may be that quick decisions sometimes need to be made about an acoustic event" (Kent, 1997, p. 226). Fourth, once speech sounds are selectively attended, the listener must localize the speech sounds relative to three-dimensional space: length, breadth, and depth. Localization also includes temporal factors: the recency and rate of the utterances. The fifth requisite to effective and efficient speech perception is identification and gross discrimination of general speech sounds: vowels and consonants. At this final speech perception requisite level, the listener identifies the language being spoken and familiar and unfamiliar sounds and words. These general auditory perceptual abilities are required for the extraction of meaning from their acoustic cues. Speech perception per se involves exclusively intangible and abstract information processing, fundamentally different from processing physical sensations.

The differences between tactile perception and speech perception illustrate the unique nature of the latter. When a person places his or her hand in a pocket and perceives objects such as a key, coin, and comb, what is perceived are the objects, and not their tactile contrasts. The person processes as meaningful the physical representations of keys, coins, and comb, and not the sensations themselves; the sensations are the objects. "Speech perception follows the same principles as all other types of sensory perception. When we perceive something, we experience the physical cause of a sensation, rather than the sensation itself. Vocal tract gestures cause speech sounds, so listeners perceive vocal tract gestures directly, without mediation" (Hawkins, 1999, p. 233). Speech perception involves a mental awareness of words and their meanings, intangible though they are.

The Auditory Cortex

In the above section on the thalamus, it was noted that auditory information is routed from the medial geniculate nucleus to the superior temporal gyrus (Heschl's gyrus) of the cortex, an important site for auditory reception. The neurologic substrate of audition from the medial geniculate body of the thalamus to the auditory cortex is extremely complex. Martin and Clark (2003, pp. 316-317) summarize the pathways:

> The medial geniculate body, located in the thalamus, is that last subcortical relay station for auditory impulses. Only one of its three main areas, the ventral division, is responsible specifically for auditory information. There is some spiral organization in this area, but tonotopicity is uncertain. Most of the fibers come from the ipsilateral inferior colliculus, and a few fibers come from the lateral lemniscus. After this point, nerve fibers fan out in the auditory radiation and then ascend to the auditory cortex. Because there are no commissural neurons at the level of the medial geniculate body, no decussations exist there.

As Figure 10-2 shows, the primary auditory cortex, also known as Brodmann area 41, is located in the parietal-temporal area of the cortex. The secondary auditory cortex, Brodmann area 42, and the auditory association cortex, Brodmann area 22, are essential cortical regions for auditory reception and association. However, there is bilateral hemispheric auditory representation and both hemispheres of the brain receive auditory input. Nevertheless, there is typically a right ear advantage in most people showing that despite the bilaterality of ascending auditory

The Brodmann localization system is a numerical method of localizing brain function based on Korbinian Brodmann's classic textbook *Vergleichende Lokalisationslehre der Grosshirnrinde in ihren Prinzipien dargestellt auf Grund des Zellenbaues* written in 1909.

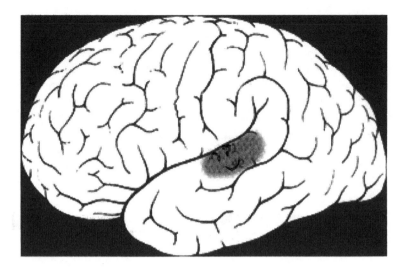

Figure 10–2. The primary auditory cortex (Brodmann's Area 41).

pathways, the contralateral pathways are still predominant, and the right ear is represented more abundantly in the left hemisphere (Durrant & Lovrinic, 1995). "At one time it was believed that the auditory cortex was the only center of auditory discrimination. It is now known that many discriminations may be mediated subcortically" (Martin & Clark, 2003, p. 317).

During the verbal exchange, the words and sentences used by Andrew are drawn from his experiences and learning, and reflect his unique perspective on the world. The semantics of the words, and the way he phrases them, are based on Andrew's life experiences. Once expressed by Andrew, Angela interprets them based on her unique perspective on the world. Angela associates the messages based on her experiences and learning, which may be close or far-removed from Andrew's. While Angela may more accurately decode some information expressed by Andrew, such as the taste of the coffee or its temperature, other ideas are less likely to be precisely decoded. Complex and abstract ideas and notions, particularly those without some physical representation, may require several communication acts to prompt Angela to appreciate Andrew's meaning optimally, and even then, there is rarely, if ever, total sharing of information. As noted above, the absolute sharing of information between speaker and listener during verbal communication is an illusion (Auditory Association Excerpt from *Connections* in Chapter 1)

The Myth of Wernicke's Area as the "Center of Language Understanding"

In the mid-1800s, a German neurologist, Karl Wernicke, identified the "sensory" or "receptive" area of communication in the
left hemisphere of the brain, particularly the temporal lobe.
(Zemlin, 1998, shows Wernicke's area also extending into the
parietal lobe.) Wernicke's area, the so-called left hemisphere's
"receptive language center" is usually described as consisting of
Brodmann areas 22, 41, and 42 (Kent, 1997) although some
authorities list the sites comprising Wernicke's area as 22, 39,
and 40. Wernicke noted that a patient with sensory aphasia has
impaired understanding of speech not attributable to hearing
loss or deafness, and may produce jargon.

Traditional thought in aphasiology attributes Wernicke's
area as the site of the brain where language is recognized, interpreted, and associated. Whereas Broca's area is the presumed
site of language expression, Wernicke's area is the site where
language is "understood." Although Wernicke's area may be an
important cortical conduit for decoding phonologic, grammatic,
and semantic features of language, attributing this site as the
"center for language understanding" is based on inexact and narrow definitions of the words "center" and "understanding" and
adds to the methodologic flawed localization movement with
respect of receptive language and especially semantics.

Attempting to localize receptive language to one or more
brain sites of a hemisphere or lobe of the brain, perhaps more
than any other attempts to localize a human cognitive function,
is theoretically unsound. Although it is a widespread practice in
the speech and hearing literature, the biggest localization flaw
lies with the vague definitions of "understanding" language and
what is meant by a brain "center."

The practice of defining Wernicke's area as the "center" for
"understanding" can be traced to early writings in communication
sciences and disorders. Wood (1971, p. 23) defines Wernicke's
area as "a region in the superior convolution of the temporal
lobe of the cerebrum identified as the center for understanding
speech heard" in Lee Edward Travis' classic textbook: *Handbook
Speech Pathology and Audiology*. Davis (1983, p. 33) notes:
"The interpretation of auditory language input in the left hemisphere is handled posteriorly to Heschl's gyrus in a region called
Wernicke's area. *Stedman's Concise Medical Dictionary for the
Health Professions* (4th ed.) defines Wernicke's area as: "The
region of the cerebral cortex thought to be essential for understanding and formulating coherent, propositional speech . . . "

(Dirckx, 2001, p. 1066). Nicolosi, Harryman, and Kresheck (2004, p.343) in *Terminology of Communication Disorders: Speech-Language-Hearing* (5th ed.) define Wernicke's area as: "Region in the superior convolution of the temporal lobe of the cerebrum which is identified as the center for understanding oral language; corresponds approximately to Brodmann's areas 22, 39, and 40." When defining the functional role of Wernicke's area, clear distinctions must be made to address the vague, imprecise attribution of Wernicke's area as the "center" for language "understanding."

Most dictionaries define "understand" as the perception of the meaning of words, appreciation of the significance of a statement, interpretion of the implications of an idea, and inferences that can be drawn from a statement (see *Oxford Dictionary* definition at beginning of this chapter.) *Webster's New World College Dictionary* (2000) makes the distinction that, although "understand" and "comprehend" are used interchangeably, understand stresses the full awareness or knowledge arrived at.

While no one would argue that Wernicke's area is important to speech perception, basic decoding of grammatic aspects of auditory input, and perfunctory semantic discernment, attributing Brodmann's areas 22, 41, and 42 as the "center" for language "understanding" is nonsensical. "A strict localizationist philosophy of brain functioning is difficult to support because no single part of the brain functions completely independently from the others. For example, although there may be certain identifiable areas of the brain important in perceiving vowels and consonants, pinpointing the mass of brain cells completely responsible, in every person, for interpreting a proverb or understanding the implications of a Robert Frost poem is absurd" (Tanner, 2003b, p. 5). Stating that Wernicke's area is the "center" for "understanding" in the brain is ambiguous and vague usage of the terms. Wernicke's area is not the center of auditory comprehension; it is simply an important conduit to the process.

However, dismissing the all-encompassing statement, "Wernicke's area is the center for understanding," as a superficial attempt to localize human verbal comprehension to a small mass of brain cells in one part of the brain should not negate the fact that hemispheric differentiation exists and there are specialized brain cells and neuronal tracts. There is a general consensus among neuroscientists that specialized motor and sensory functions occur throughout the brain, and hemispheric differentiation, if not specialization, exists in most humans. The differentiation and specialization include understanding events, constructing theories about relationships, and reading (understanding) facial expressions. Gazzaniga, Ivry, and Mangun (1998, pp. 368–369) summarize cerebral differentiation and specialization:

> The two hemispheres do not represent information in an identical manner, as evidenced by the fact that each hemisphere has developed its own set of specialized capacities. In the vast majority of individuals, the left hemisphere is clearly dominant for language and speech, and seems to possess a uniquely human capacity to interpret behavior and to construct theories about the relationship between perceived events and feelings. Right-hemisphere superiority, on the other hand, can be seen in tasks such as facial recognition and attentional monitoring. Both hemispheres are likely to be involved in the performance of any complex task, but with each contributing in their specialized manner.

Levels of Semantic Decoding

Sternberg and Ben-Zeev (2001) address understanding language in the social context of discourse. Discourses are communicative units of language larger than individual sentences, and include conversations, lectures, stories, essays, and so forth. Discourse semantics involves encoding large amounts of sensory information into meaningful representations based on the understanding of individual words and communicative contexts. Discourse-semantic decoding extends beyond basic auditory perception to discerning meaning from individual words and their contexts. The all-encompassing process of discourse decoding can be traced by analyzing levels of understanding in a stanza of Tennyson's "In Memoriam":

I hold it true, whate'er befall,

I feel it, when I sorrow most,

'Tis better to have loved and lost

Than never to have loved at all.

Current neuroscience research with normal subjects and studies in aphasiology have demonstrated the importance of Wernicke's area as the primary conduit for verbal comprehension. Nevertheless, there are five levels of understanding that can be logically postulated when a person auditorily decodes Tennyson's message that goes far beyond the functions of Wernicke's area (see Table 10–2). As will be shown in analyzing Tennyson's ode to lost love, understanding is substantially more complex than simply recognizing the individual dictionary

Table 10–2. Levels of Semantic Decoding

Decoding Level	Description
General auditory perception	Sound detection, localization, categorization, and identification
Speech discrimination	Analysis of speech acoustics and distinctive features
Denotative extraction	Derive the lexical and dictionary meanings of words
Connative extraction	Derive the personal and logical associations of words
Dynamic symbolism	Semantic assimilation

meanings of the words; auditory comprehension totally engages the listener cognitively and psychologically.

The first level of decoding a speaker's recitation of Tennyson's "In Memoriam" is general auditory perception and involving the five general auditory perceptual abilities discussed above (see Table 10-1). The listener detects the sound emanating from the speaker and selectively attends to it. The utterance is categorized as speech, separate and distinct from all other environmental sounds. The listener localizes the sound source in time and space, engages in gross identification of vowels and consonants, and attempts to determine the language being spoken. In this example, the listener recognizes the utterance as poetic in style. Consequently, he or she prepares mentally to anticipate more meaning in the utterance than if the speaker was simply remarking about the weather.

The second level of decoding a speaker's recitation of Tennyson's verse involves speech-sound discrimination. Here the listener, based on experiences with the perception of speech sounds in the past, analyzes the acoustic characteristics of each phoneme, compares them in his or her auditory memory, and attaches meaning to them. The listener analyzes each phoneme relative to the acoustic patterns of time, frequency, and energy, as well the phoneme's distinctive features. For example, the /t/ phoneme in the word "Tis" is anterior, consonantal, and coronal (blade of tongue is elevated from neutral position), while not possessing the distinctive features of back, continuant, nasal, and so forth. Interestingly, if some of the phonemes are from an unfamiliar language, the listener does not perceive their acoustic qualities and distinctive features as salient. Although phonemes from another language are grossly perceived as speech sounds, their acoustic qualities and distinctive features are relegated to background information or ignored altogether.

At the third level of semantic decoding, extracting the denotative meaning, the listener associates the individual words with his or her previous experiences. The lexical meaning of each word in Tennyson's ode to sweet sorrow is decoded by the listener in dictionary form; each word's literal meaning is recognized. At this level of decoding the auditory signal, the listener processes objective information from the speaker. The denotation of a word is its explicit primary meaning. Tennyson's verse addresses truth, love, love lost, and sorrow, and the listener denotes their meanings.

Extracting the denotative meaning of a word involves the fundamental symbol-referent relationship discussed in Chapters 5 and 6. Symbolism is associating the arbitrary relationship between a symbol with its referent. This symbol-referent relationship is the foundation of language and the essence of semantics. Some referents are tangible and concrete such as "chair." Other referents are intangible and more abstract such as "love" and "sorrow." However, as Vygotsky (1962) notes, a word does not refer to a single object, but rather to a class of objects. The class is a previously agreed-on set of parameters determined by a language society. With regard to a tangible referent such as "chair," the extension of semantic meaning to the class of objects is sometimes referred to as conceptualizing "chairness." Sternberg and Ben-Zeev (2001, p. 202) note that when you think about the single word "chair," you may also conjure the following:

- All of the instance of chairs in existence anywhere
- Instances of chairs that exist only in your imagination
- All the characteristics of chairs
- All the things you may do with chairs
- All the other concepts you may link to chairs (e.g., things you put on chairs or places where you may find chairs)

Sternberg and Ben-Zeev (2001) observe that the use of symbols to refer to the world is an economic way to manipulate information.

Although there is no clear boundary between denotation and connotation, extracting connotative implicit meaning, the

Count the number of "f's" in this sentence: "The efficiency of writing is to be one of the farthest." Most people report two because when reading the sentence, the word "of" is pronounced as a "v" rather than an "f."

fourth level of semantic decoding, involves the listener's logical associations with words. Connotations include dictionary meanings of words, and also the emotions associated with them. Connotation semantics are implied meaning of words, those logically deduced or induced from the explicit meaning. For example, the word "teacher," may denote a person who imparts information and knowledge in a school setting. The connotation of the word includes what is denoted, but also the emotive reactions of that person logically implied and suggested: someone with specialized knowledge, a mentor, a disciplinarian, and so forth. It includes the emotional associations with the word "teacher" that are unique to the person's experiences. The mood, emotion, and temperament associated with a word are parts of its connotation.

Receptive Language and General Semantics

In Tennyson's verse, the connotation of "sorrow" can include an objective meaning of profound distress associated with loss, but also a listener's specific associations with the word. It may invoke the listener's unique feelings and personal associations with the specific loss of a loved one. A person grieving over a recent lost love will have unique connotations when decoding the word "sorrow" and they may take the form of personal and intimate thoughts and feelings related to the word.

Dynamic symbolism is the fifth, and most comprehensive, level of semantic decoding. Dynamic symbolism is based on the general semantics philosophy advanced by Alfred Korzybski, a Polish mathematician and engineer. In general semantics, the statement, "The map is not the territory" illustrates the relationship between the word, the map, to its meaning, the territory. This symbol-referent relationship is highly variable. General semantics takes a non-Aristotelian relativistic view of humans as time-binding semantic reactors. According to general semantics, meanings of words are relative and the result of accumulated personal and social experiences. General semantics has evolved to become a social philosophy focusing on the effects of language on human behavior, and ways to increase self-awareness. The movement refers to itself as "up-to-date, applied epistemology" and bases its philosophy on the scientific method especially as it pertains to mathematics.

Wendell Johnson was an adherent to this philosophy, and it was the basis to his diagnosogenic theory of stuttering. According to the Institute of General Semantics home page (2005):

Wendell Johnson speculated that people who really "got into" general semantics tended to fall into two categories. There were those individuals who were naturally inquisitive and always searching for means and methods for self-awareness, understanding and improvement. And then there were those who felt compelled to find and overcome the causes underlying some type of maladjusted—either of a personal type, or a societal type.

For example, Johnson noted his own study of general semantics stemmed from his stuttering condition. For as long as he could remember, he had stuttered. He tackled his problem methodically, investigating all the available literature on the theories and treatments of stuttering. He attended the University of Iowa, graduated, then stayed on as a clinician and professor and earned his doctorate in speech pathology—and he still stuttered. Not until he read *Science and Sanity* and took his first seminar with Korzybski in 1939 did he begin to make progress in treating his own condition.

General semantics attempts to make a person continuously aware of the process of verbal abstraction.

Dynamic Symbolism and the Decoding of Discourse

Although the concept of dynamic symbolism and the decoding of discourse is based on the all-encompassing philosophy of General Semantics, it specifically addresses semantic decoding of language, particularly abstract words, and is the final stage of *The Unified Model of Communication Sciences and Disorders.* Dynamic symbolism is the process of assimilating abstract words, absorbing and integrating their meanings into the decoder's frame of reference.

Several factors must be considered to understand how the individual "understands" a particular word or discourse in his or her unique way. The individually unique sensory, perceptual, and associational processes discussed above (see Table 10-2) determine a person's ultimate dynamic symbolism and the decoding of discourse semantics. First, the decoder's unique sound detection system, the hearing mechanism, senses the available acoustic energy and is dependent on his or her sensitivity to the atmospheric pressure changes. Everyone has different hearing sensitivities, minor though they may be, and they change over the duration of a person's life span. Therefore, the nature of the raw energy for semantic decoding is the first factor affecting each person's personal and unique dynamic symbolism and the decoding of discourse.

The second personal and unique factor involved in dynamic symbolism and the decoding of discourse involves auditory perception. It includes the nature and amount of information allowed to reach a person's consciousness. As discussed above, perception is the process of gating important environmental information to reach conscious awareness and ignoring or relegating to background information all other sensory information. Auditory perception is an ongoing process of receiving environmental information and continuously adjusting the parameters of what is to be perceived. An individual's unique learning and memory experiences play important roles in this perceptual process.

The third personal and unique factor in dynamic symbolism and the decoding of discourse involves determining the denotative and connotative meanings of words, and this process also involves myriad learned verbal associations, emotions, connections with vast stores of previously acquired information, and the continuous learning of new symbol-referent relationships. Not only are new symbol-referent relationship associations made, but previous connections are continuously modified to account for changes in word meanings occurring over time. For example, the meaning of the word "liberal" changes contextually as time passes, political and social events occur, but also as a person ages, brain chemistry changes, and he or she draws on previous learning. In most instances, what is mean by the word to a person when uttered a decade ago is quantitatively and qualitatively different from what is meant by the word today. This is the essence of dynamic symbolism: changing meanings over time.

The final personal and unique factor in dynamic symbolism and discourse decoding involves all of the accumulated sensory, perceptual, and learned associations unique to an individual. This process can virtually engage the brain as a whole and the totality of a person's mind. Tennyson's powerful ode to love lost demonstrates this process. One cannot semantically decode this passage without accessing a plethora of emotional and cognitive associations, each individually unique and personal. To propose that Wernicke's area of the brain, this small mass of brain cells and the tracts leading to and from it, is the "center" for verbal "understanding" when decoding Tennyson's "In Memoriam" is inaccurate. True understanding of substantive discourse is the highest cognitive process to which a person can aspire and not limited to one center of the brain.

Auditory Processing Disorders

No diagnostic category in communication sciences and disorders is more vaguely defined than auditory processing disorders. This diagnostic category is a broad clinical entity that can include a variety of learning disabilities, attentional deficits, cognitive disorders, and specific language disorders in children. Theoretically, it can also include several types of agnosia and aphasia typically seen in adult neurogenic communication disorders. Auditory processing disorders are typically seen in children, although adults certainly can experience difficulty processing auditory information. Early signs of an auditory processing disorder show up in the child's attentional interactions with his or her parents.

The primary auditory processing disorders occurring at the perceptual level are attention deficit disorder (ADD) and attention deficit hyperactivity disorder (ADHD).

According to Westby (1998), attentional interactions reflect the child's capacity to attend to and discriminate among stimuli. They include visual tracking, smiling in response to a familiar person, laughing, and orienting toward a sound. Problems with the above in the maturing child may be the first indicators of an auditory processing disorder. English (2002) also reports early signs of an auditory processing disorder to include problems with memory, short attention span, inconsistent response to auditory stimuli, and distraction. Auditory processing disorders occur more often in boys than girls and include delayed or disordered language development and receptive language disorders, in particular.

Communication: Sharing Associations

Verbal communication is a complex process of transforming thoughts and emotions into a series of electrochemical, acoustic, mechanical, and hydraulic energy states. During this process, the speaker transforms information into a linguistic code, motorically programs the five basic motor speech processes to express it, and executes the muscular movements necessary to produce speech. The human body acts on the surrounding atmosphere to create small pressure changes which are picked up by the listener's ear and the energy is transformed from acoustic to mechanical and to hydraulic states. From hearing sensation, the listener engages in the complex process of auditory perception and completes the process when he or she mentally connects the speaker's information with his or her previously stored associations or co-occurring experiences. The speaker prompts the listener to share associations based on the information transmitted, and in this age-old communication turn-taking ritual, the listener then becomes the speaker, building on the shared experiences and association. The accuracy of communication and the satisfaction speaker and listener experience in this encounter depends, in no small part, on how well they allow the process to work.

CHAPTER SUMMARY

Auditory perception is a complex process of determining the importance of what is to be perceived, gating salient information to conscious awareness, and relegating to background information or ignoring all other auditory stimuli. The act of perception is tied to intuition, and although perception does not determine a person's reality, it plays an important part in what is ultimately brought to conscious awareness. Auditory perception is important to speech sound acquisition, and the agnosias are perceptual disorders. The auditory cortex, particularly Wernicke's area, is an important cortical conduit to decoding incoming auditory information. There are several levels of understanding auditory input, cumulating in discourse semantic decoding that can engage the brain as a whole and the totality of a person's mind.

Study and Discussion Questions

1. What is the role of the thalamus in perception? What sense is not routed through the thalamus?

2. What is the role of perception, if any, in intuition?

3. Describe the Sapir-Whorfian hypothesis and criticize it.

4. Compare the concepts of saliency and figure-ground.

5. What are the agnosias? Describe auditory and acoustic agnosia.

6. How do coping styles and defense mechanisms affect perception?

7. What role does auditory perception play in speech sound acquisition?

8. What is psychoacoustics?

9. What is the "myth" of Wernicke's area as the "center" for language "understanding?"

10. List and describe the levels of semantic decoding.

11. Discuss the philosophy of General Semantics and dynamic symbolism.

12. How is communication the process of sharing associations?

Suggested Reading

Bear, M. F., Connors, B. W. & Paradiso, M. A. (1996). *Neuroscience: Exploring the brain.* Baltimore: Williams and Wilkins.

Bois, J. S. (1966). *The art of awareness: A textbook on general semantics.* Dubuque, IA: Wm. C. Brown Company Publishers.

Martin, F., & Clark, J. (2003). *Introduction to audiology* (8th ed.). Boston: Allyn & Bacon.

Sternberg, R., & Ben-Zeev, T. (2001). *Complex cognition: The psychology of human thought.* New York: Oxford University Press.

Whorf, B. (1956). *Language, thought and reality: Selected writings of Benjamin Lee Whorf* (J. B. Carroll, Ed.). Cambridge, MA: MIT Press.

Glossary

a-: A prefix indicating the complete inability to perform a function or the absence of function.

abduction: The movement away from the body's midsagittal plane. In laryngeal functioning, the moving away from the midline of the two vocal folds; opening of the glottis.

abductor: In laryngeal functioning, the muscle that performs abduction; posterior cricoarytenoid muscle.

abstract attitude: The generalized ability to understand relationships; the ability to symbolize, understand, and categorize verbal and nonverbal information.

acalculia: The inability to perform and understand simple mathematics due to neurologic damage; not attributable to lack of education.

accent: A distinctive speech mannerism that is identifiable with a particular geographic, cultural, or dialectic group; carryover of the traits of one language to another. In phonetics, the application of stress to a syllable.

acoustic agnosia: The inability to perceive salient auditory linguistic features; auditory perceptual disorder affecting speech signals.

acoustic impedance: Opposition or resistance to sound energy transmitted through the middle ear.

acoustic reflex: Automatic contraction of the stapedius and tensor tympani muscles in response to a loud sound; stapedial reflex.

acoustics: A branch of physics dealing with the audible displacement of molecules; the physics of sound.

acquired aphasia: Loss of language occurring after birth as a result of injury or disease.

acquired hearing loss: Hearing loss that is not congenital; hearing loss occurring after birth as a result of disease or injury.

addition: In speech articulation, an unnecessary sound placed in an utterance.

adduction: Movement of a body part toward the midsagittal plane. In laryngeal function, the drawing toward the midline of the two vocal folds; closing the glottis.

adductors: In laryngeal functioning, the muscles performing adduction including the lateral cricoarytenoid, transverse arytenoid, thyroarytenoid, and oblique arytenoid muscles.

adventitious deafness: Deafness occurring after birth because of disease or injury; acquired deafness.

affricate: A phoneme consisting of a plosive and a brief fricative.

agnosia: A perceptual disorder affecting the ability to recognize and appreciate salient sensory information and usually specific to one modality of communication.

agrammatism: The loss of the ability to understand and use the grammar of a language due to neurologic damage; omission or misuse of the grammatic units of language.

agraphia: The inability to write secondary to a central language disorder and not due to lack of education, limb paresis, or paralysis; inability to express oneself in writing.

air-bone gap: An audiometric term referring to the difference in decibels that the air-conduction threshold exceeds the bone-conduction threshold at any pure-tone frequency.

alexia: The inability to read not due to visual acuity deficits or blindness and not attributable to lack of education.

allophone: A particular variation of a phoneme imposed by the phonetic environment or to suprasegmental features, such as syllabic stress.

alveolar: In phonetics, a place of articulation that refers to the ridge of tissue just behind the upper incisors: the anterior part of the superior (maxillary) dental alveolus, posterior to the incisors.

amnesia: Partial or complete inability to recognize or recall past events; loss of memory.

anomia: Loss of the ability to recall words; not limited to nouns.

anosognosia: The inability to perceive, recognize, and accept defective body parts or functions; denial of disability.

anoxia: Lack of oxygen to the brain.

anterograde amnesia: Loss of the ability to form, store, and recall new memories.

antiresonance: A significant amplitude reduction in a part of the acoustic spectrum; zero amplitude.

aperiodic: Without periodicity; irregular.

aphasia: Multimodality inability to encode, decode, and manipulate symbols for the purposes of verbal thought and/or communication; loss of language due to neurologic damage.

aphonia: Loss of the ability to vibrate the vocal cords to produce voice; without voice.

apraxia: Loss of the ability to conceptualize, plan, and sequence voluntary body movements due to a neurologic disorder.

apraxia of speech: Loss of the ability to conceptualize, plan, and sequence voluntary motor speech due to a neurologic disorder.

aprosody: Loss of the rhythm, cadence, and melody of speech.

articulation: Shaping compressed air from the lungs into individual phonemes; act of moving the vocal tract structures in such a manner that phonemes are produced.

articulator: A structure of the speech mechanism that valves the compressed air coming from the lungs.

aspiration: In phonetics, addition of the whispered glottal sound source to a phoneme. In dysphagia, ingestion of a foreign substance into the respiratory system.

assimilation: The process of combining characteristics of adjacent phonemes.

association: In cognition, the internalization of information and the process of making it personally relevant; relating of experiences, perceptions, and thoughts.

audiogram: Graph for recording air and bone conduction hearing thresholds.

audiology: Branch of science concerned with the study, diagnosis, and nonmedical treatment of hearing disorders.

auditory-acoustic agnosia: Inability to perceive differences in speech and environmental signals.

auditory agnosia: The inability to perceive salient auditory features.

auditory closure: Integration of auditory stimuli into a perceptual whole.

auditory cortex: Auditory area located in the superior temporal lobe of the cerebral cortex.

auditory discrimination: Ability to perceive differences in sounds.

auditory perception: The process of detecting salient features of input coming from the hearing mechanism; mental awareness of sound.

back consonant: Syllabic boundary produced by positioning the posterior part of the tongue with the hard palate, velum, or uvula.

back vowel: A vocal tract resonance created when the major vocal tract constriction is formed by arching the posterior tongue in the back part of the oral cavity.

Bel: A logarithmic unit of sound intensity measurement where ten decibels equal one bel; named in deference to Alexander Graham Bell.

Bernoulli principle: A fluid dynamics principle of physics that describes the decrease in air pressure associated with increased airflow velocity.

bilabial: Pertaining to two lips.

bilateral: Referring to two sides of a structure.

binaural: Pertaining to both ears.

bisyllable: A word with two syllables.

blend: Two or more consonants without a vowel separating them; consonant cluster.

body image: Awareness of one's own body and bodily behaviors; composite vision of oneself.

bone conduction: Acoustic stimulation of the inner ear through application of a vibrator to the mastoid process of the temporal bone; hearing test bypassing the air conduction mechanism.

Boyle's law: A principle of physics describing the inverse relationship of the volume of a fixed amount of gas to its pressure.

breathy: Voice quality created by excessive leakage of air when the vocal cords vibrate.

Broca's area: Motor speech area in the frontal lobe in the dominant cerebral hemisphere; cortical area important to expressive language and motor speech planning in most persons.

Brodmann's areas: A brain mapping system localizing areas of the cerebral cortex and their functions.

central deafness: Absence of hearing resulting from damage to the central nervous system.

central nervous system (CNS): The brain and spinal cord.

central vowel: Vocal tract resonance produced by positioning the tongue near the center of the oral cavity during the production of vowels.

cerebellum: A large brain structure responsible for muscle tone, balance, and coordination lying posterior to the pons and medulla.

cerebral cortex: Thin layer of gray matter surrounding the cerebral hemispheres.

cerebral dominance: Tendency for one cerebral hemisphere to be dominant for a particular function.

cerumen: Waxlike secretion in the auditory canal.

circumlocution: The substitution of a word to avoid one that is feared, forgotten, or difficult to produce; using a substitute word for the one that cannot be remembered or spoken.

clavicular breathing: Shallow breathing accomplished primarily with the upper thoracic muscles.

cleft lip: A congenital craniofacial anomaly of the upper lip involving fusion failure during gestation; may be unilateral or bilateral.

cleft palate: A congenital craniofacial anomaly involving maxillary fusion failure during gestation resulting in a complete or incomplete fissure in the hard palate, velum, and/or uvula; may be unilateral or bilateral.

clinical phonetics: The use of phonetics in the diagnosis and treatment of communication disorders.

closed-head injury (CHI): Cerebral trauma of the nonpenetrating variety in which one or more cognitive functions are impaired or destroyed; traumatic brain injury.

cluttering: A thought-organization fluency disorder characterized by short attention span, excessive rate of speech, transpositions, substitution, revisions, omissions of sounds and words, and usually accompanied by a lack of awareness of the disorder.

coarticulation: Overlapping articulatory influences during connected speech.

cochlea: Sensory mechanism of hearing in the inner ear; end organ of hearing.

cochlear implant: An electronic device surgically implanted into the ear to enhance hearing.

cochlear nerve: Auditory or acoustic branch of the VIIIth cranial nerve.

cognates: Phonemes produced in the same manner and place and differing only by voicing.

cognition: Higher mental functions that include reasoning and information processing; mental process of thinking.

compliance: In audiology, ease of energy transfer through the outer or middle ear.

confabulation: Giving answers to questions with little or no regard for their truthfulness or accuracy; making up false stories.

congenital deafness: Loss of hearing occurring before, during, or shortly after birth.

connotation: In addition to what the word denotes, the affective and evaluative associations made by the speaker or listener.

consciousness: Awareness of self and the environment.

consonant: Phoneme produced with or without voicing by movements of the articulatory structures that modify the compressed air coming from the lungs.

consummation of communication: The satisfactory completion of a communicative act.

content word: Words that carry the most meaning in an utterance such as nouns and verbs.

continuant: Speech sound produced by continuous, uninterrupted airstream modulation.

coprolalia: Unprovoked use of obscene or profane language; excessive swearing.

cortex: Any outer layer of an organ; thin layer of gray matter covering the surface of the cerebral hemispheres.

damping: The decrease of acoustic energy over time and distance because of impedance or opposing energy.

deaf: Without functional hearing.

decibel: One-tenth of a Bel; logarithmic unit for measuring loudness.

decode: The process of taking apart a signal, such as speech and language, into its meaningful component parts; analysis.

delayed auditory feedback (DAF): Time delay in perceiving one's own speech and associated with increased disfluency in normal speakers.

dementia: General cognitive deterioration including disorientation, impaired judgment, and memory defects; generalized intellectual deficit.

denasality: Voice quality characterized by lack of nasal resonance on normally nasal phonemes; reduced nasality.

denial: Refusal to perceive and recognize threatening, unpleasant, objectionable, and intolerable realities.

denotation: The objective referent for a word; unemotional and nonaffective meaning of a word.

dental phoneme: Speech sound made by approximating the lip or tongue with the upper incisors.

developmental stuttering: Fluency disorder occurring during the developmental period; incipient stuttering.

dialect: Phonologic, semantic, and/or syntactic variation of spoken language associated with geographic, social, or social-economic factors.

dichotic listening: Presentation of different signals to both ears at the same time.

difference limen: Smallest difference than can be detected between two signals; minimal perceptual difference.

diphthong: Phoneme produced by moving the articulators from one phoneme articulatory gesture to another.

diplophonia: Simultaneous vibration of the true vocal folds and the ventricular folds producing two tones.

discourse: The systematic conjoining of utterances.

disfluency: Normal breakdown in the rhythm and flow of speech caused by repetitions, prolongations, and/or pauses (*see* dysfluency).

disorientation: Inaccurate perceptions and judgments about time, place, person, and/or situation (predicament).

distinctive features: A set of phonetic attributes that distinguish one phoneme from another.

distortion: In speech articulation, the indistinct production of a sound; substitution of a nonstandard speech sound for a standard one.

Doppler effect: In acoustics, change in pitch caused by movement toward or away from the source of a sound.

dyne: The amount of force necessary to accelerate one gram a distance of one centimeter per second.

dys-: A prefix indicating impaired, faulty, deficient, defective, and/or diseased.

dysarthrias: A group of neuromuscular speech disorders; impaired speech due to neurologic and muscular deficits.

dyscalculia: In aphasia, the impaired ability to comprehend and perform simple arithmetic and not due to lack of education.

dysfluency: Abnormal breakdown in the fluency of speech (*see* disfluency).

dysgraphia: In aphasia, problems with writing not due to hand paralysis or lack of education.

dyslexia: In aphasia, the impaired ability to read not due to visual acuity deficits or lack of education.

dysnomia: In aphasia, word-finding problems; not limited to nouns.

dysphagia: Problems with the ability to chew, suck, and/or swallow.

dysphonia: Any voice impairment or defect in voice production.

dyspraxia: Impaired ability to plan and sequence voluntary movements due to a neurologic disease or disorder.

ear: External, middle, and inner aspects of the organ and structures of hearing.

echolalia: Automatically repeating or parroting something heard; automatic and unthinking repetition of that which has recently been spoken.

ego: One of the three aspects of the personality which is involved in evaluating, directing, and controlling thoughts and actions in response to reality.

egocentric: Self-centered.

encode: The process of putting an idea or thought into a signal system, such as speech and language; synthesize.

engram: A location or physical representation of a memory.

enunciate: To articulate phonemes precisely.

equal loudness contour: Sound pressure necessary to produce the sensation of equal loudness across frequencies.

etiology: The cause of something.

eustachian tube: Air passageway from nasopharynx to middle ear allowing equalizing of pressure between the two structures.

executive function: Cognitive skills involved in planning, organization, self-monitoring, and strategy formulation for complex behaviors; metacognition.

experimental phonetics: A branch of phonetics utilizing laboratory instruments and the scientific method.

expiration: During breathing, the process of expelling air from the lungs; process of letting air out of the lungs.

expressive aphasia: A type of neurologically based language disturbance involving the expressive components of language.

expressive language: Use of socially shared encoded symbols to communicate spoken, gestured, or written concepts, ideas, and emotions; expression of the speaker's psychological state.

facilitation: Enabling desired behaviors, reactions, and adjustments.

falsetto: Highest voice register produced by vibration of only the medial part of the vocal folds.

filler: An interruption of the flow of speech by sounds such as "uh," "um," and "er."

flat affect: Narrowed mood, emotions, and temperament; reduced emotion.

fluent speech: Smooth and effortlessly produced speech without hesitations, repetitions, or prolongations; act of speaking easily and effortlessly.

foreign accent: Phonetic characteristics of nonnative speakers of a language.

formant: On a spectrogram, a frequency band in which there is a relatively high degree of acoustic energy for a voice phoneme (F_1, F_2, F_3, ... F_n).

frame of reference: Beliefs, attitudes, and assumptions about the cause-effect of life events.

frequency: The number of periodic energy cycles occurring over time.

fricatives: Phonemes made by forcing air through a constricted area resulting in turbulence.

front vowel: A phoneme produced by constricting the anterior oral cavity to a greater extent.

function words: Words with grammatic functions; prepositions, articles, conjunctions, and so forth.

functional communication: The ability to express and understand basic wants, needs, and emotions.

fundamental frequency (f_0): In laryngeal functioning, average frequency of vibration of the vocal folds. In acoustics, the lowest frequency of a complex periodic sound wave.

general phonetics: The study of speech sounds.

gesture: Formal or informal movement of the body to describe or reinforce verbal communication.

glide: In speech articulation, a phoneme requiring movement of the articulators from one position to another.

glossal: Pertaining to the tongue.

glottal: Pertaining to the glottis

glottal cycle: Cycle of vibration of the vocal folds during phonation.

glottal fry: A low-pitched gravelly sound produced by the vocal cords; pulsating or creaking voice quality.

glottal opening: The space between the vocal cords.

glottal stop: A sound made by stopping and releasing the airstream at the level of the vocal folds.

glottal tone: Sound produced by the vibrating vocal folds.

grammar: Rules of the form and usage of a language.

grammatic morphemes: Units of meaning in language; function words.

grapheme: Printed or written symbols.

gray matter: Collection of neuronal cell bodies in the central nervous system; gray-colored tissue of the brain and spinal cord.

gustatory: Related to the sense of taste.

gustatory agnosia: Perceptual disorder relating to the sense of taste.

guttural: Pertaining to the throat or voice.

gyrus: A convolution of the cerebral cortex.

habitual pitch: The pitch used most often during speech; modal pitch.

hard glottal attack: Forced vocal fold initiation during phonation.

hard-of-hearing: Reduced hearing sensitivity; partial deafness.

hard palate: The bony roof of the mouth.

harmonics: In acoustics, whole number multiples of the fundamental frequency of a complex sound wave.

harshness: In voice, acoustic qualities associated with forced medial compression and hypertension of the vocal folds; acoustic qualities associated with hard glottal attacks.

hearing aid: Any device that amplifies sound to improve hearing.

hertz (Hz): In hearing, the number of compressions and rarefactions of a sound wave in one second; cycles per second.

high vowel: A phoneme produced with the tongue in a superior position relative to its neural position.

hippocampus: A brain structure that plays a role in learning and memory.

historical phonetics: The study of a language's sound system over time.

hoarseness: A combination of harsh and breathy voice qualities; raspy voice quality.

homonym: A word pronounced like another but having different meaning and often different spelling.

homonymous hemianopsia: A disorder where the patient's visual field is limited to half of his or her total visual world; blindness or visual impairment in the same half fields of both eyes.

husky voice quality: Voice quality that is breathy or whispered resulting from incomplete glottal closure.

hyper-: Prefix meaning "too much."

hyperacusis: Abnormally sensitive hearing; sounds perceived as excessively loud.

hypernasality: Excessive nasal resonance during phonation.

hypo-: Prefix meaning "too little."

hyponasality: Too little nasal resonance during phonation; densality.

id: One of the three aspects of the personality; the unconscious (subconscious) part of the psyche containing instinctual drives.

ideation: Creation of ideas into concepts.

ideational apraxia: Disruption of the ability to conceptualize and program a motor impulse.

ideomotor apraxia: Disruption of the ability to conceptualize and transmit a motor impulse purposefully while automatic acts can be done normally.

idiolect: An individual speaker's variation in phonology, semantics, or syntax.

image: Mental representation of some aspect of reality.

image-present icons: Visual processing using images that are present; involves real-time sensation, perception, and association through the visual sense.

image-stored icons: Stored images of reality in the mind used to process information without being in direct physical contact with it.

immittance: In audiology, measurements made of tympanic membrane compliance or impedance.

impedance: Resistance to the flow of energy.

incus: One of three bones comprising the ossicular chain; anvil.

inflection: In language, the alteration of a word to denote a grammatic distinction.

infraglottic: Those parts of the larynx below the vocal folds.

inhalatory stridor: A glottic sound produced during inhalation.

inner ear: Aspect of the ear where mechanical energy is transformed into hydraulic and electrochemical energy.

inspiration: In respiration, the process of taking air into the lungs.

intelligence: The adaptive abilities to reason, abstract, solve problems, and acquire and retain knowledge.

intelligibility: The ability to be understood by a listener, usually measured in percent; degree a person's speech can be understood by others.

intensity: In acoustics, the power of a sound wave.

interdental: Phoneme produced with the tongue approximating the upper teeth.

internal monologue: Communicating with one's self; self-talk or inner speech.

intrusive sound: An extraneous sound during speech.

ipsilateral: Pertaining to the same side; on the same side of the midline.

jargon: Fluent nonsensical utterances.

jitter: In laryngeal functioning, the cycle-to-cycle variation in the periods of glottal cycles; frequency instability.

juncture: In phonetics, the manner in which syllables join one another in dynamic speech.

just noticeable difference (JND): The minimal perceptual difference in characteristics between two stimuli; difference limen.

kinesthesia: In motor speech production, the awareness of movement and direction of the speech musculature.

labial: In phonetics, a phoneme produced by one or both lips; having to do with the lips.

labialization: Using the lips in the production of a sound.

labiodental: Phoneme produced by approximating the lower lip with the upper incisors.

language: The multimodality ability to encode, decode, and manipulate symbols for the purposes of verbal thought and/or communication; rule governed, socially shared code for representing concepts through the use of symbols.

laryngeal: Pertaining to the larynx.

laryngeal prominence: Anterior projection of the thyroid cartilage; "Adam's apple."

laryngopharynx: The most inferior division of the pharynx lying between the oropharynx and the trachea.

laryngoscopy: Observation of the interior of the larynx by an optic device.

larynx: The voice box.

latency: Time interval between a stimulus and a response.

lateral: In phonetics, a phoneme produced by air pressure around one or both sides of the tongue.

lax: In phonetics, sounds produced with reduced muscular tension; opposite of tense.

limbic system: A group of interconnected structures involved in learning, memory, and emotion.

lingua-alveolar: Relating to the tongue and the alveolar ridge in the production of a phoneme.

linguadental: Relating to the teeth and tongue in the production of a phoneme.

lingual: In phonetics, a phoneme made with the tongue.

lingual frenulum: Tissue running from floor of the mouth to the middle of the undersurface of the tongue.

linguapalatal: Relating to the tongue and the hard palate in the production of a phoneme.

linguavelar: Relating to the tongue and the velum (soft palate) in the production of a phoneme.

linguistic phonetics: A branch of applied phonetics which studies the sound system of a language; phonology.

linguistic relativity: The theory that language affects and facilitates perception and thought.

linguistic stress: Emphasis on certain syllables and words.

linguistics: The study of language.

lip rounding: In phonetics, production of a phoneme with the lips in a rounded position.

liquid: General term for /l/ and /r/ phonemes.

listening: Thoughtful detection, perception, and association of acoustic events.

localization: In neuroscience, the identification of areas of the brain responsible for specific aspects of physical, mental, or psychological functioning; the idea that all brain functions can be discovered and mapped.

loft register: Falsetto.

logorrhea: Continuous, excessive, fluent incoherent production of words.

Lombard effect: Tendency of a speaker to raise the volume of speech to compensate for background noise.

loudness: Psychological perception of amplitude or intensity of an acoustic signal.

low vowel: A phoneme produced by the tongue in an inferior position from the neutral position.

lower motor neurons: Motor neurons below the synapse.

lung capacity: Potential amount of air contained in the lungs; respiratory capacity.

lung volume: Space occupied by the air in the lungs at a given time; respiratory volume.

malleus: One of three bones comprising the ossicular chain; hammer.

mandible: The lower jaw.

manner of articulation: The characteristics of phoneme production by changes in airstream modulation and amount of vocal tract constriction.

masking: Noise which interferes with the detection of another acoustic signal.

maxilla: The upper jaw.

meninges: The three membranes surrounding the surface of the central nervous system; dura mater, arachnoid mater, and pia mater.

microbar: Unit of pressure; one-millionth of a bar.

midline: The center point or line.

minimal pair: Two syllables or words differing only by a single phoneme.

mixed deafness: Combination of sensorineural and conductive hearing losses.

modality: In language, any avenue or mode of communication.

modulation: In voice, alteration of voice quality and loudness during connected speech.

monaural: Pertaining to one ear.

monosyllable: Having one syllable.

morpheme: In language, the smallest unit of meaning.

morphemics: A branch of linguistics which studies the morphemes of a language.

motor cortex: The areas of the brain directly involved in control of voluntary movement.

motor neuron: A nerve which connects the central nervous system to a muscle and causes movement.

motor speech disorders: Pertaining to a group of disorders involving motor tracts and muscles; apraxia of speech and the dysarthrias.

motor strip: A term used to represent motor control areas in the precentral gyrus.

motor unit: A muscle fiber and the lower motor neuron which cause it to contract.

mutational falsetto: In males, the failure to change from the higher pitch of a child to the lower pitch of the adult male.

mutism: Completely without speech; inability to phonate and articulate.

myringotomy: A surgical procedure to open the tympanic membrane and allow reduction of pressure in the middle ear.

nasal: Pertaining to the nose; rhinal.

nasal coupling: Lowering of the velum to allow airflow through the nasal passageway.

nasal emission: Air escape from the nose during speech.

nasal release: Plosive release through the velopharyngeal port producing nasal airflow and resonance.

nasal resonance: Coupling of the nasal to the oral cavities and the subsequent modification of the glottal tone by the nasal cavities.

nasalance: Ratio of nasal to oral resonance.

nasality: Production of phonemes with the acoustic properties of nasal resonance.

nasalization: In phonetics, nasal resonance applied to any vowel when adjacent to a nasal sound; assimilated nasality.

naso-oral: Pertaining to the nose and mouth.

nasopharyngeal: Pertaining to the superior pharynx.

neologism: A made-up or invented word; established word used in an unconventional manner.

nerve deafness: Deafness resulting from disease or damage of the cochlea or auditory nerve.

neuron: In the nervous system, those cells that transmit electrochemical impulses; basic unit of the nervous system.

neuroscience: The interdisciplinary science which studies the brain, cognition, emotions, and behaviors.

neurotransmitter: A chemical involved in presynaptic and postsynaptic activation.

neutral vowel: A phoneme produced with the tongue in its neutral position.

noise: Any signal that competes with the detection and perception of a stimulus; unwanted sound.

nonfluency: Disrupted fluent speech; speech produced with complications.

nonfluent: The absence of fluent speech.

nonverbal communication: Communication without using spoken words.

normative phonetics: A branch of linguistics addressing speech standards for a given population.

obstruent: Phonemes produced with the vocal tract partially or completely occluded (fricatives, plosives, and affricates).

olfactory: Related to the sense of smell.

olfactory agnosia: Perceptual disorder relating to the sense of smell.

omission: In articulation, the lack of a phoneme in a word where one would be expected.

open syllable: A syllable ending with a vowel.

optic chiasm: The brain structure in which the right and left optic nerves converge.

optimal pitch: The pitch level best suited to an individual that produces the voice with the least exertion and most efficiency.

oral apraxia: Loss of the ability to conceptualize, plan, sequence, and execute voluntary oral nonspeech movements due to a neurologic disorder.

organ of Corti: Section of the cochlea containing sensory receptors.

organic: In medicine, the physical basis for a disorder.

orientation: Awareness of time, place, person, and situation (predicament).

oscillation: Rhythmic repetitive movements.

ossicles: Bones of the middle ear.

palsy: Paresis or paralysis of a muscle.

paralysis: A condition in which a muscle loses its ability to contract or move due to muscular deficits or neurologic lesions.

paraphasia: Aphasic word-finding and naming disorder characterized by choosing the incorrect word which either rhymes or has a semantic relationship to the correct one; literal and verbal paraphasias.

Passavant's pad: Prominence of the posterior pharyngeal wall.

perception: Awareness and appreciation of the salient aspects of a sensory stimulus; selection, organization, and interpretation of sensory stimulation.

perceptual-motor: The interaction between perception and motor activities.

peripheral: Away from the center.

peripheral nervous system (PNS): Nervous system made up of cranial nerves, spinal nerves, and the autonomic nervous system; other than the brain and spinal cord.

phonation: Any voiced sound that occurs at the level of the glottis; creation of acoustic energy within the larynx by means of vocal fold vibration.

phone: Any sound purposefully created in the vocal tract.

phoneme: A speech sound.

phonemic analysis: Speech sounds analysis in a given language.

phonetic analysis: The study and analysis of speech sounds relative to their acoustic and perceptual features.

phonetic context: The allophones that precede and follow a phoneme.

phonetic features: Elements of a sound.

phonetic power: Distance the acoustic characteristics of a speech sound will travel and remain intelligible.

phonetic variation: Phoneme differences.

phonetics: The science concerned with the description, acoustics, perception, classification, and production of phonemes of a language.

phonics: A method of teaching reading by addressing the phonetic pronunciation of letters.

phonology: The study of the sounds of a language and the way they are combined into words; study of a language's sound system.

phonotactics: Rules for sequencing phonemes in words.

physiologic phonetics: The study of the anatomy and physiology involved in speech production.

pitch: Psychological perception of frequency of vibration.

place of articulation: The characteristics of speech sounds production by contact or approximation in the oral tract of the articulators; location of greatest vocal tract constriction.

plosive: Phoneme produced with complete cessation of the airflow and often occurring with an audible burst of air on release.

polysyllabic: Having multiple syllables.

posterior: Toward the back or behind.

postlinguistic deafness: Deafness occurring after the development of speech and language.

pragmatics: Rules governing how language is used and the linguistic acts involving the context in which they are performed; social communicative functioning.

prelinguistic deafness: Deafness occurring before the complete development of speech and language.

presbycusis: Age-related hearing loss.

prevalence: The extent a disorder occurs in a population or a group; period prevalence.

projection: In psychology, attributing one's own intolerable wishes, thoughts, motivations, and feelings to another person.

propositionality: The meaningfulness and amount of content in an utterance.

proprioception: Sensory data about body position in space.

prosody: Patterns of speech such as stress, intonation, rhythm, melody, pitch, and voice quality that extend across one or more segments; fluency, cadence, inflection, and emphasis aspects of speech.

psychoacoustics: Science concerned with the psychological responses to sound.

psychogenic: Of emotional or psychological origin.

psychology: The study of human consciousness; measuring, explaining, and changing behavior in humans and other animals.

puberphonia: The voice of an adolescent.

pure tone: Sound wave having only one frequency.

quality: In voice, the perceptual correlate of complexity; spectral characteristics of a sound.

quality of life: Combination of factors that contribute to satisfaction with life.

rarefaction: In acoustics, the separation of air particles in a sound wave from their neutral positions.

rate of speech: The speed of speaking usually measured in words per minute.

receptive aphasia: A neurologically based loss of the receptive components of language: auditory comprehension, reading, gesturing.

receptive language: The decoding of phonemes, words, gestures, graphemes, and discourse.

recoil: In respiration, the tendency of the lungs to collapse; elasticity of the lungs.

recruitment: Disproportionate increase in the loudness of a particular sound.

referent: In semantics, the aspect of reality referred to by the symbol.

reflex: An involuntary reaction in response to a stimulus.

register: Pitch range and resonance properties of the voice.

residual hearing: The amount of hearing remaining in an individual with a hearing loss.

resonance: In speech, passive or sympathetic vibration of vocal tract tissue and air columns in response to a vibrating source, such as the glottis.

resonance frequency: A system's natural frequency.

resonator: In speech, a vocal tract cavity responsible for the amplification and damping of the fundamental vibrations produced at the level of the glottis.

respiration: The act of breathing; inspiration and expiration.

respiratory capacity: Potential contents of the lungs and air passageways.

respiratory tracts: Air passageways of the lungs.

respiratory volume: Space occupied by the air in the lungs and air passageways.

retrocochlear: Neural structures of the auditory system beyond the cochlea.

retroflection: In the production of the /r/ phoneme, the curling of the tongue toward the prepalatal area.

rhotic: An "r-coloring" of a vowel resonance.

schwa: A neutral vowel.

secondary stress: In multisyllabic utterances, syllables characterized by shorter duration, less loudness, and/or lower pitch than the syllable with the primary stress.

segmental analysis: Study of speech sounds in dynamic speech.

self-concept: Awareness of oneself particularly in relation to others; images and definitions of self.

self-esteem: Positive belief and feelings about one's self-concept.

semantics: Aspects of language concerned with word meaning; the symbol-referent relationship.

semicircular canals: Three bony tubes within the temporal bone which help an individual maintain balance.

sensitivity: The ability to sense and respond to a stimulus.

sensorimotor: A combination of motor activity and the sensations accompanying them.

shimmer: In voice, the cycle-to-cycle variations in amplitude of a glottal sound; amplitude instability.

short-term memory: Temporary storage of information requiring continual rehearsal.

sibilant: A consonant produced with acoustic energy in the mid-to-high-frequency ranges.

simple harmonic motion: Periodic oscillations of a body resulting in a sine wave.

simple tone: Pure tone.

simple wave: A sinusoidal wave.

sine wave: The graphic representation or waveform of simple harmonic motion or of a pure tone.

sociocusis: Progressive loss of hearing due to aging, noise exposure, and/or disease.

soft palate: The soft part at the back of the roof of the mouth; velum.

sonant: Phoneme produced with accompanying vocal fold vibration; voiced phoneme.

sound discrimination: The auditory ability to perceive the difference between two sounds, especially similar ones.

sound pressure level: Decibel level relative to 0.0002 dyne/cm^2.

spectrography: In acoustics, an instrument or computer program that analyzes the acoustic signal by passing it through a series of filters and graphically representing its frequency, duration, and intensity.

spectrum: In acoustics, graphic representation of sound showing the frequencies and amplitudes of the individual components of a wave.

speech act: The verbal expression of an intent; an act of propositional verbal communication.

speech frequencies: Frequencies at which the majority of speech energy occurs.

spirometer: Device used to record and measure air capacity of the lungs.

split-brain studies: Studies of brain functioning following disconnection of all or part of the corpus callosum.

stapes: One of three bones comprising the ossicular chain; stirrup.

stop consonant: A phoneme produced by brief cessation of airflow.

stress: In speech, the variations of intensity and force of a syllable when compared to adjacent ones.

strident: Fricative or affricate produced by directing the airstream against a hard articulator and creating high-frequency acoustic energy.

subcortical: The areas of the brain below the cerebral cortex.

subglottal air pressure (P_{sub}): Pressure below the glottis.

subglottic: Below the vocal folds.

substitution: In speech articulation, replacing the correct phoneme with another one.

supraglottic: Above the vocal folds.

surd: A sound of a language produced without accompanying vocal fold vibration; voiceless.

syllable: The basic physiologic and acoustic unit of speech.

synapse: The region where an action potential is propagated from one neuron to another by means of chemical mediation.

syndrome: A combination or cluster of symptoms that usually occur together.

syntax: Aspect of the grammatic structure of language, especially word order.

tactile: Relating to the sense of touch.

tactile agnosia: Disorder relating to the perception of touch.

tap: In articulation, a speech sound resulting from brief contact between articulators, usually the tip of the tongue and the alveolar ridge.

telegraphic speech: Communication using a minimum of function words, and many content words; similar to a telegram.

tempo: The rate or speed of speaking.

tense: In phonetics, sounds produced with increased muscular tension; opposite of lax.

thorax: The chest.

timbre: The perceptual correlate of sound spectrum; voice quality.

tinnitus: Sensation of ringing, buzzing, or humming in the ear without external stimulation.

trachea: The windpipe.

tract: Central nervous system axons having a common origin and destination.

trill: A speech sound produced by vibrating an articulator by the airstream.

tympanic membrane: Thin, sensitive membrane between the external and medial sections of the ear which transmits acoustic energy to the ossicles.

ultrasonic: Frequency of vibrations not perceived as sound; above approximately 20,000 Hz for humans.

unstressed vowel: Neutral vowel.

unvoiced: A sound produced with no vibration of the vocal folds.

upper motor neurons: Motor neurons above the synapse.

utterance: A vocal expression of a word or phrase.

velopharyngeal closure: Closing off of the nasal cavity by the velum and pharynx.

velopharyngeal competence: Adequate separation of the nasal cavity from the oral cavity by the velum and pharynx.

velopharyngeal port: A sphincter valve formed by the pharynx and velum and allowing coupling of the oral and nasal cavities; velopharyngeal sphincter.

velum: The soft palate.

verbal: Spoken words.

vibrato: Rise and fall in the pitch and loudness of the voice.

vibratory cycle: One cycle of periodic acoustic or of vocal fold vibration.

visual agnosia: Disorder relating to the perception of written words, forms, and objects.

vocal: Pertaining to the voice.

vocal cords: Vocal folds.

vocalic: A speech sound serving as a vowel or a syllabic nucleus.

voice: Any sound produced by the vibration of the vocal folds; phonation.

voice-onset time (VOT): The time between the release of an obstruent consonant and the commencing of voicing.

voiced: Sounds produced with vocal fold vibration.

voiceless: Sounds produced without vocal fold vibration.

volume: The internal capacity of a closed space. In acoustics, the loudness of a sound.

vowel: A voiced speech sound resulting from relatively unrestricted passage of the airstream though the vocal tract.

waveform: In acoustics, the graphic representation of molecular displacement.

wavelength: Distance a wave travels during each cycle of vibration.

Wernicke's area: The part of the left hemisphere of the brain serving as a primary conduit for language understanding.

white matter: The part of the brain that is white in appearance; collection of axons lying below the cerebral cortex.

white noise: Broad-band aperiodic sound levels across the audible range of hearing.

zero hearing level: Minimum sound pressure level necessary to make any frequency audible.

References

Adler, R., & Towne, N. (1978). *Looking out/Looking in: Interpersonal communication* (2nd ed). New York: Holt, Rinehart and Winston.

American Speech-Language-Hearing Association. (2003). Code of ethics (revised). *ASHA Supplement, 23,* 13-15.

American Speech-Language-Hearing Association. (2005). Code of Ethics. Retrieved June 19, 2005 from http://www.fairaccess.org/asha_ethics.htm

Aronson, A. (1990). *Clinical voice disorders: An interdisciplinary approach.* New York: Thieme.

Bear, M. F., Connors, B. W., & Paradiso, M. A. (1996). *Neuroscience: Exploring the brain.* Baltimore: Williams and Wilkins.

Bell Telephone Laboratories. (1958). *The science of sound.* New York: Folkways Records and Service Corp.

Benson, F., & Ardila, A. (1996). *Aphasia: A clinical perspective.* New York: Oxford University Press.

Benton, A. (1981). Aphasia: Historical perspectives. In M. Sarno (Ed.), *Acquired aphasia.* New York: Academic Press.

Benton, A., & Joynt, R. (1960). Early descriptions of aphasia. *Archives of Neurology, 3,* 205-221.

Berg, J. van den. (1958). Myoelastic-aerodynamic theory of voice production. *Journal of Speech and hearing Research, 1,* 227-244.

Berne, E. (1961). *Transactional analysis in psychotherapy.* New York: Grove Press.

Berne, E. (1964). *Games people play.* New York: Grove Press.

Bois, J. S. (1966). *The art of awareness: A textbook on general semantics.* Dubuque, IA: William C. Brown.

Borden, G., Harris, K., & Raphael, L. (1992). *Speech science primer: Physiology, acoustics, and perception of speech* (3rd ed.). Philadelphia: Lippincott Williams & Wilkins.

Brewer, J. (2004). *Introduction to early childhood education: Preschool through primary grades* (5th ed.). Boston: Pearson Allyn & Bacon.

Brownell, R. (2000). *Expressive one-word picture vocabulary test* (3rd ed.). Novato, CA: Academic Therapy Publications.

Bruer, J. (1999, September). "In search of brain-based education." *Phi Delta Kappan, 80,* 649-657.

Brumfitt, S. (1996). Losing your sense of self: What aphasia can do. In C. Code (Ed.), *Forums in clinical aphasiology* (pp. 349–355). London: Whurr.

Campbell, J. (1982). *Grammatical man: Information, entropy, language, and life*. New York: Simon and Schuster.

Carrow-Woolfolk, E. (1999). *Comprehensive assessment of spoken language*. Circle Pines, MN: American Guidance Service.

Cessna. (1977). *Cessna integrated flight training system: Manual of flight*. Denver: Jeppssen & Co.

Champlin, C. (2000). Hearing science. In R. Gillam, T. Marquardt, & F. Martin (Eds.), *Communication sciences and disorders: From science to clinical practice* (pp. 101–124). San Diego: Singular Publishing Group.

Chomsky, N. (1965). *Aspects of the theory of syntax*. Cambridge: MIT Press.

Chomsky, N. (1971). *Language and the mind: Problems of knowledge and freedom*. New York: Pantheon Books.

Chomsky, N. (1975). *Reflections on language*. New York: Pantheon Books.

Critchley, M. (1964). The neurology of psychotic speech. *British Journal of Psychiatry, 110*, 353–364.

Critchley M. (1970). *Aphasiology and other aspects of language*. London: Edward Aronld.

Culbertson, W. & Tanner, C. (2001a). Clinical comparisons: Phonological processes and their relationship to traditional phoneme norms. *Infant-Toddler Intervention, 11*(1),15–25.

Culbertson, W., & Tanner, D. (2001b). *Dependency of neuromotor oral maturation on phonological development*. Presentation at the 9th Manchester Phonology Meeting, University of Manchester, Manchester, United Kingdom.

Culbertson, W., & Tanner, D. (2005). *Forensic phonetics: Perspectives on subjective and objective approaches to speaker identification*. Presentation at the 4th Annual Hawaii International Conference on Social Sciences, Honolulu.

Dalston, R. M. (2000). Voice disorders. In R. Gillam, T. Marquardt, & F. Martin (Eds.), *Communication sciences and disorders* (pp. 283–312). San Diego: Singular Publishing Group.

Daniels, S., McAdams, C., Brailey, K., & Foundas, A. (1997). Clinical assessment of swallowing and prediction of dysphagia severity. *American Journal of Speech-Language Pathology, 6*, 17–24.

Darley, F. (1982). *Aphasia*. Philadelphia: W.B. Saunders Company.

Darley, F., Aronson, A., & Brown, J. (1975). *Motor speech disorders*. Philadelphia: W.B. Saunders Company.

Davis, G. A. (1983). *A survey of adult aphasia*. Englewood Cliffs, NJ: Prentice-Hall.

Denbigh, K., & Denbigh, J. (1985). *Entropy in relation to incomplete knowledge*. Cambridge, UK: Cambridge University Press.

Dirckx, J. H. (2001). *Stedman's concise medical dictionary for the health professions* (4th ed). Philadelphia: Lippincott Williams and Wilkins.

Duffy, J. (1995). *Motor speech disorders*. St. Louis, MO: Mosby.

Durrant, J. D., & Lovrinic, J.H. (1995). *Bases of hearing science* (3rd ed). Baltimore: Williams & Wilkins.

Eisenson, J. (1984). *Adult aphasia* (2nd ed.). Englewood Cliffs, NJ: Prentice Hall.

English, K. (2002). Audiologic rehabilitation services in the school setting. In R. L Schow & M. A. Nerbonne (Eds.), *Introduction to audiologic rehabilitation* (4th ed). Boston: Allyn & Bacon.

Fairbanks, G. (1954). Systematic research in experimental phonetics: A theory of the speech mechanism as a servosystem. *Journal of Speech and Hearing Disorders, 19,* 133-139.

Fitzhenry, R. I. (1993). *The Harper book of quotations* (3rd ed). New York: HarperCollins.

Gazzaniga, M., Ivry, R., & Mangun, G. (1998). *Cognitive neuroscience: The biology of the mind.* New York: W.W. Norton & Company.

Gillam, R., Marquardt, T., & Martin, F. (Eds.). (2000). *Communication sciences and disorders*. San Diego: Singular Publishing Group.

Gillis, R. (1996). *Traumatic brain injury rehabilitation for speech-language pathologists.* Boston: Butterworth-Heinemann.

Glattke, T. (1973). Elements of auditory physiology. In F. Minifie, T. Hixon, & F. Williams (Eds.), *Normal aspects of speech, hearing, and language* (pp. 285-341). Englewood Cliffs, NJ: Prentice-Hall.

Goldstein, K. (1924). Das Wesen der Amnestischen Aphasia. *Schweizer Archiv fuer Neurologia and Psychiatrie, 15,* 163-175.

Goldstein, K. (1948). *Language and language disturbances.* New York: Grune and Stratton.

Goldstein, K. (1952). The effects of brain damage on the personality. *Psychiatry, 15,* 245-260.

Goss, B. (1982). *Processing communication*. Belmont, CA.: Wadsworth.

Hall, C., & Lindzey, G. (1970). *Theories of personality* (2nd ed.). New York: John Wiley & Sons.

Hawkins, S. (1999). Reevaluating assumptions about speech perception: Interactive and integrative theories. In J. M. Pickett (Ed.), *The acoustics of speech communication* (pp. 232-282). Boston: Allyn & Bacon.

Head, H. (1926). *Aphasia and kindred disorders of speech*. New York: Cambridge University Press and Macmillian. (Reprinted in 1963 by Hafner Publishing Co., New York).

Huttlinger, K., & Tanner, D. (1994). The peyote way: Implications for culture care nursing. *Journal of Transcultural Nursing,* 5(2), 5-11.

Ihara, S. (1993). *Information theory for continuous systems*. Singapore: World Scientific.

Institute of General Semantics. (2005). *Frequently asked questions about General Semantics.* Dallas-Fort Worth, TX: Author.

Jackson, J. (1878). On affections of speech from diseases of the brain. *Brain, 1,* 301-330.

Jaynes, J. (1976). *The origin of consciousness in the breakdown of the bicameral mind.* Boston: Houghton Mifflin.

Jakobson, R., & Halle, M. (1956). *Fundamentals of language.* The Hague: Mouton.

Johnson, W. (1938). The role of evaluation in stuttering behavior. *Journal of Speech Disorders, 3,* 85–89.

Kent, R. D. (1997). *The speech sciences.* San Diego: Singular Publishing Group.

Kirshner, H. (1995). Cerebral cortex: Higher mental functions. In S. Bhatnagar, & O. Andy (Eds.), *Neuroscience for the study of communicative disorders.* Baltimore: Williams & Wilkins.

Kuhn, T. (1977). *The essential tension: Selected studies in scientific tradition and change.* Chicago: University of Chicago Press.

Ladefoged, P., & Maddieson, I. (1988). *Language, speech and mind: Studies in honour of Victoria Fromkin* (pp. 49–61). London: Routledge.

Lashley, K. (1951). The problem of serial order in behavior. In L. A. Jeffress (Ed.), *Cerebral mechanisms in behavior* (pp. 112–136). New York: Wiley.

Love, R., & Webb, W. (2000). *Neurology for the speech-language pathologist* (4th ed). Boston: Butterworth-Heinemann.

Lum, C. (2002). *Scientific thinking in speech and language therapy.* Mahwah, NJ: Lawrence Erlbaum Associates.

Luria, A. R. (1958). Brain disorders and language analysis. *Language and Speech, 1,* 14–34.

Luria, A. R. (1974). Language and brain. *Brain and Language, 1,* 1–14.

Makan, J., & Marty, D. (2001). *Cooperative argumentation.* Prospect Heights, IL.: Waveland Press.

Martin, F., & Clark, J. (2003). *Introduction to audiology* (8th ed.). Boston: Allyn & Bacon.

Maxwell, D., & Satake, E. (1997). *Research and statistical methods in communication disorders.* Baltimore: Williams & Wilkins.

Minifie, F. (1973). Speech acoustics. In F. Minifie, T. Hixon, & F. Williams (Eds.), *Normal aspects of speech, hearing, and language* (pp. 235–284). Englewood Cliffs, NJ: Prentice-Hall.

Murray, I.. & Arnott, J. (1993). Toward the simulation of emotion in synthetic speech. *Journal of the Acoustical Society of America, 93,* 1097–1108.

Nicolosi, L., Harryman, E., & Kresheck, J. (2004). *Terminology of communication disorders: Speech-language-hearing* (5th ed). Philadelphia: Lippincott Williams & Wilkins.

O'Neill, Y. V. (1980). *Speech and speech disorders in Western thought before 1600.* Westport, CT: Greenwood Press.

Oller, D. (1980). The emergence of the sounds of speech in infancy. In G. Yeni-Komshian, J. Kavanagh, & C. Ferguson (Eds.). *Child phonology: Vol. 1. Production* (pp. 93–112). New York: Academic.

Peterson, G., & Barney, H. (1952). Control methods used in a study of the vowels. *Journal of the Acoustical Society of America, 24,* 175–184.

Piaget, J., & Inhelder, B. (1969). *The psychology of the child.* [H. Weaver, Trans.]. New York: Basic Books.

Plante, E., & Beeson, P. (2004). *Communication and communication disorders: A clinical introduction* (2nd ed.). Boston: Pearson.

Potter, R., Kopp, G., & Green, H. (1947). *Visible speech*. New York: Van Nostrand.

Power, G. (2002). Communication sciences and disorders: The discipline. In R. Gillam, T. Marquardt, & F. Martin (Eds.), *Communication sciences and disorders: From science to clinical practice* (pp. 3-24). San Diego: Singular Publishing Group.

McReynolds, L., & Kearns, K. (1983). *Single-subject experimental designs in communicative disorders*. Baltimore: University Park Press.

Rockey, D. (1980). *Speech disorders in nineteenth century Britain*. London: Croom Helm.

Ruben, R. J. (2000). Redefining the survival of the fittest: Communication disorders in the 21st century. *Laryngoscope, 110*, 241-245.

Ruthrof, H. (2000). *The body in language*. New York: Cassell.

Ryalls, J., & Behrens, S. (2000). *Introduction to speech science: From basic theories to clinical application*. Boston: Allyn & Bacon.

Sacks, O. (1990). *Seeing voices: A journey into the world of the deaf*. New York: Vintage Books.

Sapir, E. (1921). *Language*. New York: Harcourt, Brace & World.

Schuell, H. (1965). *The Minnesota test for differential diagnosis of aphasia*. Minneapolis: University of Minnesota Press.

Schuell, H., Jenkins, J., & Jimenez-Pabon, E. (1964). *Aphasia in adults: Diagnosis, prognosis, and therapy*. New York: Hoeber.

Scientific American Science Desk Reference. (1999). New York: John Wiley & Sons.

Searle, J. (1969). *Speech acts: An essay in the philosophy of language*. London: Cambridge University Press.

Shannon, C. E. (1949). *The mathematical theory of communication*. Champaign/Urbana: University of Illinois Press.

Sies, L. (1974). *Aphasia: Theory and therapy*. Baltimore: University Park Press.

Small, L. (2005). *Fundamentals of phonetics: A practical guide for students* (2nd ed.). Boston: Pearson, Allyn & Bacon.

Sowa, J. F. (2000). *Knowledge representation: Logical, philosophical, and computational foundations*. Pacific Grove, CA: Brooks/Cole.

Sternberg, R., & Ben-Zeev, T. (2001). *Complex cognition: The psychology of human thought*. New York: Oxford University Press.

Tanner, D. (1996). *An introduction to the psychology of aphasia*. Dubuque, IA.: Kendall/Hunt.

Tanner, D. (1999). *The family guide to surviving stroke and communication disorders*: Austin, TX: Pro-Ed.

Tanner, D. (2001, December). The brave new world of the cyber speech and hearing clinic. *ASHA Leader, 6*(22).

Tanner, D. (2003a). *Forensic aspects of communication sciences and disorders*. Tucson, AZ: Lawyers and Judges.

Tanner, D. (2003b). *The psychology of neurogenic communication disorders: A primer for health care professionals*. Boston: Allyn & Bacon.

Tanner, D. (2003c, Winter). Eclectic perspectives on the psychology of aphasia. *Journal of Allied Health, 32*, 256-260.

Tanner, D. (2003d). *Exploring communication disorders: A 21st century introduction through literature and media*. Boston: Allyn & Bacon.

Tanner, D. (2006). *Case studies in communication sciences and disorders*. Upper Saddle River, NJ: Pearson Merrill Prentice Hall.

Tanner, D., Culbertson, W., & Secord, W. (1997). *The developmental articulation and phonology profile* (DAPP). Oceanside, CA: Academic Communication Associates.

Tanner, D., & Derrick, G. (1981). The treatment of stuttering in Arizona public schools. *Journal of the Arizona Communication and Theatre Association, 12*(2).

Tanner, D., & Gerstenberger, D. (1996). Response to grief? Responses to commentaries. In C. Code & D. Muller (Eds.), *Forums in clinical aphasiology* (pp. 328–331). London: Whurr.

Tanner, D., Sciacca, J., & Cotton, S. (2005). *Science and logic in diagnosis and treatment of communication disorders*. Presentation at the 4th Annual Hawaii International Conference on Social Sciences, Honolulu, Hawaii.

Tanner, D., & Tanner, M. (2004*). The forensic aspects of speech patterns: Voice prints, speaker profiling, lie and intoxication detection*. Tucson: Lawyers and Judges.

Time Almanac. (2005). Borgna Brunner, Editor in Chief. Needham, MA: Pearson Education.

Timler, G., Olswang, L., & Coggins, T. (2005, January). "Do I know what I need to do?" A social communication intervention for children with complex clinical profiles. *Language, Speech, and Hearing Services in Schools, 36,* 73–85.

Titze, I. R., & Story, B. H. (2002, Fall). Voice quality: What is most characteristic about "you" in speech. *Echoes, 12*(2), 1,4.

Tosi, O. (1975). *Personal correspondences.* Institute of Voice Identification, Department of Audiology and Speech Sciences, Michigan State University, East Lansing, MI.

Tosi, O. (1979). *Voice identification: Theory and legal applications.* Baltimore: University Park Press.

Trousseau, A. (1865). *Clinique Medicale de l'Hotel-Dieu de Paris* (2nd ed.). Paris: J.B. Bailliere.

Velasquez, M. (2002). *Philosophy* (8th ed.). Belmont, CA: Wadsworth/Thomson Learning.

Vygotsky, L. (1962). *Thought and language.* New York: MIT Press and John Wiley & Sons.

Webster's New World College Dictionary. (4th ed.). Foster City, CA: Books Worldwide.

Weinstein, E., Lyerly, O., Cole, M., & Ozer, M. (1966). Meaning in jargon aphasia. *Cortex, 2,* 165–187.

Weinstein, E., & Puig-Antich, J. (1974). Jargon and its analogues. *Cortex, 10,* 75–83.

Weisenburg, T., & McBride, K. (1935). *Aphasia.* New York: Commonwealth Fund. (Reprinted in 1964 by Hafner Publishing Co. New York).

Wepman, J., & Jones, L. (1961). *Studies in aphasia: An approach to testing*. Chicago: University of Chicago Press.

Westby, C. E. (1998). Communicative refinement in school age and adolescence. In W. O. Haynes & B. B. Shulman (Eds.), *Communication development: Foundations, processes, and clinical applications*. Baltimore: Williams & Wilkins.

Whorf, B. (1956). *Language, thought and reality: Selected writings of Benjamin Lee Whorf* (J. B. Carroll, Ed.). Cambridge, MA: MIT Press.

Wiig, E., Secord, W., & Semel, E. (1992). *Clinical evaluation of language fundamentals—Preschool*. San Diego: The Psychological Corporation, Harcourt, Brace.

Wise, R. J. S., Greene, J., Büchel, C., & Scott, S. K. (1999). Brain regions involved in articulation. *Lancet, 353,* 1057-1061.

Wood, K. (1971). Terminology and nomenclature. In L. E. Travis (Ed.), *Handbook for speech pathology and audiology*. Englewood Cliffs, NJ: Prentice-Hall.

Zemlin, W. (1998). *Speech and hearing science* (4th ed.). Boston: Allyn & Bacon.

Zimmerman, I., Steiner, V., & Pond, R. (1992). *Preschool language scale-3*. San Antonio, TX: The Psychological Corporation.

Index

A